CW01185091

KALWANT BHOPAL

Race and Education
Reproducing White Supremacy in Britain

A PELICAN BOOK

PELICAN
an imprint of
PENGUIN BOOKS

PELICAN BOOKS

UK | USA | Canada | Ireland | Australia
India | New Zealand | South Africa

Penguin Books is part of the Penguin Random House group of companies whose addresses can be found at global.penguinrandomhouse.com

Penguin Random House UK

First published 2024
001

Text copyright © Kalwant Bhopal, 2024

The moral right of the author has been asserted

Book design by Matthew Young
Set in 11/16.13pt FreightText Pro
Typeset by Jouve (UK), Milton Keynes
Printed and bound in Great Britain by
Clays Ltd, Elcograf S.p.A.

The authorized representative in the EEA is Penguin Random House Ireland, Morrison Chambers, 32 Nassau Street, Dublin D02 YH68

A CIP catalogue record for this book is available from the British Library

ISBN: 978-0-241-53732-9

Penguin Random House is committed to a sustainable future for our business, our readers and our planet. This book is made from Forest Stewardship Council® certified paper

www.greenpenguin.co.uk

To Martin, Dylan, Yasmin, Deva and Sachin

Thank you for making my life complete

Contents

LIST OF TABLES	1
ACKNOWLEDGEMENTS	3
INTRODUCTION	5
CHAPTER 1 A Critical Race Perspective	25
CHAPTER 2 Schools and Everyday Racism: 'It's Just Banter'	51
CHAPTER 3 Higher Education: 'Unspoken White Noise'	87
CHAPTER 4 White Elites and Educational Advantage: 'Once Privileged, Always Privileged'	123
CHAPTER 5 Equality Whitewash: A Hierarchy of Oppression and the Performativity of Whiteness	157

CHAPTER 6
Race Equality Training: For Whose Benefit?   191

CONCLUSION   221

NOTES   241

INDEX   265

SENSITIVE CONTENT WARNING

Please note that this book contains occasional words and phrases that might be triggering for some readers.

List of Tables

1.	UK-domiciled students by ethnic group, 2019–2020	92
2.	UK-domiciled students by ethnic group and undergraduate qualifiers	94
3.	UK first-degree undergraduate qualifiers by ethnic group, 2019–2020	96
4.	UK-domiciled graduate outcomes by leaving destination and ethnic group, 2019–2020	97
5.	UK professors in higher-education institutions by gender and ethnicity, 2019–2020	159
6.	UK senior managers in higher-education institutions by gender and ethnicity, 2019–2020	160

Acknowledgements

There are many people who have contributed to the ideas presented in this book. I would like to thank my colleagues in the School of Education and the Centre for Research on Race and Education at the University of Birmingham, particularly David Gillborn, with whom I have had the opportunity and immense pleasure to work with. Thanks also to John Preston, Martin Dyke, Claire Pitkin and Holly Henderson for allowing to me to share and discuss my ideas. I am particularly grateful to the students and members of staff I interviewed as part of my research at schools and universities for giving generously of their time and allowing me to share their stories. All of the ideas in this book have been presented at numerous seminars and conferences around the world. I am grateful for all the comments and questions I have had about my work, some of which have been negative at times, but all of which have helped me develop my intellectual scholarship.

Thanks to everyone at Penguin, especially Casiana Ionita who invited me to write the book, Hana Teraie-Wood for her support and excellent editing skills, and Kate Parker for the copyediting. It has been a pleasure to work with you!

Thank you to my four children – Dylan, Yasmin, Deva

and Sachin – who continue to help me develop my scholarship and keep me on my toes by constantly pushing me to question my intellectual ideas; for their advice on the book and chapter titles and topics to be covered; for their courage in dealing with the brutal everyday realities of racism; and for always making me appreciate what is truly important. You make my life better every single day. Special thanks to Dylan for his advice during countless conversations about the contents of the chapters, the theoretical focus, the link to policy discourse, the intersectional nuances of understanding racism, and for his suggestion of including more details on the experience of ethnic minority students and staff in schools.

Thank you to my partner – of thirty years – Martin Myers, for his love, strength, unquestioning support, intellectual prowess and endless discussions about the scholarly ideas presented in this book. I am hugely grateful to him for his superb editing skills, and for reading the manuscript several times and providing excellent feedback.

Thanks to my wonderful mum, Swaran Kaur Bhopal, for her strength, courage and love. To my siblings for their kindness, love and laughter. During the final stages of writing this book, sadly my dad, Gian Chand Bhopal, passed away. He was eighty-one years old and taught me to work hard and never give up. I miss him terribly and think about him every day. Rest in power, Dad – you will never be forgotten.

Introduction

In this book, I want to explore how race affects the educational experience of ethnic minority groups in Britain by analysing how institutions and processes work to perpetuate racism in education. In the pages that follow, I work from the premise that racism is a given in society, and is central to explaining how education reinforces systems and structures of Whiteness and White privilege that benefit White people. I specifically focus on schools and higher-education institutions in the United Kingdom, and examine how the impact of (White) policy-making perpetuates White supremacy in this country. Drawing on my own empirical data, and that of others, I use research on schools and universities in Britain to show how this inequality works in practice.

For the past thirty years I have devoted my academic career to researching and writing about education and racism, an undertaking that had its genesis in my own experiences of racism in Britain, and the ways in which it has intertwined with my personal and academic life. My parents emigrated to England from India in the 1950s and I was the first child in my family to be born in the UK. I grew up watching *Coronation Street* and eating fish and chips every Friday night. But from an early age I experienced racism and never felt completely accepted by White British society. It started with my parents: I vividly remember my father getting stopped and questioned by the police on a regular basis because he drove an expensive car, as if to suggest that Asian people could not afford to own such vehicles or indeed be allowed to drive them. At primary school, I was already viewed as an outsider and was often taunted by my classmates with slurs such as 'You smell of curry, you Paki'. As a teenager, the racism continued, and I even remember crossing a busy street on one occasion and being shouted at by a White policeman in a police car: 'Get out of the road, you Paki.' My encounters with racism have followed me into adulthood and I have lost count of the number of times I have been asked, 'Where are you from?' When I respond with 'London', I'm inevitably asked again, 'No, where are you *really* from?' I have been told, 'You must be used to the hot weather where you come from', and that I don't need sunscreen because, of course, brown skin does not burn. More bizarrely, I've been complimented by random strangers who have told me, 'Your English is so good.' I've also been ignored – and sometimes encountered overt hostility – in shops, bars and restaurants where White people are greeted warmly and politely. None of these are one-off or unusual examples. They are regular everyday occurrences. My name has been shortened to 'Kal' without my consent. I have been asked if it's OK to call me Carol because Kalwant is too difficult to say or spell.

As someone from an ethnic minority, I encounter covert and overt racism every single day of my life. Having been deeply affected by racism, I decided to enter academia as a career, naïvely thinking it would be a safe haven, inclusive and tolerant.

How wrong I was; I have experienced both overt and covert racism throughout my academic career. I was racially bullied in one organization for five years and this had a profound effect on me. I found myself not only questioning my right to belong in the White space of higher education, but even the validity of my scholarship. I was made to feel like an outsider by other, White academics. My research on racism was denigrated by my peers and not seen as worthy. In meetings, fellow academics would avoid eye contact with me and my views were dismissed. Publicly, my research was often excluded from seminars and conferences. I was constantly reminded that higher education was a White space reserved for Whites only. I ultimately left the university in question, but instead of giving up, the experience made me determined to show how racism continues to persist in all aspects of our lives – including in higher education. This was one of the reasons I decided to then focus my research on racial discrimination in education. I wanted to understand how schools and universities were complicit in perpetuating racism, and how it could be challenged and addressed.

In this book, I work from the premise that racism is a commonplace feature of everyday life, determining how ethnic minority groups are treated. I aim to show how schools and higher-education establishments implicitly perpetuate racism and disadvantage ethnic minority groups in the UK, while at the same time benefiting White people by perpetuating Whiteness and White privilege. Because of its vital influence on individual life chances and choices, education provides a key lens through which we can view the workings of racism and racist practices. Educational success is a crucial indicator of social mobility, access to the labour market, earning potential and one's likely position in society. Those who succeed in education hold the keys to status and power; they are more likely to pursue careers that have a significant impact on society owing to their influence in the media, politics or the law. By the same token, those who do not succeed in the education system are less likely to have their views heard or their interests addressed. Without a proper insight into the educational experience of different groups, therefore, we cannot gain a true understanding of the workings and inequalities of the society in which we live.

The main focus of this book is an examination of the experiences of ethnic minorities within the British education system. But before we explore this, it's worth saying a few words about who we mean when we talk about ethnic minorities. There have been several attempts in academia and elsewhere to try to group them under one label, with BME (Black and minority ethnic) or BAME (Black, Asian and minority ethnic) being the main terms in current use. (Other alternatives include 'people of colour', 'global majority' and 'minoritized communities' – terms that are more popular in the United States.) Neither of these terms appeal to me, because they are not sufficiently inclusive: BME prioritizes the experiences of Black groups, and BAME prioritizes those of Black and Asian groups. They also homogenize the experiences of a diverse range of people and disregard the disparities and diversities that exist *within* and *between* these different groups.

Furthermore, these labels do not necessarily use *Black* as a political term that encompasses *all* people of colour (including those from Indian, Pakistani and Bangladeshi backgrounds) who continue to encounter racial discrimination and have historically suffered under colonialism and imperialism. Using 'Black' as an all-encompassing political term could be a move towards a united fight against racism. In the 1970s, it was used in anti-racist campaigns by Caribbean, African, Arab and Asian communities to express a united front in their common struggles against racism.[1] This worked to strengthen a politics of solidarity between the different groups to challenge everyday racism in all areas of society, from employment and housing to the media, health and education.

Some have argued that the term 'Black' does not include South Asian groups as it denies South Asian identity,[2] while others have argued that many South Asians do not define themselves as Black, and many Black Africans and Black Caribbeans do not regard them as such either, as I was to discover for myself.[3] It is important to remind ourselves that race itself is a social construct and the terms 'Black' and 'South Asian' are fluid, essentialist and intertwined in a range of diverse social, economic and historical interpretations. Moreover, their meaning can vary according to the context, whether social, cultural or political.

As a university undergraduate, my politics as an Asian woman were linked to the political term 'Black' and the emergence of Black feminism in Britain, which acknowledged the importance of intersecting strands such as race and gender. However, my own identity as a Black woman was questioned. When I was a first-year undergraduate, my presence in the Black Student Society was queried by a Black Caribbean man, who said I should not be part of the group because I was not Black. Black in this context did not signify a political spectrum; it was simply a racial dividing line. Given the changing discourses in identity politics, it is no longer appropriate to define myself as Black. I am thus a British Indian woman of South Asian heritage who experiences oppression based on my race, gender and class.

Throughout the book, I use the term *ethnic minority* to refer to all ethnic groups except White British ones, employing it is an inclusive term that does not prioritize one group over another. I am aware of the complexity of the term, however, and when discussing individual cases, I refer to specific ethnic minority groups where appropriate.

This book brings together the findings of a number of research projects I have conducted over the past five years. From my own experiences of racism at school and university, and the experiences of my children, I wanted to examine how, despite the existence of anti-bullying policies, racism still profoundly affects the lives of ethnic minority groups. I am especially interested in how the racist language used by students in schools and higher education is simply dismissed as 'banter' by White students and teachers, and how policy-making intended to address racism is enacted in such a way that is addresses *perceptions* of racism rather than *actual* racism, by which I mean stereotypes that are often used to make judgements about individuals (Black students being perceived as aggressive, for instance, and Asian female students as passive) rather than real, individual acts of racism (such as the use of racist slurs). Given my own experiences of racism in higher education, I am also interested in exploring how higher education is perpetuated as a White space in which ethnic minority staff are positioned as outsiders and ethnic minority students are marginalized and racially profiled.

As I've already mentioned, I embarked on a career in academia under the assumption that universities were progressive, liberal places with social justice at the heart of their agendas. However, based upon extensive evidence and my own experience, I quickly discovered the prevalence of different forms of racism in higher-education institutions. My own encounters with racism in higher education have occurred at times when I have least expected them. Invited to present a keynote speech at a particular university, in which I was presenting statistics on the ethnic minority awarding gap, I was interrupted by a White woman who questioned the validity of my statistics and said they were wrong. During my speech, I was also interrupted by a White male professor when I mistakenly read one line of statistics from the wrong PowerPoint slide. He took it upon himself to correct me, and explain my data to the audience, *while I was still speaking.* I doubt such things would have happened if I were a White woman or indeed a White man: when White academics present their research about race and racism, it is rare to hear of them being interrupted or their data openly disputed. Such was the embarrassment of some audience members that, unbeknown to me, some had complained and a few days later I received an apology from one of the pro-vice-chancellors. I shared the experience on Twitter (now X), and while I received some understanding comments from friends and strangers, it also generated a flurry of responses dismissing the racial element, suggesting instead that 'you get interrupted because you are a woman' or 'because you are working class'. Such responses were of course missing the point, and in fact highlighted further how most White groups simply ignore *individual acts* of racism (rather than structural and institutional racism – outlined below) as a key factor in how individuals are treated and judged (never mind the lack of value accorded to the scholarship on race by an ethnic minority woman).

When my work has found explicit evidence of racism, this has resulted in countless abusive emails and Twitter (now X) messages. On many occasions, the response to it has been 'How do you know it's racism?' or 'Are you sure this is down to racism?' A lot of academics appear to share this default setting of doubting research that provides evidence of racism – a position that they do not hold in other contexts. When I have presented research on gender and evidence of sexism, I have never been asked, 'How do you know it's sexism?' When race is mentioned, by contrast, it provokes a degree of discomfort and awkwardness that seems unique to the subject. As a result, I have concluded that many White people feel personally challenged when faced with evidence of racism and consequently seek to discredit it.

Beyond their personal discomfort, there are bigger questions. Underpinning my research is the need to question, disrupt and challenge historical depictions of oppression in their presentation of imperialism, colonialism and slavery. Such depictions are often presented as old news, terrible failings by earlier generations and unrelated to the world we live in today. This post-racial view of society should be disputed, as racism is still encountered in the present day and has its roots in those historical patterns of White oppression. Personal experiences and my own academic research have contributed to an interest in how a discourse of denial surrounding race and racism has become a defining feature of contemporary society in Britain and America, leading to a denial of the relevance today of past White oppression. These sorts of claims tend to emerge from those on the right, and, because they can be shown to be empirically wrong, are perhaps easier to challenge. However, there are also other forms of denial, such as questions about how one really knows whether it's about race, or the conflation of race and racism with inequalities of class and gender. These forms of denial are often voiced by progressive people on the Left and people committed to social justice. Every time I hear such protestations, I recall how critical race theory emerged in the US in the 1960s as a result of Black legal scholars wishing to challenge their liberal (White) colleagues who acknowledged inequalities of gender and class but seemed unable to recognize the specific and significant impact of racism.

There are other forms of denial, too. In this book, I identify a hierarchy of oppression in the British education system in which race almost always takes a back seat to other types of inequality, such as gender and class. I will also show how policy-making has specifically addressed gender inequalities at the expense of ethnic minority groups and in which White women have been the main beneficiaries. Historically, greater attention has been paid to the feminist agenda and to increasing access to education for the White working class, with little thought given to racial inequalities. This historical imbalance has perpetuated the myth that addressing racial inequalities is less important, which is a particularly pernicious form of denial and one that has a huge impact on educational outcomes for ethnic minority pupils. A longstanding watchword of my research has been that a failure to acknowledge racism results in a failure to act upon it.[4]

Unfortunately, one consequence of conducting research on racism is that racists notice it. In my book *White Privilege: The Myth of a Post-Racial Society*, published in 2018, I unpicked how Whiteness and White privilege work to deliberately perpetuate a system that excludes and disadvantages ethnic minority groups in all areas (including education, the labour market and level of income). I demonstrated that, far from living in a post-racial society, racism continues to permeate all of its institutions, from schools, colleges and universities to popular culture, the media and the social sphere. In my book, I argued that racism works to deliberately perpetuate a system of White supremacy, and provided a comprehensive account of the workings of racism in society today. After *White Privilege* was published, I received countless abusive emails and Twitter (now X) messages and was accused by some of racism towards White groups and 'starting a race war'. I was even threatened by one correspondent over the book's title: 'White privilege doesn't exist and for your own safety, the quicker you realize that the better.' Some of the abusive emails and messages that I received were so offensive that they can't be printed here, but they all served as excellent examples of the aggressive, vulgar assumptions that racists have towards individuals from ethnic minority groups: that they have lower IQs; they do not work hard enough ('Blacks don't work as hard and can't be bothered'); they do not belong here ('You should go back to where you came from'); and they are robbing the White working class of job opportunities ('What about those white working-class blokes who can't get jobs because all you immigrants have taken them?'). This abuse not only confirmed the kinds of views that racists hold, but it also terrified me into thinking about my own safety and that of my family, and led to countless sleepless nights, and many phone calls to the police.

Despite receiving such abuse, I have continued to investigate how racist practices work as a form of oppression for the perpetuation of White supremacy, and in this current volume I aim to show how it takes place in educational institutions. Such outpourings of abuse confirm racism has never gone away. Yet it is the more nuanced, ambiguous examples of racism that I explore in this book which are, arguably, the most effective means of perpetuating White forms of privilege today.

Everyday Forms of Racism

Racism and racial discrimination, both covert and overt, continue to affect people from ethnic minorities on a daily basis in the UK. Compared with White groups, they are more likely to be unemployed and paid less when in employment, to live in poverty, suffer from poor health and be disadvantaged in the criminal justice system.[5] Black groups in particular experience significant racial disadvantage in their daily lives. A recent report published jointly by the House of Commons and the House of Lords found that Black people in the UK do not believe their human rights are equally protected compared with those of White people, and they are not confident that they would be treated in the same way as a White person by the police.[6] Recent evidence of this proves their point: from April 2020 to March 2021 there were 52.6 searches for every 1,000 Black people, compared with 7.5 searches for every 1,000 White people.[7]

While there have been attempts by the British government

to address these inequalities – such as the Race Relations (Amendment) Act (2000), which includes a definition of institutional racism,[8] and the setting up of the Equalities and Human Rights Commission and the Equality Act (2010), which includes race as a protected characteristic – these have resulted in little significant change. Published in 2017, the Race Disparity Audit, commissioned by the prime minister of the time, Theresa May, outlined key areas in which ethnic minority groups were disadvantaged, with regard to such issues as income, education, employment, housing, health and access to the criminal justice system.[9] In many respects, this report simply confirmed existing evidence of racial inequalities and, despite its rhetoric of inclusion, resulted in little change in practice.

The Covid-19 pandemic has also highlighted racial inequalities in terms of access to education, healthcare, employment and the criminal justice system.[10] People from ethnic minority groups were more likely to die from Covid-19,[11] and were less likely to be able to self-isolate due to such factors as poverty, financial difficulties, overcrowded accommodation and being employed on a zero-hours contract.[12] They were also more likely to consistently report a loss of income and require financial assistance during the pandemic compared with people from White groups.[13] Racial discrimination was evident in the number of individuals from ethnic minority groups reporting racial attacks or abuse or being treated unfairly because of their ethnicity.[14] During lockdowns following the announcement of measures to restrict social gatherings, ethnic minority people were disproportionately more likely to be fined for breaching lockdown rules compared with those from White groups.[15] The pandemic simply exacerbated existing racial inequalities, particularly those entrenched by structural and institutional racism.

Racism and Education: Business as Usual

Educational outcomes for individuals from ethnic minority groups show how the inequalities are both shocking and stark. Ethnic minority students are more likely to fall behind in terms of educational achievement compared with their White peers. After Gypsy, Roma and Travellers of Irish heritage,* Black Caribbean pupils achieve the lowest Attainment 8 score[16] and they are the least likely to achieve three good A levels (at grade A or above) compared with those from other ethnic groups, followed by Pakistani and Bangladeshi pupils.[17] Ethnic minority pupils are also more likely to be placed in lower sets (regardless of educational achievement); they are more likely to be excluded or expelled and to face harsher punishment compared with their White peers.[18] Furthermore, ethnic minority pupils regularly report racist bullying by teachers and fellow pupils in the form of slurs based on racial stereotypes.[19]

Despite this, the narrative presented in policy-making and the right-wing media (such as on television and in newspaper

---

* Gypsy, Roma and Travellers of Irish heritage experience the worst educational outcomes of all ethnic groups due to racism from their teachers and peers. I have discussed this extensively elsewhere (see Kalwant Bhopal and Martin Myers, *Home Schooling and Home Education: Race, Class and Inequality*, London: Routledge, 2018). However, in the current volume I focus specifically on how racism affects the lives of those who are visibly identified as outsiders *because* of the colour of their skin, and how this leads to overtly racist assumptions about people from Black and Asian groups.

articles and opinion pieces) has continually centred on the idea of the 'White working-class victim', masking racial inequalities and ignoring the underachievement outlined above of individuals from disadvantaged minority groups.[20] Researchers from the influential think tank on race the Runnymede Trust have argued that pitting the interests of the White working class against those of other ethnic minority groups simply ignores the larger and more important questions of structural disadvantage that contribute to the causes of inequality.[21] Poor ethnic minority children may be disadvantaged because of their class, but *in addition* they are disadvantaged because of their race. They experience the same disadvantages as the White working class, but they encounter on a daily basis different forms of racism – which is often ignored.

While the Equality Act (2010) introduced protected characteristics (such as race), it has in effect diluted the importance of racial inequality in particular, with race now understood as one protected characteristic among many others.[22] This policy has allowed issues of race to take a back seat to other types of inequality, with schools shifting their attention to generic diversity policies that divert attention from racism,[23] a topic that I will explore in Chapter 3.

In the UK, schools themselves are predominantly White spaces. While a quarter of all pupils are from an ethnic minority background, this is not reflected in the teacher population. Teachers and head teachers are more likely to be White. In November 2021, only 14.9 per cent of teachers were identified as being from an ethnic minority background, and only 8.1 per cent of Asian and 9.3 per cent of Black groups were in leadership positions.[24] Compared with the high numbers of students from an ethnic minority background, this figure is relatively low. Furthermore, ethnic minority teachers experience regular incidents of racism, which has a significant impact on their teaching and career progression.[25] In addition, schools themselves are ill equipped to teach about our diverse history, not least because the school curriculum continues to be dominated by an ethnocentric viewpoint that focuses solely on the history and culture of White groups.[26]

Inequalities for ethnic minority students continue into higher education, where they remain under-represented at the more prestigious universities, are less likely than their White peers to obtain a higher-class degree, and encounter racism on a regular basis.[27] Such inequalities continue into the labour market, in which students from ethnic minority groups are more likely to be unemployed six months after they graduate compared with their White peers.[28] In addition, they are also more likely to be employed in insecure jobs with lower pay.[29]

Ethnic minority staff working in higher-education institutions also regularly report being subjected to racism by their colleagues and students.[30] They are less likely to be professors or occupy senior managerial positions, and are more likely to earn less and be on a fixed-term or zero-hours contract compared with their White colleagues.[31] There is also evidence to suggest that policy initiatives introduced to address gender inequalities have specifically disadvantaged ethnic minority women. My research has shown that White women have been, and continue to be, the main beneficiaries of equality policy-making in higher education (which I look at in more detail in Chapter 5).

INTRODUCTION

The Reproduction of Educational Racism

In this book, I explore how Whiteness shapes our educational spaces in the UK, and I analyse how this contributes to, and drives, different types of racism – structural, institutional and individual – in society today. Taking each of these terms in turn, *structural racism* may be defined as the historical and cultural legitimization of policies and practices that perpetuate White supremacy through the preferential treatment of White groups over those from Black and minority ethnic backgrounds. The 1999 Macpherson report into the murder of the Black British teenager Stephen Lawrence gave prominence to *institutional racism* in relation to the Metropolitan Police but the term has since been applied to all public bodies. In the report, institutional racism is defined as: 'The collective failure of an organisation to provide an appropriate and professional service to people because of their colour, culture or ethnic origin. It can be seen or detected in processes, attitudes and behaviour which amount to discrimination through unwitting prejudice, ignorance, thoughtlessness and racist stereotyping which disadvantage minority ethnic people.'[32] Structural and institutional racism may be manifested through *individual acts of racism*, in which an internalization of White privilege translates into forms of behaviour that oppress ethnic minority individuals, often based on stereotypes.

The power of Whiteness, and the value attached to it within different organizations, is taken for granted by White people and is consequently not regarded as significant. However, Whiteness should be understood as having much greater reach; it is, according to Canadian geographers Audrey

Kobayashi and Linda Peake, 'a normative identity in which power and privilege are translated by controlling dominant values and institutions and in particular by *occupying space* within a *segregated* landscape'. As Kobayashi and Peake observe, the White space is one in which accepted White practices are the norm and to which ethnic minority groups must adhere in order to be successful.[33] As we will see, educational spaces appear inclusive but are deliberately set up and arranged to benefit White groups and disadvantage those from ethnic minority backgrounds. In the pages that follow, I will demonstrate how this takes place in schools and in higher education – in spaces that are identified as inclusive, but in reality are designed to be exclusive.

This book is divided into six chapters in which I look at how racism works at different levels within the UK education system. Each chapter provides key evidence (based on statistics or educational policy) to demonstrate how racism continues to dominate the experiences of ethnic minority groups in education. This is accompanied by excerpts from interviews with students and academic staff, conducted as part of my own research, to illustrate how racism is encountered in everyday life.

In addition, this book draws on the ideas of key thinkers who have been significant in advancing my understanding of racial injustice. I specifically draw on critical race theory to show how racism is ubiquitous and how, every single day, it promotes Whiteness and White privilege. Developed in the US in the 1990s, critical race theory contends that racism is a normal feature of society. Such racism is intentional rather than accidental, and it works to protect the interests of White groups and to perpetuate White supremacy.[34]

INTRODUCTION

In each chapter, I use critical race theory to examine how the experiences of ethnic minority students in our schools and higher-education institutions are defined by structures shaped by White privilege and White supremacy, and how, as a result, our education system is built on a completely false vision of meritocracy and equality. Instead, policies, practices and procedures reinforce the idea that Whiteness is the norm, thereby determining who does or does not belong; who is successful and who is not; and who is included and who is not. Such processes work in multiple ways to control ethnic minority groups. In Chapter 1, I outline and explain in detail the main principles of critical race theory, including *racial realism* (the idea that racism is normal and endemic in society), *interest convergence* (when White groups will only invest in equality policy-making when it benefits them more than those from ethnic minorities), *intersectionality* (understanding inequalities through co-existing and interacting forms of identity, such as race, class and gender) and *Whiteness*, *White supremacy* and *Whiteness as property*, which work together as forms of power for White groups to secure their dominance over ethnic minorities through status, political power and material resources.

In Chapter 2, I examine the shocking realities of everyday racism faced by ethnic minority pupils in schools. I focus in particular on how policy-making has failed to address racial discrimination encountered by ethnic minority pupils at school, and how in fact policy-making has created a culture of fear in which ethnic minority pupils are demonized as outsiders. I also include extracts from compelling interviews with ethnic minority students (aged 16–18) to demonstrate how overt racism is an everyday occurrence and a normal part of school life. And I show how racist language and racial slurs are dismissed as banter by White students, and consequently become an overlooked form of everyday racism experienced by ethnic minority students.

Chapter 3 looks at higher education and examines how it continues to be a normative White space in which ethnic minority students are still racially marginalized. In this chapter, I discuss the Black Lives Matter protests in particular and their impact on higher education. I argue that, far from being a significant 'moment' that addressed racial injustice, and despite high-profile commitments to enact change, higher-education institutions continue to perpetuate White privilege within a system of White supremacy.

In Chapter 4, I focus on elite White groups to explore how privilege stems from first attending a private, fee-paying school and then an elite university, before entering a labour market in which elites are rewarded for their privilege. Through such processes of White privilege, White groups are able to maintain and reproduce their elitism through a system of White supremacy that works to exclude ethnic minorities.

Chapter 5 considers equality policy-making in higher education. It argues that, far from having a beneficial effect, these policies have created a hierarchy of oppression in which racial equality is always given a lower priority than other forms of equality deemed more 'worthy', such as gender. Furthermore, the burden of tackling racial inequalities tends to fall on the shoulders of individuals from ethnic minorities – it is treated as their problem and one for them to solve – which benefits White groups while disadvantaging the very people it is meant to serve.

In Chapter 6, I examine how 'diversity' has become the new buzzword for addressing racial inequalities. I show how, in reality, positive outcomes of 'diversity' initiatives are few and far between, and how so-called 'diversity' is in fact used instead as a performative, rather than practical, tool in schools and universities to maintain the superior position of White groups and reinforce the inferior status of ethnic minorities. 'Diversity' schemes often assume that ethnic minorities lack the qualities that White groups possess, and encourage them to mirror White models of success in order to navigate these racist institutions, rather than asking the institutions themselves to address their own racist practices and behaviours.

In the final chapter, I outline solutions for a more equitable system. I argue that there is an urgent need to make significant and bold changes to address the continued persistence of racial inequality, not just in education, but in society as a whole. This book offers one way forward and its contribution will be to outline and raise awareness about the shocking evidence of racial discrimination at all stages of the educational journey. At the same time, I aim to demonstrate that education offers a means by which White hierarchies can be dismantled and disrupted, so that we can work towards building a society that is truly equal in every way. Education matters, and everyone should have access to it so that its transformative power can be experienced by all.

CHAPTER 1
A Critical Race Perspective

Since the eruption of the Black Lives Matter protests in 2020, Britain, alongside many other countries around the world, has been forced to address issues of racial injustice wherever they may be found, including in education. Our universities and schools were (and continue to be) criticized for their lack of ethnic minority teachers and academic staff in senior roles in particular, as well as for their curricula and the way young students from ethnic minorities progressed, or did not progress, through the system. As a result, efforts have since been made by educational establishments to address racial inequalities – for instance, by increasing the presence of Black academics at universities, both in academic and professional support roles. But how can we assess the true impact of such changes on education and society as a whole?

In this chapter, I outline how a critical race perspective can help us examine these questions, and how it can be used to demonstrate how our educational structures continue to perpetuate and reinforce racism and White supremacy. The key principles of critical race theory (or CRT) that I draw on, and which I will be explaining in more detail, are: racial realism, interest convergence, Whiteness, White supremacy, Whiteness as property and intersectionality. In addition to outlining how CRT works, I will also discuss how recent public debates in the UK and the US have distorted our understanding of it, creating a sense of moral panic in which White groups believe *themselves* to be the victims of racial politics at the hands of such a theory. I do so by analysing the report of the Commission on Racial and Ethnic Disparities,[1] which demonstrates how politicians weaponize the subjects of race, education and inequality in order to advance their own political agendas – no matter what the evidence shows.

What Is Critical Race Theory?

Critical race theory is an intellectual and social movement that seeks to understand and analyse racial inequalities in society. It originally developed in the US from critical legal scholarship, a field of study devoted to looking at how the law is inextricable from social issues, as a response to the inadequacy of civil rights litigation as a means of addressing racial inequalities. Developed by a group of critical legal scholars – including Derrick Bell (the founding father), Kimberlé Crenshaw, Richard Delgado, Lani Guinier, Angela Harris and Charles Lawrence – CRT was created to analyse how racism works as a form of social and economic oppression. In many respects, it was a backlash to the progressive Left and civil rights protest that seemed to focus on inequalities associated with class and gender in education, housing and the labour market. Bell and his fellow scholars felt that because race and racism was only understood as an element of class inequality, rather than a specific issue in itself, this had made little or no difference to advancing racial equality. In developing CRT, Crenshaw gave a definition of it: 'We would signify the political and intellectual location of the project through [the term] "critical", the substantive focus through "race" and the desire to develop a coherent account of race and law through the term "theory".[2]

In the UK, critical race theory as an academic discipline came about through intellectual and scholarly exchanges between academics who wanted to work out how racial injustices could be identified and tackled. It gave academics from both White and ethnic minority groups a springboard from which anti-racism scholarship could be launched as a legitimate form of scholarship in its own right. CRT first emerged in the UK with the influential work of David Gillborn,[3] who looks at how it can help us establish how educational policy-making and practice in Britain might function as a form of White supremacy. Other eminent CRT scholars include Kevin Hylton, who uses CRT to analyse racism in sport; John Preston, who analyses Whiteness and class in education; and Paul Warmington, who looks at Black British intellectual spaces.[4]

Critical race theory provides a way of understanding the relationship between power and racism, and of looking at how they have worked together to reinforce systems of oppression. In this sense, CRT does not see racism as the result of single, individual acts but rather as the outcome of the way society was built to keep White groups in superior positions in the workplace and society as a whole, at the expense of ethnic minorities.

CRT rejects the idea that race is a biologically fixed social category, arguing instead that it is socially constructed and based on a performative identity that changes in different social contexts and according to different social interactions.[5]

CHAPTER 1

Consequently, race is understood differently at different times and in different locations through a process of racialization. As Noel Ignatiev points out, this ability for racial meaning to change over time can be illustrated by the example of Irish migrants in the United States – who were once regarded as Black in the nineteenth century but were later seen as a White group.[6]

In his book *Faces at the Bottom of the Well*, Derrick Bell explores the permanence of racism.[7] In one chapter, 'The Space Traders', he presents an allegorical tale set in the future in which aliens land on earth and claim that they can solve all of the socio-economic problems experienced by Americans by providing each person with enough income, food and fuel to last them a lifetime. However, this must involve a 'trade': in return for all this, they must give up to the aliens all the Black people in America. The government and the majority of White citizens are in favour of the deal, apart from liberal political groups and civil rights leaders. While there is some concern that the country would lose revenue and cheap labour provided by Black people, there is also trepidation that the aliens might return for other marginalized and powerless minority groups. As the citizens are unable to come to a decision, a 'democratic vote' is cast that results in the deal being agreed to, and the entire Black population is sacrificed. As Bell's narrator powerfully observes: 'There was no escape, no alternative. Heads bowed, arms now linked by slender chains, Black people left the New World as their forebears had arrived.'[8]

This shocking and disturbing tale reminds us of the tragedy of slavery, a legacy that Bell clearly felt had not disappeared and would continue into the future. The story underlines this by reminding us that Black people are still treated as inferior because of the colour of their skin, *because they are Black*. It shows how White groups will do anything they can for their own benefit and will continue to maintain their superiority, whatever the cost. It also reminds us how racism is normalized in society, and how, unless it is addressed head on, racial equality will never be achieved.

The Key Tenets of Critical Race Theory

RACIAL REALISM

The main premise of CRT is to acknowledge that racism is normal. It is normal in the sense that assumptions of White superiority may be found in political, legal and educational structures throughout the world. In his book *The Racial Contract*, Charles Mills notes that racism is not a local or regional anomaly, but rather it is embedded in a global history shaped by slavery and imperialism. It is, he says, a form of 'global White supremacy [that] is itself a political system, a particular power structure of formal and informal rule, privilege, socioeconomic advantages, and wealth and power opportunities'.[9] Because it is assumed to be a normal or a natural feature of social structures, it often goes unchallenged or unnoticed. When evidence of systemic racism is identified – in the awarding of university degrees, for example – that evidence is often ignored because it is assumed to be a *normal* outcome. The ability to normalize inequalities is central to processes that quietly reproduce them, and there is thus a need to identify and challenge these inequalities in order to work towards changing the status quo.

CHAPTER 1

INTEREST CONVERGENCE

Drawing from his experience in civils rights law, Derrick Bell argues in *Faces at the Bottom of the Well* that legislative progress has done nothing to address racism, because it is a fundamental aspect of society; it is 'permanently embedded in the psychology, economy, society and culture of the modern world'.[10] When legislation was introduced to address racial inequality, as Bell notes elsewhere, this took place only through interest convergence – the process by which White groups will tolerate or accommodate Black groups gaining racial equality *only* when such interests converge with their *own* interests and benefit them *more*. In addition, according to Bell, even when there are times when interest convergence is seemingly effective, it will only achieve so much if it does not threaten the superior position of White groups. Ultimately, therefore, the main beneficiaries must be White groups. Consequently, policy-making always furthers the interests of White people, and White people *only*. As an example of interest convergence, Bell cites the *Brown vs Board of Education* case that ended segregated schooling in the US.[11] According to Bell, despite ostensibly being a landmark civil rights victory, the legislation did not end segregation in full but instead primarily benefited a range of national and global White policy interests. Initial gains were stalled and de facto racial and socio-economic segregation continued, as it does today. Schools remain racially and socially segregated in the US; those in predominantly Black areas are under-resourced, while those in areas populated chiefly by White people are much wealthier. An unintended consequence of

Brown vs Board of Education was the closing of some schools, rather than their desegregation. In addition, the ruling created a system of White leadership in which White groups were the ones who had power in how schools were run and how education was controlled. Thus, *Brown vs Board of Education* is a prime example of interest convergence, where race equality policy is enacted to give the illusion of progress, when, in reality, only White interests are served and nothing changes.

WHITENESS, WHITE SUPREMACY AND WHITENESS AS PROPERTY

Critical race theory also examines how Whiteness and White privilege work to benefit White groups and oppress ethnic minority people by maintaining White supremacy. Whiteness, in a racial context, is based on the identity or quality of being White, and White supremacy is the idea that Whiteness dominates as the superior race in a society to the exclusion of other racial and ethnic minority groups. David Gillborn argues that all White groups are part of the systems that perpetuate White supremacy, and while they may differ from each other in certain respects, the one thing they have in common is that they benefit from their Whiteness – whether they like it or not.[12] Hence Whiteness is a crucial factor in assessing how power structures work intentionally to oppress and marginalize ethnic minority groups, because, while the concept of Whiteness does not assume that all White people are the same, it does presume that all White people are implicated in acts of White supremacy, *simply because they are White.*

Peggy McIntosh, an American feminist and anti-racist

scholar, first introduced the term *White privilege* in the 1980s. She described the benefits it conferred on White people as being 'like an invisible weightless knapsack of special provisions, assurances, tools, maps, guides, codebooks, passports, visas, clothes, compass, emergency gear and blank checks'.[13] White privilege is thus based on taken-for-granted advantages that individuals possess based on their White identity. While it often comprises characteristics and entitlements that go unnoticed by the White people who possess them, White privilege is never imagined, masked or hidden. It is always out in the open and clearly visible to other ethnic groups, experienced by them as small, everyday slights and rebuttals. It is encountered as microaggressions, when comments or behaviours, whether deliberate or unintentional, betray deep-seated hostility to ethnic minority people. White people benefit from their White privilege through their Whiteness on a daily basis, and in doing so disadvantage and oppress ethnic minority groups.

Various definitions of *Whiteness* have been useful in assessing how White privilege works as a form of exclusion and oppression. Commentators have defined it as 'a social construction that embraces white culture, ideology, racialisation, expressions and experiences, epistemology, emotions and behaviours... normalized because white supremacy elevates whites and whiteness to the apex of the racial hierarchy',[14] a 'standpoint... that is usually unmarked and unnamed',[15] observing how 'normative assumptions of whiteness that remain unspoken and often in the background... profoundly shape white attitudes and beliefs about racial others'.[16] Zeus Leonardo, a prominent scholar in Whiteness studies, notes how '"Whiteness" is a racial discourse, whereas the category "white people" represents a socially constructed identity, usually based on skin colour'.[17] In this sense, Whiteness is a *worldview* and a specific racial perspective that is, Zeus continues, 'supported by material practices and institutions ... white people are often the subjects of whiteness because it benefits and privileges *them*'.[18] White people, in other words, are the main beneficiaries of Whiteness. By contrast, the American CRT scholar Robin DiAngelo defines White supremacy as a culture:

> White supremacy describes the culture we live in, a culture that positions white people and all that is associated with them (whiteness) as ideal. White supremacy is more than the idea that whites are superior to people of color; it is the deeper premise that supports this idea – the definition of whites as the *norm* or standard for human, and people of colour as a deviation from that norm.[19]

While race is socially constructed, it continues to remain the mechanism through which White privilege and racial inequalities are perpetuated, reinforced and maintained.[20]

Whiteness as property, or the control of property by White groups, is a form of power that gives White groups specific entitlements. Cheryl Harris, who was one of the first scholars to write about this, defines it as 'the legal legitimation of expectations of power and control that enshrine the status quo as a neutral baseline, while masking the maintenance of white privilege and domination'.[21] She argues that the Black experience of chattel slavery, in which Black bodies were regarded as a legal form of property, still resonates and determines the social standing of ethnic minorities today. According to Zeus Leonardo and Alicia Broderick, it allows White groups to secure their dominance over ethnic minority groups through social status, laws, political power and control of material resources. In education, such dominance by White groups is manifested in the unequal treatment of ethnic minority groups in educational policies and as reflected in outcomes.[22]

INTERSECTIONALITY

The concept of intersectionality is important when analysing educational inequalities because it allows us to see how ethnic minority students, marginalized because of their race, may *also* experience disadvantages based on their other identities, such as social class, gender, sexuality and disability. The concept was developed by leading critical race theorist Kimberlé Crenshaw to counter the prevailing idea that a single axis of identity was sufficient to explain an individual's experiences of oppression. She wanted to show how, for Black women, race might intersect with other factors, particularly those relating to gender, sexuality, disability and social class.[23] Crenshaw argued that to understand the unfair treatment of Black women, race alone cannot explain their experiences:

> Consider an analogy to traffic in an intersection, coming and going in all four directions. Discrimination like traffic through an intersection may flow in one direction, and it may flow in another. If an accident happens in an intersection, it can be caused by cars traveling from

any number of directions and sometimes from all of them. Similarly, if a Black woman is harmed because she is in the intersection, her injury could result from sex discrimination or race discrimination.[24]

Crenshaw applied intersectionality to an anti-discrimination law to examine how competing and interlocking identities affected Black women's lives and experiences. Her aim was to highlight how the 'focus on the intersections of race and gender only highlights the need to account for multiple grounds of identity when considering how the social world is constructed'.[25] The concept of intersectionality has been a key element in CRT in showing how race and racism remain central to understanding systems of oppression. This is important for emphasizing the marginal nature of ethnic minority experiences, but also to show how interlocking identities are crucial in understanding and analysing them.

In the UK, intersectionality has been used by Black feminists to challenge White feminism for only representing the experiences of middle-class White women.[26] According to the sociologist Nira Yuval-Davis, the benefit of intersectionality as a form of analysis is that it 'is the most comprehensive, complex, nuanced and does not reduce social hierarchical relations of power into one axel of power, be it class, race or gender'.[27] More recently, the concept has been used to examine disadvantages in relation to the Covid-19 pandemic as a means of assessing the extent to which intersecting inequalities have affected individuals from ethnic minority groups and their ability to survive the pandemic. Intersectionality can thus be seen an important analytical tool for examining the complex and multiple systems of structural inequality and privilege that exist in society today.[28]

The Backlash: White Lives Matter *More*

In 2020, following the murder of George Floyd by a White police officer in the US, the Black Lives Matter protests sparked a renewed interest around the world in addressing racial inequalities. In the UK, this led to the toppling of the statue of slave trader Edward Coulson in Bristol[29] and a wider acknowledgement of the impact of racism in society and how to address it across multiple spheres, from education, the labour market and the criminal justice system to housing and income distribution. While the Black Lives Matter protests brought racism to the forefront of political, social and economic agendas, it also triggered a backlash by those on the Right. In a desperate bid to suggest that the Black Lives Matter movement was itself the perpetrator of racist rhetoric, they countered with variations on the same theme, including All Lives Matter or White Lives Matter. Beyond simply missing the point of the original slogan, which highlighted the lack of value attached to Black lives and the need for racial injustice to be recognized and acknowledged, these dissenting voices chose to interpret the movement as a direct attack on White groups, labelling supporters of Black Lives Matter as, among other things, 'lockdown-busting statue-toppling anarchists'.[30] As Nesrine Malik has observed, such responses to Black Lives Matter were designed to water down the vital need for racial equality and social justice, and to portray demands for them as existential threats to society rather than attempts to secure universal basic human rights for marginalized groups.[31]

In the UK, following the 'moment' of the Black Lives Matter protests, fifty-nine Conservative MPs and seven members of the House of Lords formed the 'Common Sense Group', issuing the pugnacious statement: 'we are ready for a culture war and we are confident that our policy agenda will help win it'.[32] The group accused the National Trust of being 'coloured by cultural Marxist dogma' and in the grip of 'elite bourgeois liberals' when it conducted an inquiry into alleged links between the Trust's properties and the slave trade.[33] In September 2020, the then culture secretary Oliver Dowden informed museums that they would no longer receive public funding if they took down statues,[34] and at the same time schools in England were told by the Department of Education that they were not allowed to teach using materials produced by anti-racist groups.[35] Such ideas were further reinforced by Prime Minister Boris Johnson, who in his conference speech in October 2020 proclaimed, 'We are proud of this country's culture, history and traditions', and suggested that the Labour Party supported those who 'want to pull statues down, to rewrite the history of our country, to edit our national CVs, to make it look more politically correct'.[36]

In the same month, Kemi Badenoch, Minister for Women and Equalities at the time, addressed MPs in the House of Commons in a debate about Black History Month, which takes place in October each year to mark the contribution to British history by people of African and Caribbean backgrounds. Badenoch declared that teaching children about White privilege as an uncontested fact broke the law and that the government did not want children being taught about 'white privilege and their inherited racial guilt'. She specifically criticized CRT:

> I want to speak about a dangerous trend in race relations that has come far too close to home in my life, which is the promotion of critical race theory, an ideology that sees my blackness as victimhood and their whiteness as oppression. I want to be absolutely clear that the government stands unequivocally against critical race theory. Any school which teaches these elements of political race theory as fact, or which promotes partisan political views such as defunding the police without offering a balanced treatment of opposing views, is breaking the law.

She went on to state that schools had an obligation and statutory duty to remain politically impartial and should not openly support 'the anti-capitalist Black Lives Matter group'.[37]

Badenoch was responding to the Labour MP Dawn Butler, who had been calling for the decolonization of the history curriculum in schools to account for the harmful legacies of imperialism and colonialism. Badenoch then continued:

> We should not apologise for the fact that British children primarily study the history of these islands, and it goes without saying that the recent fad to decolonise maths, decolonise engineering and decolonise the sciences that we've seen across our universities – to make race the defining principle of what is studied – is not just misguided but actively opposed to the fundamental purpose of education.[38]

This perspective was given some support later that year by Amanda Spielman, head of Ofsted – the independent body that inspects the education, care and training services of schools in the UK – who maintained that the curriculum was already broad and gave schools sufficient flexibility: 'The curriculum is there to serve many purposes, one of which is to make children feel represented, but there are so many others.'[39] Spielman made these comments despite research suggesting that British pupils complete their GCSEs and leave school without ever having studied a novel or a play by a non-White author.[40]

By presenting critical race theory and the teaching of White privilege in schools as a threat to Whiteness and British identity, Badenoch failed to confront decades of racism towards ethnic minorities and the dark history and brutal violence of colonialism and imperialism. Perhaps more pertinent was the impact of having a Black person making this argument on behalf of the government. In this instance, *who* delivers the message is as important as the actual message itself. As Derrick Bell has observed, when a Black person takes the side of White groups in criticizing Black people, that person is given 'enhanced standing' for doing so, even when they have no expertise or experience in what they are criticizing.[41] As the mouthpiece of the government, Badenoch not only gave considerable weight and credibility to the views held by those in her party and elsewhere – that racism is not an issue – but she also made them feel good about themselves. By espousing such views, as a Black woman in the cabinet, she was legitimizing the idea that racism is not relevant in society and should not be studied in schools.

CHAPTER 1

Critical Race Theory: 'Anti-American Propaganda'

Similar assaults were already taking place in the US, with Donald Trump attacking anti-racist teaching and banning anti-diversity training for federal contractors, in a process that has continued after his term as president. Since January 2022, a total of 32 states in the US have introduced bills that restrict the teaching of CRT, while 13 states have actually enforced the bans and created restrictions through legislation.

The language used by Trump and Badenoch, declaring CRT as 'un-American' or 'un-British', is just one example of the perpetuation of the White nationalism and White supremacy entrenched in a racist, imperialist and colonial past. Their attack on those who teach CRT, and the suggestion that they are betraying their real identity as 'American' or 'British', allows the violent history of each country to remain unchallenged, and to accept the racial inequalities in society as integral to our nationhood.

Although Black Lives Matter raised awareness of racial inequality, it has led to little (if any) significant changes in terms of addressing it. In some respects, it has reinforced solidarity among White groups, who have, by briefly engaging in protest about racial equality and racial justice, reasserted their position and their White privilege. As Derrick Bell says, it is an unfortunate fact that all of history verifies that advances in racial equality are short-lived.[42]

The CRED Report: A Critical Race Theory Analysis

In 2020, in response to the murder of George Floyd, the then prime minister, Boris Johnson, established the Commission on Race and Ethnic Disparities (CRED) to investigate why racial disparities existed in the UK, and I have used critical race theory to analyse the use of statistics and language in their most recent report, published in March 2021, which specifically focuses on education. I have done this in order to demonstrate how institutional and structural racism is dismissed and ignored by the government as a key factor in educational outcomes and achievement in the UK. Tony Sewell, the chair of the Commission, summarized the main finding of the report in the following way: 'Put simply we no longer see a Britain where the system is deliberately rigged against ethnic minorities. The impediments and disparities do exist, they are varied, and ironically very few of them are directly to do with racism. Too often "racism" is the catch-all explanation and can be simply implicitly accepted rather than explicitly examined.'[43] For many people who have experienced racism directly or indirectly, this was a jaw-dropping claim, and as a result the report made headline news. For many critical race theorists, however, it sounded a very familiar note.

CLASS VS RACE?

One key claim of the report is that factors other than racism are more significant when explaining racial inequalities in the UK. The report concludes that 'evidence shows that geography, family influence, socio-economic background, culture and religion have a more significant impact on life chances than the existence of racism. That said, we take the reality of racism seriously and we do not deny that it is a real force in the UK.'[44] The report then outlines, in some detail, evidence of racial disparities in education, employment, health and the criminal justice system, but by emphasizing the impact of other factors over and above race – despite finding evidence of institutional racism and racial inequalities – the report deliberately fudges the significance of race and racism, and instead chooses to interpret it as a minor issue that does not interfere with those other factors. This, of course, cannot be the case: race and racism affect every part of society, and cannot be separated from other social issues – and so the report, through its language, deliberately obfuscates the significance of racial inequality, thereby serving as a strategy to neutralize the very issue of racism in the UK.

SCHOOLS

The report goes on to state that the main determinant of unequal educational outcomes is socio-economic status:

> Taking the threshold of strong GCSE passes in English and maths, the White British group ranks 10th in attainment. The Chinese and Indian ethnic groups outperform the White British group on this measure by wide margins. New evidence indicates that attainment is closely related to socio-economic status – once this is controlled for, all major ethnic groups perform better than White British pupils *except for Black Caribbean pupils* (with the Pakistani ethnic group at about the *same* level).[45]

By applying critical race theory, one can see that while the report is attempting an intersectional approach – by drawing attention not just to race but also to class – it is in fact furthering the interests of White groups through the process of interest convergence. The point at which the data is 'controlled' for socio-economic status is when it is *reinterpreted* in a way that benefits White groups. By controlling for socio-economic status, or by prioritizing its significance, the data analysis effectively ignores the racism that might contribute to the low socio-economic status of some ethnic minority pupils. Consequently, a family who has experienced racism all their lives – in education, the housing and labour market, healthcare provision, etc. – is utterly disregarded. If you spoke to them, they might point out that racism has been an overarching feature of their lived experience and one that has had a direct impact on their children's education.

In the CRED report's analysis, however, it is more likely that this family's combined experience of racism over time is presented simply in terms of their current low socio-economic status. This helps White people, because by excising the specific impact of racism as a factor from the data, it becomes possible to promote a narrative in which the White working class are identified as the most disadvantaged group. This can then be leveraged to inform educational policy that directly benefits White groups – for instance, by funnelling scarce financial resources towards White pupils. In October 2021, seven months after the publication of the CRED report, the House of Commons published another report, entitled *The Forgotten: How White Working-Class Pupils Have Been Let Down and How to Change It*.[46] Its recommendations, such as greater investment in extracurricular activities and summer schools for White working-class pupils, are to be implemented in the next couple of years.

While statistics can be useful for establishing patterns of inequality, they can, of course, be misinterpreted and introduce bias. An interest in social class may have intended or unintended consequences for an analysis of educational inequality; in the case of the CRED report, there is a clear sense that it was seeking answers that suited the political discourse of the government at the time. First of all, it provided a basis on which to exempt the government from responsibility for racism, by suggesting that it was a characteristic of the past, and secondly, it established the grounds on which investment could explicitly be made in the future of White working-class people – a narrative that sits comfortably with electoral objectives, as outlined above.

At times the language of the CRED report is confusing, not least when it discusses terminology. For example, it calls for a disaggregation of the term BAME – Black, Asian and minority ethnic – which is used to describe minority groups in the UK, in order to better represent different ethnic experiences rather than homogenizing them. However, the report consistently uses terms that *do* homogenize ethnic minority groups and which treat them as single entities without highlighting the differences *within* these groups (the different educational outcomes of Asian groups, when disaggregated, demonstrate how Pakistani/Bangladeshi groups perform worse than Indian groups, for instance). The report also claims that terms such as 'White privilege' and 'White fragility' imply that 'it is White people's attitudes and behaviours that primarily cause the disadvantage experienced by ethnic minorities' rather than other factors.[47] This claim is made despite the rather startling finding of the report that 76 per cent of Black people and 59 per cent of all ethnic minorities 'believe [that] there is "White privilege"'.[48]

Perhaps more significantly, the report focuses on 'fairness' rather than 'equality'. Fairness is referred to numerous times in the report, while equality barely gets a mention. There are a large number of well-established metrics that are used to measure inequality, such as the Gini coefficient, proposed by the Italian statistician Corrado Gini, which measures wealth inequality, or the UK government's poverty metric of 'people in relative low income'. All of these tend to have defined parameters. In addition, the Office for National Statistics provides a wealth of useful guidance for measuring inequality. Fairness, however, is a rather more ambiguous concept that, to date, has not been defined in measurable terms. Such ambiguity thus provides a useful means by which the CRED report can avoid using evidence of racism in order to confirm its existence. By focusing on fairness rather than outcomes and by avoiding defined measurements of equality, it becomes possible to place emphasis on 'other factors', such as geography, class and family background, rather than race. In effect, both the apparently objective statistical data and the more subjective accounts of empirical evidence are shifted into an ambiguous grey area where it is possible to manipulate them. Statistical data is thus *controlled* to create interpretations favoured by the report's political masters, and language that is well defined is replaced with terminology that encourages a subjective interpretation, giving rise to ambiguity and misinterpretation and leading to racial inequalities being overlooked.

In other places in the report, there is an emphasis on language that promotes a *deficit model* of inequality – in which the individual is thought to lack the skills, knowledge or motivation to succeed. The report makes great play of 'the power of agency',[49] which in principle sounds positive and empowering, but in practice works on the assumption that it is up to the individual to do better and work harder. It does not acknowledge the impact of structural, institutional and individual racism in schools or on student outcomes. Instead, it places the blame on the families *themselves* for poor educational achievement. This results in such erroneous conclusions as the underachievement of Pakistani girls with high socio-economic status being attributed to 'traditional attitudes to gender roles, lower perceived benefits of daughters relative to sons' education, and threats to respectability and modesty expressed by parents in Pakistan also apply[ing] in England'.[50] These findings are partially qualified by the use of the conditional tense – they 'may' be attributed to these factors – but the authors of the report do not investigate the impact of racism in schools on girls from a Pakistani or Bangladeshi background or the high expectations of Pakistani or Bangladeshi parents that their daughters will succeed in education and enter the labour market.[51] Gendered racial stereotypes like these are used to perpetuate racism in which Pakistani culture is seen as patriarchal, backward and 'other' and judged in relation to a middle-class normative White mindset that is seen as progressive, egalitarian and forward-thinking.

Responses to the CRED Report

Following the publication of the CRED report, many organizations and individuals working in the field of race equality challenged its findings. The Commission and the report were mired in various controversies, including rumours that the government's top race adviser had resigned over the report's publication,[52] that it falsely listed 'academics and consultants' who were not consulted by the Commission[53] and that large sections of the report were rewritten by Munira Mirza, then head of the Policy Unit at No. 10 Downing Street.[54] Perhaps the most damning critique came from the Runnymede Trust:

> The very suggestion that government evidence confirms that institutional racism does not exist is frankly disturbing. A young Black mother is four times more likely to die in childbirth than her white friend. A young Black man is 19 times more likely to be stopped and searched by the Metropolitan Police than his young white neighbour and those with Black or Asian 'sounding surnames' have to send in twice as many CVs as their white counterparts, with the same qualifications, to receive the same jobs.[55]

And when discussing the report's findings on education in particular, the think tank observed:

> Regarding educational attainment, it is telling to note that the Government ascribes much of the success of ethnic minority children to 'minority aspiration'. Certainly, there is no government policy that we are aware of to which

the success of 'minority aspiration' can be attributed. As such, this is a clear acknowledgement by the Commission that immigrants and ethnic minorities are often left to pull themselves up by their bootstraps, urging their children to over-achieve in school, precisely because there is not the necessary institutional support available to them.[56]

The historian David Olusoga criticized the authors of the report for their lack of understanding of the slave trade in particular:

> Determined to privilege comforting national myths over hard historical truths, they give the impression of being people who would prefer this history to be brushed back under the carpet . . . Shockingly, the authors – perhaps unwittingly – deploy a version of an argument that was used by the slave owners themselves in defence of slavery 200 years ago: the idea that by becoming culturally British, black people were somehow beneficiaries of the system.[57]

Three weeks after the report was published, the Office of the High Commissioner for Human Rights openly condemned it and called upon Prime Minister Boris Johnson to reject the findings, noting how

> The report cites dubious evidence to make claims that rationalise white supremacy by using the familiar arguments that have *always justified racial hierarchy*. This attempt to normalise white supremacy despite considerable research and evidence of institutional racism is an unfortunate sidestepping of the opportunity

to acknowledge the atrocities of the past and the contributions of all in order to move forward.[58]

Despite these criticisms, the report did appear to find support in some sections of the media, as reflected in this expansive headline in the *Daily Mail*:

> Landmark report slams 'divisive' barbs about 'White Privilege' as it says racism is a 'real force' in the UK but poorer white boys are often the most disadvantaged, where people live has more impact on prospects, and Britain is NOT 'institutionally racist'[59]

And, under the headline 'We finally have proof that the lines dividing us are based on class not race', the *Sun* reported:

> SO, it's official. The most important report into racial inequality in the UK for decades has concluded that there is NO PROOF for structural or institutional racism in our country.
>
> Instead, Britain stands as a beacon of integration and fairness. Who compiled the report and wrote up its findings? Boris Johnson? Nope, the brilliant black educationalist Tony Sewell.[60]

Comments of this kind that use the CRED report as their evidence reinforce the perception that the UK is no longer a racist society, that racism has been dealt with and is a thing of the past. And as we saw earlier, for such views to be expressed by a Black person, as the compiler and co-author of a report that does not acknowledge institutional racism, lent the report greater credibility. Such rhetoric simply provides justification to right-wing commentators as to why the government no longer needs to focus on racial inequalities or invest in tackling them; and, more worryingly, it nurtures the idea that racism is an individual problem rather than a structural or institutional one.

As we have seen in the analysis of this report, critical race theory provides an invaluable tool for analysing how racial inequalities form part of the educational system and society more generally. As outlined in this chapter, public debates in Britain and the US have distorted the findings of CRT, arguing instead that it is White groups who are the victims of racial politics. My examination of the CRED report, using a CRT approach, demonstrates that such dangerous rhetoric has perpetuated a discourse that dismisses an acknowledgement of structural, institutional and individual racism in the UK. Instead, the report emphasizes again the argument that it is White groups who are the real victims of racial inequality. This rhetoric is weaponized by the government to denounce a 'culture war' against 'woke liberals' who believe that institutional racism exists, and consequently it is legitimatizing an acceptable form of White racism, which permeates policy-making and works to ensure that White groups continue to be advantaged, whatever the cost.

CHAPTER 2
Schools and Everyday Racism
'It's Just Banter'

A stark reality of the British educational system is that children from Black, Pakistani and Bangladeshi backgrounds are more likely to fall behind in their schooling compared with White groups.[1] They are more likely to be placed in lower sets and to be excluded from school, and less likely to progress to more prestigious universities or better-paid employment.[2] Despite increasing numbers of ethnic minority pupils, schools remain predominantly White institutions: teachers and head teachers are more likely to be White and those teachers from ethnic minority backgrounds regularly report racist incidents. This, coupled with a White-centred curriculum, disadvantages ethnic minority pupils, who feel they have few role models and are taught a curriculum that does not represent their own experiences.

The most distressing aspect of school life for ethnic minority students is the overt racism they face on a daily basis, which is rarely challenged by their teachers. Such racism is tolerated by the pupils, but when they do complain, they are often accused by their peers of being overly sensitive, or by their teachers of confusing racism with bad behaviour. When I was at school, I remember regularly being told to 'go back to your own country, you Paki' and asked, 'What's that Paki smell?' My White friends would refer to their local shop as the 'Paki shop'. Sadly, decades later, my research shows that little has changed and that these kinds of incidents persist in schools. In the experience of ethnic minority pupils, the privilege of Whiteness works to reinforce their position as outsiders who will never be accepted in the White school environment.

In this chapter, you will hear their voices, through my interviews I conducted with them. And by drawing upon data obtained during my research, I will show how schools are complicit in perpetuating racism, through policy-making and by dismissing complaints about racism as 'banter' or minor behavioural infractions. In this way, racist behaviours become the norm, experienced on a daily basis by ethnic minority pupils and rarely taken seriously or indeed challenged by teachers.

Before I show you how this works on a day-to-day level, I will take you through some of the key background data on the ethnic minority population in British secondary schools today, and the main challenges that students and teachers face when it comes to striving towards a more inclusive and equal learning environment.

The School Population

Government statistics from 2020 indicate that there are just under 9 million pupils in England, attending 24,360 schools, and 33.2 per cent are from an ethnic minority background, a figure that has been steadily growing since 2003. In primary schools, a total of 33.9 per cent of pupils are from an ethnic minority background (a slight increase from 33.5 per cent in

2019), and in secondary schools the figure is slightly lower, at 32.3 per cent (though a slight increase from 31.3 per cent in 2019). The number of ethnic minority pupils attending special schools also shows a slight increase, from 29.5 per cent in 2019 to 30.2 per cent in 2020. Those from an Asian background are the largest ethnic minority group in state-funded primary (17.6 per cent), secondary (11.6 per cent) and special schools (10.3 per cent).[3] Despite this steady increase and despite making up a third of the school population, research suggests that schools are unable to fully support the needs of ethnic minority students.[4] Many of them are underachieving and continue to experience racism daily, with a significant impact upon their educational achievement and outcomes.[5]

Educational (Under) Achievement

ATTAINMENT 8 SCORES

Since 2021, the Department of Education has used a new measure to analyse the results of pupils at mainstream state-funded schools, known as 'Attainment 8'. Attainment 8 has been used to calculate a school's progress by measuring how well its pupils perform at Key Stage 4 at age sixteen. Each grade is ranked from the highest score of 9 to the lowest of 1. The eight subjects that are used to measure 'Attainment 8' consist of English and maths and six other subjects, including three from the English Baccalaureate – the sciences, a language and history or geography – and three from other GCSE subjects or approved technical qualifications. A pupil's 'Attainment 8' score is measured by adding up the individual points of their eight subjects (with English and maths counted twice). A school's 'Attainment 8' score – used purely by the

CHAPTER 2

Average 'Attainment 8' score (out of 90) by ethnicity

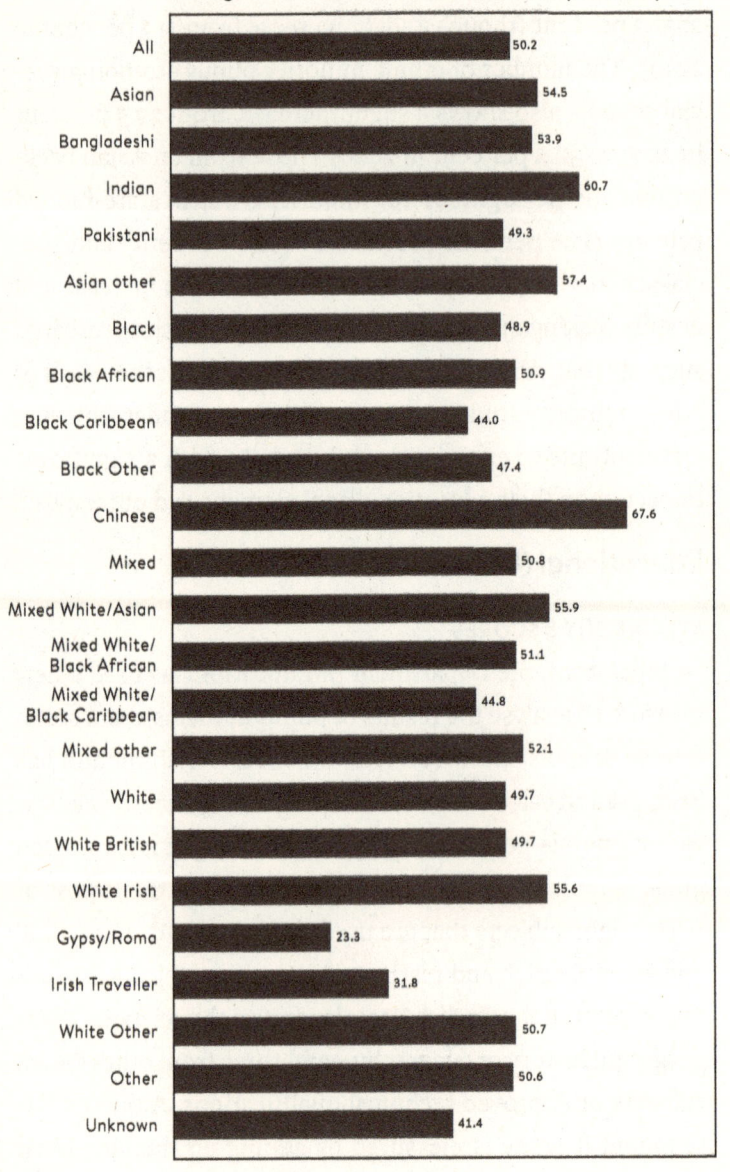

Ethnicity	Score
All	50.2
Asian	54.5
Bangladeshi	53.9
Indian	60.7
Pakistani	49.3
Asian other	57.4
Black	48.9
Black African	50.9
Black Caribbean	44.0
Black Other	47.4
Chinese	67.6
Mixed	50.8
Mixed White/Asian	55.9
Mixed White/Black African	51.1
Mixed White/Black Caribbean	44.8
Mixed other	52.1
White	49.7
White British	49.7
White Irish	55.6
Gypsy/Roma	23.3
Irish Traveller	31.8
White Other	50.7
Other	50.6
Unknown	41.4

school to assess its standards, and not shared with pupils – is the average of all of the eligible pupil scores combined.[6]

For the period 2019–20, as shown in Graph 1, the national Attainment 8 data indicates that racial inequalities continue to persist in educational achievement, albeit with big discrepancies between different ethnic groups. While pupils from certain ethnic minorities, notably those of Chinese and Indian backgrounds, performed particularly well at GSCE level during this period, other ethnic groups, by contrast, achieved the lowest scores. As Graph 1 shows, it is Gypsy/Roma and Irish Traveller pupils (classified here as White)[7] who remain the most disadvantaged, followed by Mixed White/Black Caribbean and Black Caribbean pupils. While there are many reasons why this might be the case, a wealth of evidence indicates that these pupils are more likely to be placed in lower sets, based on teacher prejudice; they are more likely to be excluded from school, experience racism, or be offered less support compared with White pupils.[8]

A LEVEL GRADES

Recent data from the Department of Education also suggests that inequalities in gaining good A level grades are related to ethnicity.[9] This is important because the grades that young people achieve during this period have a significant impact on the choices that they make at this age, such as entrance into

Graph 1
Average 'Attainment 8' score (out of 90) by ethnicity in England for 2019–20

Source: 'Key stage 4 performance: academic year 2019/20', *Ethnicity Facts and Figures*, GOV.UK

the labour market or gaining a place at university. As Graph 2 shows, among all ethnic groups Chinese students were most likely to have gained three A grades or higher (25.7 per cent), followed by Indian students (15.5 per cent). There is evidence to suggest that Chinese and Indian students perform better compared with other groups due to their cultural and family background (irrespective of their social class), which includes a significant emphasis on professional careers and high educational achievement, a committed work ethic and access to support networks within and outside the family.[10] In addition, teachers are more likely to view Chinese and Indian students as model pupils who are more likely to succeed compared with other ethnic groups and to provide them with greater academic and emotional support in their schooling.[11] This suggests that examining educational outcomes for different ethnic minority groups is both nuanced and complex and that there are differences *within* and *between* the groups.

Black students were least likely among all ethnic groups to have gained three A levels at grade A or above; this was the lowest percentage of all ethnic groups (5.5 per cent). A total of 11.2 per cent of students from mixed ethnic backgrounds gained three A grades or above, followed by White (11.0 per cent) and Asian students (11.0 per cent), and lastly, 10.2 per cent of students from the 'Other' ethnic category gained three A grades or above. Students from Gypsy/Roma and Irish

Graph 2
Percentage of students receiving three A grades by ethnicity in England for 2018–19

Source: 'A level and other 16 to 18 results: 2018 to 2019 (revised)', *Ethnicity Facts and Figures*, GOV.UK

Percentage of students receiving 3 A grades by ethnicity

Ethnicity	Percentage
Asian	11.0%
Bangladeshi	7.8%
Indian	15.5%
Pakistani	7.3%
Asian other	11.8%
Black	5.5%
Black African	6.1%
Black Caribbean	3.4%
Black other	5.4%
Chinese	25.7%
Mixed	11.2%
Mixed White/Asian	15.3%
Mixed White/Black African	8.3%
Mixed White/Black Caribbean	6.2%
Mixed other	11.8%
White	11.0%
White British	11.0%
White Irish	13.8%
Gypsy/Roma	0.0%
Irish Traveller	0.0%
White other	11.5%
Other	10.2%
Unknown	23.4%

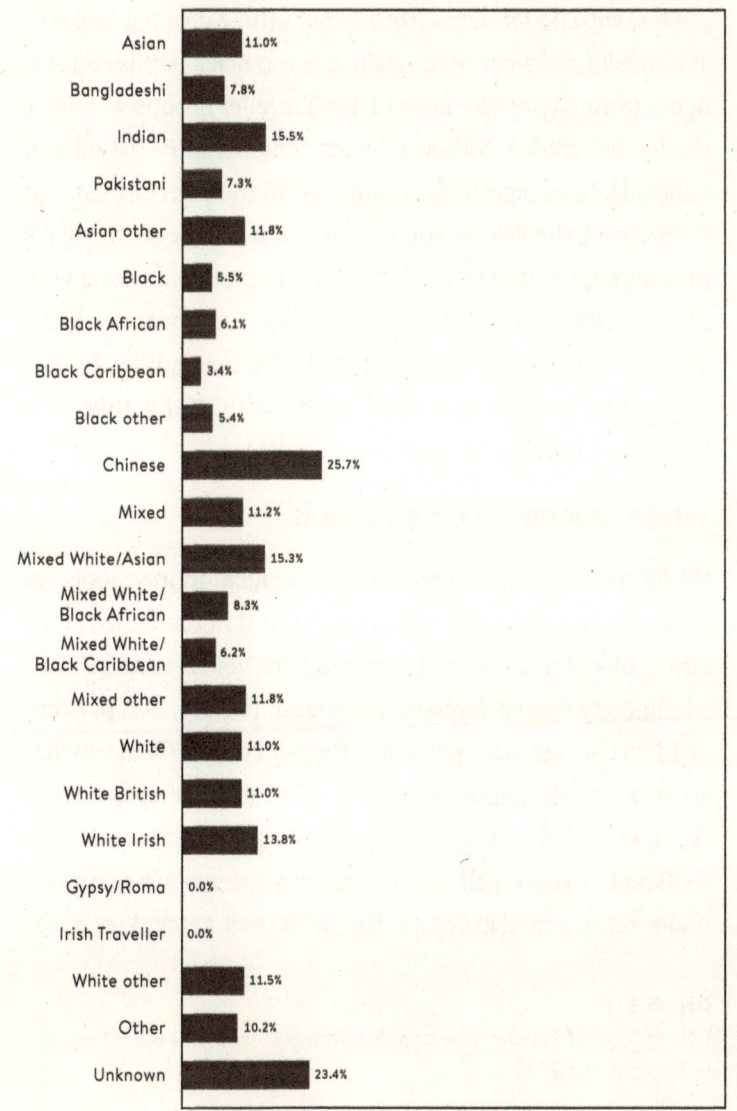

Traveller groups were the least likely to get at least three A grades, with no students from either ethnic group doing so – at a shocking 0.0 per cent. Again, it is the Black pupils and students from Gypsy/Roma and Irish Traveller groups who have the lowest grades, followed by students from Pakistani and Bangladeshi backgrounds. Compared to their performance at GCSE level, the White group as a whole has done better. Black African pupils have fared less well, however, and, along with Black Caribbean and Mixed White/Black Caribbean students, are among the most disadvantaged. The inequalities in outcomes for these groups, which start with GCSEs, thus continue to be reflected in A level results.[12]

White Teachers, White Schools

While around a third of the student population in schools are from an ethnic minority background, this is not reflected in the ethnic mix of teachers and head teachers, who tend to be overwhelmingly from a similar background. In 2019, 85.7 per cent of all teachers in state schools in England were White, which is an over-representation compared with the working-age population as a whole (78.5 per cent according to the 2011 Census). As Graph 3 shows, all ethnic minority groups are massively under-represented in comparison with their percentage in the

Graph 3
Percentage of teachers by population workforce and ethnic group in England for 2019

▪ Teacher workforce
▪ Working age population (2011)

Source: 'School workforce in England: November 2019', *Ethnicity Facts and Figures*, GOV.UK

Percentage of teachers by population workforce and ethnic group in England

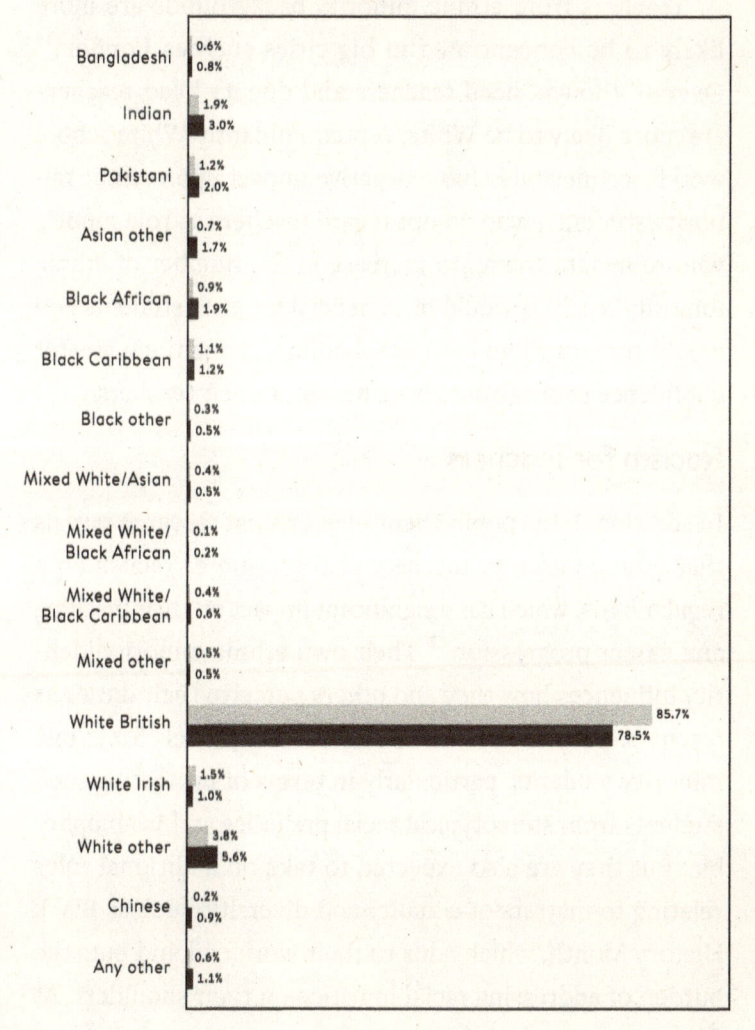

Ethnic group	Population	Workforce
Bangladeshi	0.6%	0.8%
Indian	1.9%	3.0%
Pakistani	1.2%	2.0%
Asian other	0.7%	1.7%
Black African	0.9%	1.9%
Black Caribbean	1.1%	1.2%
Black other	0.3%	0.5%
Mixed White/Asian	0.4%	0.5%
Mixed White/Black African	0.1%	0.2%
Mixed White/Black Caribbean	0.4%	0.6%
Mixed other	0.5%	0.5%
White British	85.7%	78.5%
White Irish	1.5%	1.0%
White other	3.8%	5.6%
Chinese	0.2%	0.9%
Any other	0.6%	1.1%

national working-age population. The school workforce is predominantly White and, as other data shows, female.[13]

Teachers from ethnic minority backgrounds are more likely to be concentrated in big cities such as London.[14] Overall, though, head teachers and deputy head teachers are more likely to be White. A predominantly White school workforce inevitably has a negative impact upon ethnic minority students, who do not regard teachers as role models who represent them. An increase in the number of ethnic minority teachers would be beneficial for such students and would support them in their schooling, giving them greater confidence to speak out about racism to their teachers.

Racism for Teachers

In addition to the pupils themselves, recent research reveals that ethnic minority teachers also encounter racism on a regular basis, which has a significant impact on their teaching and career progression.[15] Their own ethnic minority identity influences how they and others perceive their duties as teachers. They too see themselves as role models for ethnic minority students, particularly in terms of protecting such students from stereotypical racial prejudice and Islamophobia. But they are also expected to take on additional roles relating to matters of equality and diversity, such as Black History Month, which adds to their workload and puts the burden of addressing racial injustice on their shoulders. At the same time, whether out of conscious or unconscious bias by fellow teachers, as my research has found, they are not encouraged to apply for promotion, often being told they are not good enough or that they do not have the qualities needed to be a leader. This has a significant impact on their self-esteem and contributes to their considering leaving the profession.[16] Research suggests that ethnic minority teachers are best placed to teach in culturally responsive ways, but within this, they have to negotiate their own role in a predominantly White environment.[17] Teaching in a culturally responsive way ensures a student-centred approach to learning, which helps unpick how a student's cultural background and identity, and particularly the influence of racism, has affected their educational experience. However, ethnic minority teachers also experience what amounts to racial 'battle fatigue', characterized by 'the psychological, emotional, physiological energy and time related cost of fighting against racism'.[18] Such pressures take their toll and can be a contributing factor in why they might not being recommended for promotion to a leadership role instead of their White colleagues, as well as making them more likely to leave the teaching profession due to stress.[19]

According to a Runnymede Trust report from 2019: 'Structural barriers such as racism, including assumptions about capabilities based on racial/ethnic stereotypes, were everyday experiences for ethnic minority teachers. In particular, ethnic minority teachers spoke about an invisible glass ceiling and widespread perception among senior leadership teams that ethnic minority teachers, "have a certain level and don't go beyond it".'[20] Such processes work to reinforce schools as predominantly White spaces, with pupils being taught by White teachers. This impacts on the lack of ethnic minority role models for all pupils and reinforces the idea that the teaching workforce is and should be White.

Ethnic minority teachers also report a lack of clarity and transparency on recruitment and promotion processes.[21] A recent survey conducted by the National Association of Schoolmasters Union of Women Teachers found that, out of 400 ethnic minority teachers, 59 per cent said they had encountered on a daily basis attempts to belittle them for their racial identity and 46 per cent said they were not confident about reporting incidents of racism to their managers.[22] The impact this has on young ethnic minority people is that they too are less likely to want to choose teaching as a career. The knock-on effect is, of course, on ethnic minority pupils, who will suffer in the long term, as they will not be taught by a diverse teaching body and will not feel their needs are represented or supported in the classroom.

In addition to being taught a White curriculum, ethnic minority students are left feeling that the education system as a whole does not serve them or their needs. This has a marked effect on their schooling and level of academic achievement, which in turn affect future life opportunities and social mobility. In order to diversify the school workforce, the government must commit to increasing funding and support to encourage those from ethnic minority backgrounds to take up teaching as a career, particularly in relation to providing pupils with positive role models. In addition, clear guidelines are needed to address structural, institutional and individual forms of racism, along with a recognition that the lack of career progression has a significant impact on ethnic minority teachers who want to pursue leadership roles.

Everyday Racism at School

Between 2016 and 2021, schools recorded more than 60,000 racist incidents that had occurred at their premises. These were defined as 'any situation perceived to be racist by the alleged victim or any other person, including unintentional racism'. This is probably just the tip of the iceberg, as, in 2012, schools were advised by the government that they had no legal duty to report racist incidents to local authorities, and in 2017, they were no longer obliged to record any form of racist bullying.[23]

As a result, no accurate data is available on the numbers of racist incidents that take place in schools. Furthermore, those that are recorded are done so at the schools' discretion. This suggests that schools have an inaccurate picture of the level or type of racism that is taking place under their watch. This inconsistent approach disadvantages ethnic minority pupils and leaves them in a vulnerable position, because if schools are not recording incidents of racism, they are also unlikely to have measures in place to address racism effectively.

Despite these gaps in the data, we know that ethnic minority students experience racism in schools on a daily basis. There is evidence to suggest that it takes many different forms.[24] Ethnic minority pupils encounter racism from both their peers and teachers. Sometimes it can be direct and overt, such as being subject to racist name-calling; at other times it can be covert, such as through individual microaggressions or insidious systemic and institutional inequality. Recent research conducted by the YMCA, based on a survey of focus groups consisting of 557 Black people aged 16–30, found that young Black people experienced racism in every aspect of their lives, particularly at school and in the workplace.[25] The overwhelming majority of respondents (95 per cent) said they had heard and witnessed the use of racist language at school, and 78 per cent had heard and witnessed it in the workplace.

Furthermore, 49 per cent felt that racism was the biggest barrier to achieving success at school and 50 per cent said that it was due to teacher perceptions and stereotypes of them as being perceived as 'too aggressive'.[26] A total of 54 per cent of respondents felt that they would be discriminated against during the recruitment process for a job. The findings also suggest that young Black people felt that they were more likely to be excluded or expelled from school compared with their White peers, which is confirmed in national data. They also felt that they would be placed in the lowest sets, regardless of their academic achievements. Recent data suggests that, in some local authorities, exclusion rates are up to six times higher for Black Caribbean students in English schools compared with their White peers. Gypsy, Roma and Traveller children are also more likely to be excluded, with Roma children nine times more likely to be suspended in some areas. Exclusion rates for mixed White/Black Caribbean students in some areas are four times higher than for their White peers.[27] Other examples of racism include Black children being racially abused and punished at school for their hairstyles.[28] The YMCA report also found that 49 per cent of young Black people felt they would have to change their hair in order to be accepted at school, a figure that rose to 82 per cent for Black university students. It is unsurprising, then, that racism encountered at school will affect an ethnic minority pupil's future experiences as an adult, leading to lower self-esteem and even depression.[29]

An Inclusive Curriculum?

While race is often at the forefront of public media attention (albeit negatively), it is rarely directly addressed in the classroom.[30] When race is discussed as a subject, it is often treated as an 'add-on', rather than an integral part of a lesson or module; and when it is taught, ethnic minorities are often represented in negative terms as 'victims' of their stories. The evidence indicates that, in Britain, our whole curriculum reflects the values and beliefs of White groups and, as we have seen, is taught by predominantly White teachers. One example of this is the teaching of British history in schools, which consistently ignores the contribution of ethnic minority groups and their own history. The British Empire is taught with a focus on national unity but without examining how the empire was built on the oppression of ethnic minorities. When slavery is taught, the focus is on White abolitionists rather than the impact of slavery on ethnic minorities. When the Second World War is covered, the number of ethnic minority soldiers who fought is not discussed, and the curriculum does not even mention the British civil rights, or Black Power, movement of the 1960s and 1970s. Schools are ill equipped to teach Black history,[31] often signalling their commitment to racial equality through one-off events such as Black History Month, rather than embedding Black history within the curriculum and culture of the school.

As a result, ethnic minority pupils do not see themselves,

or the stories of their ancestors, represented in history books. Instead, they are presented with a Whitewashed version of history that portrays White groups in positive and favourable terms. If the history of ethnic minorities continue to be treated as extraneous or marginal, then they will always be seen as outsiders in our schools and in our society. When teachers do consider teaching about race in the classroom, they often do so from a colour-blind perspective or do not provide a critical take on the subject, assuming that it does not affect people's lives, and they teach from a White viewpoint, using images and figures from White history,[32] rather than material that reflects ethnic minority experience.[33] This is myopic and counterproductive, as research has found that when teachers use a diverse range of materials to teach students, this has a positive impact on ethnic minority pupils, specifically in relation to their own history.[34]

Recently, there has been a more vocal challenge to the teaching of history from a colonial perspective. In 2021, just under 270,000 members of the British public signed a petition to teach Britain's colonial past as part of the compulsory curriculum.[35] The UK government still resists the call to do so, arguing that the curriculum is broad, balanced and flexible. In 2020, in her address to the House of Commons, Kemi Badenoch declared, 'our curriculum does not need to be decolonised, for the simple reason that it is not colonised'.[36] The following year, the CRED report characterized the decolonization movement as a negative force mostly concerned with banning White authors and pulling down statues, arguing that, in a post-racial United Kingdom, it was right to celebrate Britain's Commonwealth and heritage. In the future, children should be taught a 'new story' of the 'slave period not only being about profit and suffering but how culturally African people transformed themselves into a re-modelled African/Britain'.[37] Far from decolonizing the curriculum, the government seems to suggest that it is in urgent need of recolonization.

In the absence of any attempt by the government to change the curriculum and make it more inclusive, more than 660 schools have signed up to the diverse and anti-racist curriculum developed by Hackney Council in London.[38] It supplies material to any school across the country to teach pupils about the Windrush generation and about activism, identity and diversity in the arts and sciences. Other non-governmental initiatives include the Black Curriculum campaign, which also provides access to inclusive teaching resources.[39]

What children learn at school has a significant impact on how they view the world. Decolonization is important because it ensures that children are able to see all ethnic minority groups represented in a positive way and to understand the contribution they have made to the UK. One way of doing this could be to encourage collaboration between students of all ethnic backgrounds, with a focus on the experiences of ethnic minority students, in order to promote anti-racist learning in the classroom. This should directly inform teacher development and training so that an inclusive pedagogy – or method and practice of teaching – is at the heart of children's learning. Teachers themselves must consider their own teaching and examine the impact of colonialism on students and their learning, so that a diverse curriculum is the norm rather than an exception.

One way in which this can take place is by adopting a critical race perspective. If teachers were taught critical race theory, they would recognize that racism lies at the heart of our society and therefore should be central to the school curriculum as it has a significant impact on the educational experience of all students. It would also help White teachers understand how their ethnic minority colleagues have had to work to navigate the predominantly White world of education, and how more work is needed to create a more inclusive and diverse environment.[40] As we saw above, ethnic minority teachers are more likely to employ a culturally responsive approach in their teaching,[41] to act as positive role models for ethnic minority students, with high expectations of their students, and to challenge racial inequalities in the classroom.[42] Furthermore, such teachers are committed to encouraging their students to succeed and see themselves as key agents of change in this regard.[43] However, as I mentioned before, ethnic minority teachers also continue to experience racism from their colleagues and students, with many reporting that they receive little or no training on how to teach in ways that are responsive to race, diversity and inclusion.[44] Teachers generally remain unprepared and are offered little training on how to tackle race and racism at school.[45] My own research has found that White teachers are not taught how to examine their own positions of White privilege and Whiteness in relation to teaching race and racism in the classroom and dealing with incidents of racism.[46] A school curriculum that does not include the diverse history of different ethnic minority groups teaches and perpetuates White privilege, while reinforcing the superiority of White culture and history. We need to do more to support these teachers, so that they can be the agents for change that they wish to be – and receive the support they deserve from all their White colleagues – so that together they can drive a curriculum that is more inclusive and less hegemonic.

A Critical Race Pedagogy

While much of the teaching in the UK is lacking in terms of diversity and the inclusion of the culture and history of ethnic minority groups, in America the development of a critical race pedagogy – or a method of teaching race – has been used in classrooms since the post-civil rights era to challenge and question the Eurocentric Western power structures that continue to operate in educational settings.[47] Critical race pedagogy (based on critical race theory) places race and racism at the forefront of teaching to validate the experiences of ethnic minority students and challenge dominant cultural perspectives and ideologies.[48] This approach has proved to be very effective in the US as it foregrounds the experiences of ethnic minority students as a form of *empowerment to resist racism*[49] and includes an anti-racist and culturally responsive approach to teaching.[50] Such an approach confronts existing educational policies and curricula by questioning their focus on ethnic minorities as the problem, challenging their colour-blind perspective (which treats everyone the same, without reference to their race, culture or ethnicity) and openly interrogating White privilege.[51] Consequently, the experiences of ethnic minority students become central to inclusive teaching practices.[52] Placing the experiences of ethnic minority students at the forefront of this form of teaching ensures that they feel empowered as experts of their own history. By drawing on the experiential knowledge of ethnic minority students, students and teachers alike are able to evaluate incidents in their own lives in the context of their own educational experience and place in history.[53]

However, when the educational status quo is questioned, educators who challenge oppressive racist structures may face a variety of different challenges from White students and White educators.[54] This includes a denial of racism, a topic that can incite anger and resentment in White students.[55] I have argued elsewhere that such feelings of resentment are based on threats to White privilege and Whiteness.[56] Such feelings are triggered when White students feel they must defend the concept of a meritocracy and argue that they have achieved their successes purely through hard work, rather than favourable treatment or through a system that continues to perpetuate White privilege.[57] Some White students do not accept that educational (or other) structures are racist and, furthermore, deny a legacy and history of racist oppression, refusing to accept that individual students of colour may have *actually* experienced racism in the classroom.[58] This discourse of denial takes place when racism in the classroom is simply dismissed as bad behaviour and suggests that White students are unlikely to challenge a system that benefits them personally and from which they derive immense privilege.[59] A critical race pedagogy challenges precisely this, as it highlights how educational structures perpetuate racism and racist practices in the classroom. It also ensures that the staff body is diverse and representative of different ethnic minorities, in order that students of colour are exposed from a young age to role models from their own ethnic background and an inclusive group of teachers.[60]

My research has shown how schooling in Britain explicitly works to serve and uphold Whiteness and White privilege through teacher representation and the curriculum. The experiences of ethnic minority students and teachers are understood, contextualized and interpreted within the White racial space of schools, which are populated by predominantly White teachers, White administrative staff and White students. In a predominantly White educational system, the existence of racism is thus denied, overlooking the longstanding history of struggle for equality in Britain. Our history of educational inequality has shaped the context in which ethnic minority students and teachers are portrayed as 'others' and 'outsiders'. In the following section, I will demonstrate how this is manifested in the daily experiences of children at school.

Hillside School* and the Normalization of Racism

Between 2019 and 2021, I conducted research at a secondary school to explore students' experiences of racism in our education system today. I carried out thirty-two interviews with pupils from different ethnic minority groups in years 11, 12 and 13 (ages 16–18), all of whom were either taking their GCSEs or in the first or second year of their A level studies. The school is located just outside a large city in the south east of England. In the past, it was predominantly White but had recently seen a significant increase in the number

---

* The name of the school and the names of its pupils are all pseudonyms.

CHAPTER 2

of students from a Black, Asian or Eastern European background. I conducted interviews over a two-year period, between 2019 and 2021, before and after the eruption of the global Black Lives Matter movement. What follows are excerpts from my interviews, which demonstrate what I discovered about race and education in the school at that time.

ACCEPTABLE RACISM: 'JUST GET OVER YOURSELF'

When I spoke to the students, all of them talked about the overt racism they had experienced at school. According to them, racism was not hidden, but out in the open. Ryan, who was from a Black Caribbean background, said that this was related to the fact that there were not many ethnic minority students at the school, so the White students had 'strength in numbers'.

> I get called names all the time; it varies from me being the 'darkie' in the class who is called upon to comment on everything to do with race – like anything about Black music or that I might know where to buy weed like I'm some kind of drug dealer. It happens because there's not many of us who are different in the class - or the school - so all the White kids think it's cool to say offensive things to us, and then they get away with it. It's because there's more of them [*White students*], they're in the majority and we're not. So it means we can't do much to challenge it [*racism*].

Ryan described his friendship group as 'mostly White', including two Asian girls, but on the whole, he was in the minority. He referred to a specific incident where his friends would often use racial slurs towards him, and when he complained to them about this, he was seen as being 'too sensitive' and told to 'get over' himself.

> I hear my friends even say racist things all the time! They seem to forget that I'm not White and that [*names of two female friends*] are Indian – are they so ignorant? There was a time when they would call me the N-word and they thought it was cool. I told them I didn't like it, and they just laughed at me and said I was too sensitive and needed to get over myself. That hurt a lot because I felt I should have said more, kicked up a fuss, but I was too embarrassed to say anything because I thought: they're my friends and I don't want to draw attention to myself. I kind of hated myself for that.

Ryan described how these friends who used racial slurs simultaneously declared their anti-racism on social media after the murder of George Floyd.

> I was very confused because these same friends were the ones who were saying that they thought it was really bad about what happened to George Floyd; they would use the N-word to me and then they would put #BlackLivesMatter on their Snapchat stories like they were really right-on anti-racists. To me, it felt kind of insulting; they were putting it on their social media stories because everyone else was and it was seen as the cool thing to do – yet they didn't see their racism towards me as being a problem or as being two-faced.

Similar themes were also highlighted by Juliette, who was of White and Indian heritage. Her friends often called her

CHAPTER 2

derogatory and racist names such as 'Paki', which they described as mere 'banter'. When she complained, her friends also responded by telling her that she was too sensitive and it was a 'joke'.

> All of my friendship group is White; I'm the only non-White person in the group and my friends call me racist names all the time. When I did mention it to them, they just laughed and said they didn't mean it because they're not racist. It's just banter and it's a joke, they said. I felt very hurt by this and also felt ashamed of my heritage and then felt embarrassed that I felt ashamed. It was because I wanted to be accepted in that group. Part of that is because I don't have much choice in the friends I can have here because it's mainly White – we are in the minority, so there isn't any choice. If I don't want to be on my own and have friends, then I have to put up with it.

Juliette described how her friends made her feel ashamed of her mixed-heritage identity:

> When I thought about it, I knew it was my friends who made me feel ashamed. I'm not ashamed of my heritage, it's who I am, but I wanted to be accepted and they made me feel bad about my mixedness. They also say they're not racist, but they use racist words all the time, but then if we were out somewhere and someone was racist **to me**, I know they would stick up for me. They don't see their own behaviour as being racist, they see it as a joke, but in other people they see it as racist. I think maybe they see me as White or forget that I'm mixed. [*original emphasis*]

Echoing Ryan's observation, Juliette also spoke about how her friends did not see themselves as racist and would call others out for being so.

> If they were called racist, they would be so offended by that because they don't see themselves as being racist in any way. But they think it's OK to use racist slurs against me and then go on Black Lives Matter marches and be publicly vocal against racism.

Despite their experiences, neither Ryan nor Juliette felt comfortable complaining to the school about the racism they had encountered. However, Rohit, who was British Indian, described complaining about an incident that happened when he first started at the school.

> One of the younger kids in year 7 [*aged twelve*] called me 'the brown boy' and I went a bit crazy, I admit. I ran over to him and was so angry and I asked him what he said, and he got kinda scared. The teachers got involved and they phoned my parents. I think the teachers were OK about it, but I don't think it made any difference, to be honest. The boy was just told off and he would probably use that [*phrase*] again.

For these ethnic minority students, racism was an everyday occurrence and something they simply had to put up with. The racism they encountered on a daily basis was part of their 'normal' school experience. By dismissing racist slurs as 'banter', White students at the school wielded their White privilege as a form of power to ensure that ethnic minority students *knew their place*. At the same time, White students justified their racism at school by displaying public support for anti-racism through #BlackLivesMatter on social media. For them, there was acceptable racism – that took place inside the school – and unacceptable racism, that took place outside the school. They felt it was acceptable to say racial slurs to ethnic minority students because they were their friends, while at the same time they condemned racism on a wider level by rallying behind the global Black Lives Matter protests that provided them with social status through social media sites.

The Whiteness and White identity of staff and students also worked to exclude students from ethnic minority backgrounds in different ways. By leaving this behaviour unpunished, the staff upheld this idea of 'acceptable' and 'unacceptable' racism and perpetuated a discourse of denial on the presence of racism at the school. According to respondents, the staff also reproduced existing societal racial inequalities at the school through the use of racial profiling and stereotyping. This was reinforced by the curriculum and government policies such as Prevent, which create hierarchies of different cultural practices in which Whiteness always is always positioned at the top. Such a racial hierarchy excludes students of different ethnic minority backgrounds to varying degrees, and places ethnic minority pupils *in opposition to* White students.

Racist language always confirms and reaffirms the normative hegemonic practices of society through Whiteness and White privilege. By silencing students' complaints about racial slurs, and failing to acknowledge the existence of overt racism, the school affirmed the importance of Whiteness. *Individual* acts of racism were thus a result of structural and institutional racism perpetuated at the school. As such, the school *enabled* White students to reinforce their sense of White privilege by maintaining hierarchical structures of race. They were *complicit* in this process.

RACIAL STEREOTYPES

The students I spoke to also discussed how the teachers' views of ethnic minority students conformed to specific stereotypes, and how they expected them to be the 'mouthpieces for all ethnic minorities'. Farah, who was Pakistani and the only ethnic minority student in her class, reflected on how she was picked on by the teacher in a religious education class because she was from an ethnic minority.

> It was quite embarrassing really. We were talking about differences in society and how the Black Lives Matter movement has made everyone think about racial injustice, and when Miss J. mentioned it, she just looked at me and everyone else did too. She volunteered me to talk about differences and I was so embarrassed. She put me on the spot and asked me about the racism I experienced. When I told my dad, he was very angry and wanted to phone the school, but I didn't let him. It was the way she just assumed that I would want to talk about it in front of the whole class publicly – just because I am the only Asian person in the class.

Many students who had experienced racism did not want to make formal complaints because they were afraid of drawing attention to their difference and feared reprisals from their peers and their friendship groups. As Juliette observed:

> I already look different to everyone around here, so why do I want to draw more attention to myself by complaining about it? It will only come back on me, because I will be seen as overly sensitive and making a drama out of something they don't think is a thing.

Racist behaviour is often defined as a form of bullying and included in anti-bullying policies. The behaviour policy at Hillside School, however, consisted of a four-page document that did not mention the word racism once. Instead, it referred to 'harassment' and 'respect'. There was no indication of how pupils would be punished if they used racist language. Instead, the policy stated that any 'bad behaviour' would result in a permanent or fixed-term exclusion. In addition, the school also had an 'equality and diversity policy' that related *only* to the staff and not to the students. My research in general has found that making complaints about racism rarely has any effect, resulting in little change in policy or student behaviour. When incidents of racism are raised, these are often dismissed as 'bad behaviour', with a refusal to acknowledge racism, and White students themselves don't regard their own behaviour as racist and instead blame ethnic minority pupils for being overly sensitive. In this process, those making the complaints (the victims) are deemed the problem. Behaviour policies (which do not include any reference to racism) are a simple 'tick-box' exercise in which racism is either ignored or dismissed and rarely proven.[61] In this way, education is a White space in which racism is either ignored or excused. Racism becomes and is a normal reality for ethnic minority pupils in their schooling experience.

Jayden, who was of mixed White and Black ethnicity, described this process when his parents complained about the racism he experienced in year 11 (aged sixteen).

> There was an incident when one of the boys said he didn't want our school changing and getting more mixed ethnically because he said it was better for some schools to stay as they were and it was best for the area. When I challenged him on this, he said something like, you and your natty-hair friends will just then all stick together and be in a gang. At the time I didn't think anything of it, but my dad went to the school and complained. But it kind of backfired because the teacher said it was unacceptable what the kid had said, but she said it didn't have anything to do with race. This annoyed my dad so much. After that, I had to be careful about my own behaviour because all the teachers knew what had happened and **I felt I was the one being watched and punished** for it. So, it probably wasn't worth complaining in the first place. [*original emphasis*]

Jayden went on to describe how complaining about racism made little if any difference to the regular occurrence of racism he experienced, specifically because the behaviour was not defined as racist or even punished.

> It made no difference when we complained because the racism just carried on, no difference at all. It was sometimes hidden, but mostly it was out in the open. The boys – and girls – who used racist language did it because it made them look big and important, and they knew it was annoying me and upsetting me, but they carried on

anyway. It's also because they didn't get punished for it, because the teachers said it wasn't racist. That was why they carried on, because they knew the teachers wouldn't say anything to them.

Many of the pupils I interviewed discussed how White students used racism, through racist slurs, as a 'badge of honour', a form of power and control. When complaints about racism were made, little changed and, consequently, ethnic minority students stopped complaining because they could no longer see any point in doing so. As Jayden said:

After a while, you kind of just get used to it. I can't be bothered to go through all that rigmarole of complaining and nothing changing. What's the point?

When teachers fail to interpret racist behaviour as racist – for example, by dismissing it as 'banter' or 'just teenagers being teenagers' – they are failing to acknowledge that racial slurs are in effect acts of symbolic violence. Ann Ferguson, an American philosopher who has conducted research into the experiences of male Black pupils at school, defines this as 'painful, damaging, mortal wounds inflicted by the wielding of words, symbols and standards'.[62] White students use racial slurs as part of the cultural and normative hegemony of the school, and it is through this symbolic violence that White students assert their White privilege and perpetuate White supremacy. The leading French sociologist Pierre Bourdieu defines it as 'a *gentle* violence, imperceptible and invisible even to its victims, exerted through the most part by the purely symbolic channels of communication and cognition (more precisely, misrecognition), recognition or even feeling'.[63] I emphasize the word 'gentle' because symbolic violence in schools through name-calling is interpreted by White students as unthreatening because it is seen purely as 'banter' or a joke. The teachers' disengagement from this 'gentle violence' perpetuates White privilege and the sense of 'otherness' felt by ethnic minority students as part of their everyday school experience. It results in the school environment being a *White* space in which a racial discourse of exclusion is normal. As a result, it creates a space in which White students are empowered to overtly denigrate and oppress ethnic minority students, whose protestations are silenced or ignored.

'IT'S COOL TO BE BLACK (OR BROWN)'

Despite this racism at the school, ethnic minority students also discussed how their White friends adopted Black cultural identities through their dress and language. Priya, who was of British and Indian heritage, described it as 'White kids pretending to be Black to look cool'.

> I think it's mad in how they want to be Black but, at the same time, they use quite offensive racist language. They use the N-word and the P-word and they try and dress like they're from 'da hood', as they say. They say things like 'wha gwan' like they know what it means and where it comes from. To me they pretend to be Black because they think it's cool; they do it to be different because they don't want to be just a basic White girl or White boy. But at the same time, they would never want to be Black because they don't want the racism

which comes with being Black. I find that offensive and insulting.

Priya also spoke about how her White female friends used fake tans to look brown and how they commented on her skin colour.

> They all go and get their fake tans and tell me, 'Oh, look at your lovely skin, you don't need to get a tan,' but they think I think that's cool, but I don't. I feel sorry for them because they want to hide their Whiteness, but they won't want all the disadvantages we have of being brown. We can't hide our brownness or our blackness. We can't have it both ways, like they can. They want to put on a fake tan to look brown, but I can't change the colour of my skin but they can.

White students are able to use their Whiteness as a form of privilege at all times, yet at the same time they can pick and choose when to adopt the language, mannerisms and appearance of ethnic minority students, to appear 'cool'. The power of the White gaze – seeing things from a White point of view – and the power of Whiteness enables White students to select different aspects of ethnic minority identity that they define as 'cool', without experiencing the racism that ethnic minority students encounter on a daily basis. This sense of entitlement works as a form of White privilege to perpetuate the superior position of being White, enabling White students to have the *choice* to 'try on' selective elements of ethnic minority identity to give them status among their peers.

As we see here, racialized stereotypes are used to position ethnic minority students as 'other', while also identifying some of their perceived characteristics as 'desirable' and 'cool', such as language, dress and appearance. White pupils assume they are entitled to appropriate such characteristics for their own self-gratification. At the same time, they still label ethnic minority students as 'undesirable' and disrespect them by casually deploying racist remarks and telling them to 'get over themselves' when they complain. Their racialized bodies are thus understood as either acceptable and attractive or unattractive and unacceptable, according to the vagaries of White students.

(WHITE) EDUCATIONAL ACHIEVEMENT

The students I interviewed at the school also described subtle forms of racism in relation to how they were perceived by their teachers. They spoke about the number of teachers who showed overt favouritism towards White students. As Priya commented:

> I'm not pally pally with the teachers; I'm not their best friend like the White girls are. The teachers show favouritism to all the White middle-class, well-spoken students, because they see them as being good pupils, even though they're not that bright. They see me as trouble because I question them, but when the White kids do it, they see them as being inquisitive.

White, middle-class students are seen as the 'ideal' students. Ethnic minority students who do not fit into this mould, or who question the teachers, are seen as 'troublesome', despite their academic achievements. As Anya, an Indian student, observed:

> The teachers and the students have stereotypes of Black students and Asian students, and they expect you to behave like that stereotype. A lot of the White students think that the Black boys smoke weed and are hard, but that is just a stereotype, and I think teachers have stereotypes as well. The whole system works on those stereotypes; it just perpetuates what the teachers think is a good student – those who are White.

Being bright at this school did not provide ethnic minority students with a safety net and protection from racism and White privilege. Ethnic minority students were often compared with White middle-class students, who were used as a measure of a success. This is an example of how a normative White framework defines what academic achievement is in such a school. In addition, the stereotypes about Black boys being aggressive and overly masculine, as well as not being interested in academic success, serve to justify the racist behaviour towards them by White students and White teachers. This shows how racialized discourses of the 'other' are used in schools to divide and rule and to separate the 'good', or White, students from the 'bad', or ethnic minority, students.

The types of racism that emerge in British schools are similar to those described by sociologists Eduardo Bonilla-Silva and Tyrone Forman as a new race talk that 'has emerged in the reproduction of White supremacy and allows Whites to appear "not racist", preserve their privileged status, blame Blacks for their lower status and criticize any institutional approach such as affirmative action that attempts to ameliorate racial inequality'.[64] White groups can excuse their racist behaviour, because such behaviour is perceived as part of the normality of society. It is not unusual or exceptional; it is not questioned but part of the everyday behaviour of White groups. In this sense, racism has become normalized. What seems extraordinary here is not that racism happens in schools, but that it happens *openly*.

The Consistent and Implicit Presence of Racism

From my research at Hillside School, along with other research that I have discussed in this chapter, it is clear that secondary schools in the UK remain predominantly White spaces, where the majority of teachers, head teachers and the school population are White. Beyond this, the schools also create an environment in which ethnic minorities are seen as 'other', and are confronted by a culture that caters only for White students – in the lack of ethnic minority teachers, a curriculum that centres on the White experience and a toleration of the kind of day-to-day behaviour that allows racism to flourish. Racism is thus an everyday occurrence for ethnic minority pupils, and a constant and readily identifiable feature of British schools. When ethnic minority students complain about racism, they are silenced. Such silencing is used as a form of power to keep Black and minority ethnic students *in their place*.

While the White students I interviewed recognized the importance of global movements towards racial equality, such as Black Lives Matter, they were also complicit in normalizing racism in their school. In turn, ethnic minority students recognized that the school's structures and processes created a climate in which racism was accepted. Despite the presence of anti-bullying policies, the school was complicit in perpetuating racism, which was either dismissed or went unpunished. From this, we can see how schools work as enclaves of White privilege that propagate Whiteness as the dominant culture in our society. They are complicit in this process. Schools like Hillside must acknowledge racism openly, and make significant changes to their culture and rules in order to counter the everyday racism experienced by ethnic minority pupils and to create an environment in which they are able to feel safe and can flourish.

CHAPTER 3
Higher Education
'Unspoken White Noise'

Historically, in the UK, attending university was a privilege reserved for the limited few. In order to gain a place at a higher-education institution before the mid-twentieth century, one would have to be either exceptionally bright and lucky, or, most likely, a student from one of the most selective private schools – which would usually be for elite members of society: those who were male, privileged and White.

However, in recent years this has changed dramatically. The higher-education entry rate among eighteen-year-olds increased from 24.7 per cent in 2006, to 30.7 per cent in 2015, reaching a peak at 38.2 per cent in 2021, before falling slightly to 37.5 per cent in 2022.[1] Yet despite these successful attempts at widening participation, attendance at certain universities continues to be divided along race and class lines. How this happens, and how racism plays out in higher education, is what we will explore in this chapter.

The Dearing Report: Widening Participation

Following the publication of the Dearing Report in 1997,[2] the New Labour government introduced a widening-participation agenda intended to increase the numbers of disadvantaged students entering higher education. Tony Blair set a target of 50 per cent of young people entering higher education in the twenty-first century.[3] Since then, the focus has shifted from expanding access to higher education to student retention and outcomes.[4] This was in part related to the introduction by New Labour of student fees and loans. Although the fees were, at that time, capped at £1,000, this significantly shifted the costs of higher education from public taxation to private funding by the students themselves.

The transition to regarding students as consumers of education resulted in a shift in focus at universities towards providing a value-for-money experience, mirroring a trend in other consumer activity beyond education. Towards the end of their final term in office, Labour commissioned the Browne Review to consider all aspects of higher education, including how universities should be funded. The review recommended lifting the cap on student fees while providing financial support for students from families earning below £60,000 per year. It also noted that there had been 'less progress on widening access to the most selective institutions, for students from lower income backgrounds, despite efforts by these institutions to improve the situation'.[5]

In 2010, the Conservative–Liberal Democrat coalition government set out their plans to widen participation by focusing on 'unlocking social mobility', which was meant to ensure access to higher education for marginalized groups.[6] Drawing on the Browne Review findings, the cap on fees was increased to £9,000, to be funded through student loans repayable on the basis of future earnings. This was followed by the publication of the white paper *Higher Education: Students at the*

Heart of the System, which set out plans to improve social mobility through the introduction of a National Scholarship Programme.[7] This provided financial support for students from low-income backgrounds through bursaries while they were at higher-education institutions. In 2014, the Higher Education Funding Council for England and the Office for Fair Access introduced their national strategy for widening participation, to ensure 'that all those with the potential to benefit from higher education have equal opportunity to participate and succeed, in an institution that best fits their potential, need and ambitions for employment or further study'.[8]

In practice, higher-education policy by successive governments has not delivered on its aims of widening participation. Despite the increasing numbers of students in higher education, vast inequalities still persist. My research has found that, in particular, students from working-class and ethnic minority backgrounds are much more likely to attend a less prestigious, post-1992 university.[9] Meanwhile, students from a White middle-class background are more likely to attend one of the elite, Russell Group universities.[10] Moreover, although attending a more prestigious university adds value when entering the job market, the fees are the same as for a less prestigious institution. Bearing in mind the fact that students from poorer backgrounds are more likely to borrow money to fund their studies, and thus incur greater debt than wealthier students,[11] from my research, it is clear that ethnic minority students from a poor, non-traditional working-class background are the ones who end up paying more while gaining less from their time at university compared with those from a White middle-class background.[12]

In 2015, the Conservative government published the green paper *Fulfilling Our Potential: Teaching Excellence, Social Mobility and Student Choice*, which set out specific targets on reducing inequality in education by 2020.[13] This included doubling the proportion of students from disadvantaged backgrounds and increasing by 20 per cent the numbers of students from ethnic minority groups entering higher education. According to the report published in 2016 by the Social Mobility Commission: 'universities have a key role to play in improving social mobility, and . . . while many institutions have done good work, the sector as a whole needs to raise the scale of its ambition'.[14] The report also acknowledged significant inequalities in access to higher education:

> A steep socioeconomic gradient in access means that being born into a wealthy family is still a high predictor of accessing the most prestigious universities, gatekeepers to the highest paying jobs. While a private school student has a 1 in 20 chance of entering Oxbridge, a student from a poor background still has odds closer to 1 in 1,500.[15]

This is shocking, if hardly surprising, for it emphasizes how wealth can be used to buy privilege, and how it is reproduced from school, through higher education to the labour market. It also shows clearly how education is no longer a right, but indeed has become – and, perhaps, always has been – a privilege.

In 2017, it was announced that a new independent body, the Office for Students (OfS), would be introduced to 'promote equality of opportunity' to ensure that universities did not just increase the numbers of students from disadvantaged backgrounds, but also provided evidence that they would be supported while at university and beyond. This would include addressing drop-out rates and boosting the number of students finding employment in the labour market.[16] In 2019, the OfS focused its attention on addressing student outcomes,[17] with evidence to suggest that students from ethnic minority backgrounds were less likely to do well at university and gain a good degree, compared with their White peers.[18] While the OfS served a useful purpose in highlighting important inequalities such as this, it also simply reinforced the role of the student as consumer. In the process of regulating and controlling university standards, it has turned higher education into a capitalist enterprise selling services, goods and commodities for financial gain. This includes its coercive function of financially penalizing universities that do not adhere to its rigid rules. Put simply, the OfS has turned higher education into a business.

The Experience of Ethnic Minority Students in Higher Education

Ethnic minority students remain disadvantaged at every stage of their higher education, as my research has shown, affecting their access to different types of higher-education institutions and their time in higher education and leading to inequalities in progress and outcomes compared with White students.[19] While the numbers of ethnic minority students attending higher-education institutions has seen a year-on-year increase, they remain under-represented in selective, more prestigious institutions such as Oxford and Cambridge and other Russell Group universities.[20] Ethnic minority students are less likely to leave higher education with a 2:1 or first-class degree compared with their White peers, and they are more likely to drop out of higher education.[21] My research has also found that ethnic minority students regularly report encountering covert and overt forms of racism from their peers and lecturers, including stereotypical assumptions based on their ethnic identity. Black male students are seen as aggressive and intimidating, South Asian female students are regarded as passive and obedient and Muslim students as potential terrorists. Furthermore, ethnic minority students do not feel the curriculum represents their experiences, but instead favours those from a White background.[22]

In 2019–20, in a survey by Advance HE, a charity promoting excellence in higher education, a total of 98.3 per cent of all UK-domiciled students disclosed their ethnicity, of which 25.3 per cent identified as Black, Asian or minority ethnic (or BAME, the term used by Advance HE in their yearly statistical reports) – see Table 1.[23] Since 2003/2004, there has been an 82.3 per cent increase in the numbers of students identifying as Black, Asian or from a minority ethnic background. There has been a year-on-year increase for students from all ethnic minority groups, but it is Asian and Black students who represent the most significant growth. Yet despite the increase in numbers, these students continue to be disadvantaged in higher education, particularly those from Black and Pakistani/Bangladeshi backgrounds.

Student Outcomes

There are differences in outcomes for ethnic minority students compared with White students. In 2019–20, as shown in Table 2, White students were more likely to receive a 2:1 or first-class degree (86.0 per cent) compared with 75.2 per cent

Ethnicity	No.	%
White	1,407,720	74.7
BAME total	477,355	25.3
Asian total	203,425	10.8
Bangladeshi	29,910	1.6
Indian	64,995	3.4
Pakistani	66,160	3.5
Other	42,360	2.2
Black total	144,035	7.6
African	109,390	5.8
Caribbean	27,265	1.4
Other	7,380	0.4
Chinese	15,785	0.8
Mixed	79,845	4.2
Other total	34,265	1.9
Arab	14,345	0.8
Other	19,920	1.1
All students	1,885,075	100

Table 1
UK-domiciled students by ethnic group, 2019–2020

Source: Advance HE, *Equality in Higher Education: Students Statistical Report 2021* (London: Advance HE, 2021)

of BAME students – indicating an awarding gap of 10.8 percentage points.* While there has been an increase in the numbers of Black and Asian students, it is Black and Pakistani/Bangladeshi students, as shown in Table 2, who remain the most disadvantaged in in terms of higher-degree outcomes. As Table 3 shows, BAME students are also less likely to complete their studies compared with White students (86.6 per cent compared with 90.0 per cent).[24]

In terms of graduate outcomes, inequalities for ethnic minority groups continue to persist. Fifteen months after completing their degrees, as Table 4 shows, White students were more likely to be in full-time employment (59.7 per cent) compared with those from ethnic minority backgrounds (51.6 per cent). Nearly twice as many ethnic minority leavers were more likely to be unemployed fifteen months after graduating, compared with White groups (9.7 per cent compared with 5.6 per cent). However, the proportion of ethnic minority graduates who were in some form of further study was higher compared with White groups (19.0 per cent compared with 17.4 per cent).[25]

As all the data shows, getting a degree does not necessarily improve life chances and future mobility for ethnic minority students. In fact, the inequalities they experience continue into the labour market. The reasons for this may be due to the racism they encounter from their peers and

---

* The degree-awarding gap is the difference in top degrees (a first or 2:1) awarded to different groups of students based on their prior educational achievement. In other words, it is a comparison of outcomes for like-for-like students. The largest differences are found by ethnic background, as shown in Table 2.

Ethnicity	No.	%
White	204,655	86.0
BAME total	58,750	75.2
Asian total	26,995	77.5
Bangladeshi	3,875	73.8
Indian	9,260	82.7
Pakistani	8,440	75.4
Other	5,420	75.2
Black total	14,725	66.3
African	11,140	65.9
Caribbean	2,885	68.6
Other	700	62.3
Chinese	2,115	83.8
Mixed	11,140	82.4
Other total	3,735	75.4
Arab	1,495	76.8
Other	2,240	74.5
All students	263,405	83.4

Table 2
UK-domiciled students by ethnic group and undergraduate qualifiers

Source: Advance HE, *Equality in Higher Education: Students Statistical Report 2021* (London: Advance HE, 2021)

Ethnicity	No.	%
White	237,860	75.2
BAME total	78,120	24.8
Asian total	34,850	11.0
Bangladeshi	5,250	1.6
Indian	11,195	3.5
Pakistani	11,190	3.5
Other	7,210	2.2
Black total	22,220	7.0
African	16,895	5.3
Caribbean	4,200	1.3
Other	1,125	0.3
Chinese	2,570	0.8
Mixed	15,530	4.5
Other total	4,950	1.5
Arab	1,945	0.6
Other	3,005	0.9
All students	315,980	100

Table 3
UK first-degree undergraduate qualifiers by ethnic group, 2019–2020

Source: Advance HE, *Equality in Higher Education: Students Statistical Report 2021* (London: Advance HE, 2021)

Full-time work	White no	White %	BAME total no	BAME total %
Professional full-time	109,430	47.2	26,645	40.2
Non-professional full-time	24,620	10.6	6,245	9.4
Unknown full-time	4,285	1.8	1,345	2.0
All full-time	138,335	59.7	39,235	51.6

Table 4
UK-domiciled graduate outcomes by leaving destination and ethnic group, 2019–2020

Source: Advance HE, *Equality in Higher Education: Students Statistical Report 2021* (London: Advance HE, 2021)

lecturers at university (as discussed below), the curriculum they study, and the marking and assessment practices of their institutions – which disadvantage them in relation to their White peers.

Racism in Higher-Education Institutions

Despite the much higher profile given to the issue in recent years, racism continues to persist in higher-education institutions. A recent report published by the Equality and Human Rights Commission (EHRC) found that racial harassment is commonly encountered by students on university campuses, with around a quarter of all ethnic minority students (24 per cent) reporting that they had experienced some form of racial harassment since starting their course, 20 per cent having been physically attacked and 56 per cent harassed in other ways. More worryingly, the report found that the higher-education sector does not fully understand how to address racism and staff and students lack the confidence in knowing how to deal with incidents of racism. This is further compounded by their not wanting to report racial harassment due to the university's inability to follow correct procedures for dealing with complaints.[26] Consequently, as my research has consistently found, ethnic minority staff and students are less likely to report racism if they feel their complaints are not taken seriously or dealt with adequately.[27]

According to a report published in 2020 by Universities UK, 'individual change, or change at a single university, is not enough. We must acknowledge the institutional racism and systemic issues that pervade the entire higher education sector, in all institutions, if we are to bring about meaningful change.'[28] Building on the earlier EHRC report into racial harassment, this report lists twelve recommendations for addressing systemic racism in higher-education institutions. These include developing strategies for dealing with racial harassment, collecting data on it and regularly reviewing policies and procedures, and ensuring that individuals are aware of the sanctions in place if they breach guidelines on expected behaviour (whether online or in person). Recent research carried out by the *Guardian*, based on freedom of information requests sent to 131 universities, revealed that students and staff made at least 996 formal complaints of racism between 2014 and 2019. Of these complaints, 367 were upheld, which resulted in at least 78 student suspensions/expulsions and 51 staff suspensions, dismissals and resignations. The investigation also found that significant numbers of ethnic minority staff and students were discouraged from making an official complaint and so dropped their allegations or instead settled for an informal resolution. In addition, White staff were often reluctant to acknowledge or address racism, dismissing racial slurs as mere 'banter' or a demonstration of their right to freedom of expression. Complaints were received from all sectors of higher education, including Russell Group and post-1992 universities.[29]

Of the 996 complaints, 461 were made against students (the majority of which were made by other students) and 535 were made against staff. Approximately half of the complaints made against staff were by students and 144 by fellow members of staff. The *Guardian* report also found that 'more than a quarter of the universities surveyed lacked centralised records of racism complaints. Some did not specifically record racist incidents, lumping them together with other forms of discrimination, harassment and bullying.' There was also some variation in how racism complaints were recorded, with some universities reporting that they had only started to record complaints in the last year or two and others reporting that they recorded them for either staff or students but not for both. Furthermore, only one university provided anti-racism training for all staff, while more than half did not provide any. These statistics are the tip of the iceberg and do not represent the full extent of racism in higher education. As my research has found, complaints procedures in higher education are often not fit for purpose, and when complaints about racism are made, the victims of racism are portrayed as villains for complaining about racism. In addition, complaints about racism are not taken at face value, and often dismissed as just a clash of personalities.[30]

I would argue that this data suggests that addressing racial harassment is not, and has never been, a priority for higher-education institutions. In my research, I have consistently found that racism continues to be a secondary concern for higher-education institutions compared with other issues, such as sexual harassment, for which universities have introduced more systematic procedures to deal with complaints (though these are also far from perfect).[31] The lack of simple, coherent guidelines for all higher-education institutions on how to address racial harassment suggests a piecemeal, ad hoc approach rather than delivering a clear message that failure to adhere to such guidelines would result in serious penalties – financial or otherwise. Just as the OfS has introduced penalties for higher-education institutions who fail to show how they have addressed the ethnic minority awarding gap, so too should penalties be introduced for higher-education institutions that fail to tackle systemic racism in their ranks. Exploring ways of combating endemic structural, institutional and individual racism should be seen as part of a long-term goal to create systemic change, the need for which has consistently been evidenced in my research.

Examples of racism in universities that affect ethnic minority students include a Black student at the University of Manchester being accused of 'looking like a drug dealer' and pinned to a wall by security guards during demonstrations about the university's handling of the coronavirus pandemic in November 2020,[32] and allegations of racism at St Andrews University that same year, in which thirty-eight students complained anonymously about the racism they experienced on campus, such as one Black student being called a 'negro'.[33] This shows how higher education is seen as a space in which it is fair game for White students and members of the university workforce to overtly vocalize and demonstrate their racism towards ethnic minority students. As in schools, White privilege manifests itself through White students believing such behaviour is acceptable, that it will go unchallenged and unpunished, and is supported by their peers.

Decolonizing the Curriculum?

In recent years, there have been renewed calls to address the ethnocentric White curriculum, often driven by student activism and protest. In 2014, UCL (University College London) set up a panel discussion, 'Why isn't my professor black?', to question the lack of Black professors in higher-education institutions.[34] This was followed a few months later by the 'Why is my curriculum white?' campaign that aimed to tackle the Eurocentric focus of academic studies and challenge the lack of diversity found in the reading and teaching content of the higher-education curriculum.[35]

Other movements addressing the exclusion and racism experienced by ethnic minority students have included the 'I, too, am Oxford' and 'I, too, am Harvard' campaigns, both dating from 2014. 'I, too, am Oxford' emphasizes how students of colour at Oxford are 'othered'. The campaign includes a demand that discussions about race are taken seriously and result in real institutional change for students. The movement grew from the 'Skin Deep' project, which involved photos of students displaying messages of how they felt about being a minority student at Oxford.[36] 'I, too, am Harvard' first began as a photo campaign highlighting the faces and voices of Black students at Harvard University: 'Our voices often go unheard on this campus, our experiences are devalued, our presence is questioned – this project is our way of speaking back, of claiming this campus, of standing up to say: We are here. This place is ours. We, TOO, are Harvard.'[37]

Other activist projects include the 'Rhodes Must Fall' movement, which began in 2015 with protests at the University of Cape Town demanding the removal of a statue of Cecil Rhodes, before spreading to other campuses in South Africa. A former prime minister of the Cape Colony in the late nineteenth century, Cecil Rhodes is now recognized as a White supremacist and colonial oppressor. The University of Cape Town subsequently removed his statue within a month of the campaign starting.

This campaign continued at the University of Oxford, where another statue of Rhodes remains on the side of the Rhodes building, part of Oriel College, in the High Street. The Rhodes building and statue were funded by Rhodes himself through financial provisions in his will. The statue is now seen as celebrating Rhodes racist legacy as a colonial oppressor, something that has been acknowledged since by the university. It is a legacy that has also been fostered through the prestigious 'Rhodes Scholarship', providing funding each year for 100 international students to study at Oxford. In June 2020, there were further protests against the statue following the Black Lives Matter protests. Academics have also been vocal about removing the statue, with more than a hundred academics refusing to give tutorials for students attending Oriel College. After commissioning a review of evidence, the governing body of Oriel College voted to formally the statue before applying for planning permission to have it taken down. However, the college later backtracked on its decision, citing prohibitive costs and complexities in the planning process. Instead, they erected a contextualizing plaque to provide some explanation of the sensitivity issues they faced.[38] Members of the 'Rhodes Must Fall' movement thus remain 'determined to decolonise the space, the curriculum and the institutional memory, and to fight intersectional oppression within Oxford'.[39]

Other prominent movements to address issues of race and racism include the Goldsmiths Anti-Racist Action campaign, founded by members of Goldsmiths College at the University of London, who held a 137-day sit-in occupying Deptford Town Hall. The sit-in ended on 27 July 2019, when campaigners agreed on a way forward with senior managers to address issues of racial inequality, which included decolonizing the curriculum and introducing 'cultural competency' training for all staff.[40]

'Decolonizing the curriculum', however, has since become an agenda item in which all higher-education institutions have been *forced* to demonstrate public displays of inclusion without making any significant or meaningful changes to their own racist practices. Following the murder of George Floyd, many higher-education institutions released statements on their websites and Twitter (now X) pages declaring their commitment to addressing racism. These emphasized they were not racist institutions and would take incidents of racism very seriously. For a brief period, social media was awash with statements along the lines of 'The University of X does not tolerate racism and supports the #BlackLivesMatter movement' or 'We stand against racism and our university will ensure that racism in any form is not tolerated'. Such rhetoric seemingly ignored the glaring evidence that these same universities were not addressing issues of race and racism in their own backyards. Universities with poor records of hiring ethnic minority lecturers and professors, with the worst awarding gaps in the UK and with a reputation of failing to support staff and students who had been racially harassed all declared their commitment to the cause. The obligatory branding of institutional social media feeds with #BlackLivesMatter slogans clearly served a number of useful functions for many universities. It was one means of distancing themselves from their own local racism by joining the global outrage at events in the US. Such public displays of anti-racism were also an effective marketing tool, allowing a university to align itself with the zeitgeist of anti-racist feeling. Keen to portray a *public* image of inclusion and be part of the 'historical moment', universities used George Floyd's murder and the Black Lives Matter protests for their own ends. Feminist theorist Sara Ahmed describes how the anti-racist rhetoric of universities are invariably 'nonperformatives': they are 'speech acts that commit the university to equality' but they '"work" precisely by not bringing about the effects that they name'.[41] By doing so, they give the illusion of anti-racism in such a way as to reproduce the racist structures at the heart of the institution.

Work on decolonization is not new. An early proponent of the concept was the francophone Afro-Caribbean thinker Frantz Fanon, who said that 'decolonization is always a violent phenomenon' that 'sets out to change the order of the world'.[42] Speaking about the occupation of Algeria by the French, as a supporter of the Algerian War of Independence, he saw political decolonization as a conflict between the colonizer and the colonized that calls for a 'complete calling into question of the colonial situation' in which 'the proof of success lies in a whole structure being changed from bottom up'.[43] So the process of decolonizing is a political act in which systems of power and knowledge are overtly challenged and transformed.

Calls to decolonize the curriculum in the UK grew after the Black Lives Matter protests in which universities were forced to rethink their White, ethnocentric approach. Campaigns such as the aforementioned 'Rhodes Must Fall' in Cape Town and Oxford highlighted and brought to people's attention the role that colonialism, empire and slavery play in shaping the curriculum and educational practices. The Black Lives Matter protests questioned higher education as a key site in which White, Western colonial scholarship is generated and considered the norm and where a Eurocentric White perspective governs academic learning. Despite the Black Lives Matter protests, in 2020 just a fifth of UK universities had committed to reforming their curricula due to the history of colonialism. In response to freedom of information requests sent out to universities, the *Guardian* found that, out of 128 universities, only 24 said they were committed to decolonizing the curriculum, with just 11 saying they were committed to reform across the whole institution.[44] Attempts to decolonize the curriculum after the Black Lives Matter protests were a result of senior management responding to a current 'moment' in which they were *forced* to address racial injustices. Yet again, addressing racism became a box-ticking exercise – this time in response to public demands – with a push to recruit more diverse fee-paying students.[45] In this way, universities are able to sell themselves as diverse and fair, with social justice and inclusion at the heart of their agendas – so that students (and their parents) would be more inclined to send their children to (pay for) such institutions. While there may be pockets of advancement in efforts to decolonize the curriculum (such as reforming reading lists and teaching practices), on the whole, it is business as usual. Consequently, universities drag their heels and do little to make any significant changes. In addition, there can be resentment from White colleagues if funding is diverted to address racial injustices rather than other inequalities that they feel are more worthy (relating to gender or sexuality, for instance). On the surface, universities show they are investing in decolonization but, in reality, the structure and institutions of White privilege and White supremacy remain intact and individual acts of racism go unchallenged.

Where universities have made any efforts to make reforms, they have tended to interpret 'decolonizing the curriculum' as diversifying and changing reading lists by adding ethnic minority authors, introducing modules about race and decolonization and attempting to diversify their workforce. Yet many of these attempts do little to challenge the larger racist structures, and the curriculum is expanded without a proper review of the cultural and historical context of the new material.[46] At the same time, some senior managers engage in attempts to decolonize the curriculum because it benefits them and their university more so than the groups at which it is aimed. According to Derrick Bell, these kinds of short-lived victories show interest convergence in action and reflect little or no progress in decolonizing the curriculum at all.[47] Instead, such changes at universities tend to converge with a particular historical moment, such as Black Lives Matter – and their requirement to keep up with cultural opinion and lure in more fee-paying students – but leave coloniality and White supremacy intact.

Transitions from Higher Education: The (White) Labour Market

Race also affects the type of university a student attends and the decisions they make after they graduate. As we saw above, White students are more likely to leave university with a 2:1 or first-class degree than their ethnic minority peers. They are also less likely to study at less prestigious, 'lower tariff', post-1992 universities, which tend to focus more on teaching than research.[48] My own research has found that one reason for this is that ethnic minority students (particularly those from Black and Pakistani/Bangladeshi backgrounds) are more likely to attend a local university owing to financial or cultural constraints.[49] Such institutions tend to be located in and around large cities, which reflect further regional inequalities owing to such areas being poorer and more socially deprived. Both before and after entering higher education, the same students face further disadvantages due to a lack of access to resources – social, cultural and economic – compared with their better-off White peers.[50] All of these factors have an impact on the decisions students make after they complete their studies, affecting how easily they can find a job, especially a well-paying one, with a knock-effect on social mobility and future life chances.

When ethnic minority students finish their studies in higher education, they face 'ethnic penalties' in the labour market. They are more likely to be employed in insecure jobs with lower pay compared with their White peers, with Black and Pakistani and Bangladeshi groups being the most disadvantaged. This is equally the case when socio-economic differences and degree outcomes have been taken into account.[51] When ethnic minority students do attend 'high-tariff' higher education institutions, they continue to experience inequalities in the labour market compared with their White peers.[52] But whatever the type of higher education institution an ethnic minority student might attend, and even if they gain a higher-class degree, it does not mitigate for the racism and discrimination they face when they enter the labour market.

Even when ethnic minority graduates seeking employment have the same qualifications as those from White groups, they are still more likely to be unemployed or employed in lower-quality jobs with greater insecurity and lower pay.[53] Ethnic minority applicants are more likely to be rejected in the early stages of job applications,[54] with evidence to suggest that some employers reject candidates with non-British-sounding names. They also face discrimination based on types of qualifications, proficiency in English and social class.[55] The overt discrimination faced by ethnic minority groups may explain the reasons why some decide to become self-employed[56] or use community-based cultural and social networks to seek employment, where they feel they will not experience racial discrimination.[57] In addition, ethnic minority groups tend to become self-employed through economic necessity compared with White groups.[58] Even within ethnic minority groups there is some variation in access to the labour market via community-based social networks, with individuals from Chinese and Indian groups more likely to have access to such networks compared with those from Pakistani or Bangladeshi backgrounds.[59] Furthermore, ethnic minority groups who experience discrimination when looking for a job are more likely to experience discrimination once they are employed.[60] It is Black and Pakistani/Bangladeshi groups who are the most disadvantaged in this regard; they are more likely to earn less compared with their White peers and suffer the biggest pay gaps.[61] As a result, some ethnic minority graduates may decide to stay longer in education owing to their awareness of the discrimination they will face in the labour market.[62] And as and when they do seek employment, they are likely to encounter racism and discrimination, both at point of entry to the labour market and during employment.[63]

Despite improvements in both participation and outcomes for ethnic minority groups within higher education, this is not reflected in the labour market. As ethnic minority groups are more likely to work in jobs for which they are over-qualified, their educational qualifications are often disregarded by employers. Six months after graduation, ethnic minority workers experience a significant gap in employment and earnings compared with White groups, even when the type of degree and socio-economic background are taken into consideration.[64] Overt racism thus continues from higher education into the labour market. Racism is and continues to be a pernicious force in society – and education is just one aspect of it.

Everyday Experiences of Racism in Higher Education

In this section, I focus on research that I conducted in 2021–2 with ethnic minority students enrolled in higher education. The aim of the study was to explore to what extent ethnic minority students experienced racism at university, how they felt about their future choices after they graduated and the amount of support that was available to them in helping them to find their feet in a predominantly White environment. I carried out forty-three interviews with ethnic minority students* from a variety of universities throughout the

---

* Respondents were from a range of different ethnic backgrounds; they self-identified as Black British, British Indian, British Pakistani/Bangladeshi and mixed heritage, and all were born in the UK. All of their names are pseudonyms.

UK, from post-1992 to Russell Group, in their final year of undergraduate study.

EVERYDAY POLITE RACISM

For the ethnic minority students I spoke to, racism of every kind – structural, institutional and individual – was a normal, everyday reality. The majority of respondents spoke about how the racism they encountered was 'normal' – something that they had experienced at school, and which had continued into higher education. As Jonathan, who was Black, observed:

> It's here, yes, it's everywhere. I think it's just something that we have to get used to. Racism is everywhere and it's because the public narrative gives it credence and allows it to happen, so people think it's OK to be racist. These days, it's more acceptable to be racist. I think the way things have progressed – or not progressed – around race has made it more OK to say racist things and for people to see that as a legitimate view. It's no longer hidden any more. If you confront people about their racist views, they come back with their freedom of speech argument. They say they can say what they want, because it's their right to express their views and that in itself is where we are.

Other students spoke about how people assumed that higher-education institutions must be liberal and progressive, and thus exempt from racism and racist practices, *because* they were universities and liberal sites of learning. As Omar, who was Pakistani, commented:

> It's very naïve for people to think that just because you're at a university there isn't any form of racism; it's just more hidden. The lecturers can just tone it down, but it manifests itself in other ways – like you get marked down compared to the White students who aren't that bright anyway, you don't get included in things. There are assumptions made about you that are based on ignorance and stereotypes. It's silent, but you know it's there [*racism*]. It's hidden but out in the open at the same time. I would say it's a polite way of being racist, so people are able to excuse it and get away with it.

Respondents also discussed racism based on stereotypes, such as a fear of Black masculinity, which was shown by some lecturers. Priya, who was Indian, felt stereotypes about Black male students were used to portray them as threatening.

> There are some of the White lecturers who kind look a bit intimated by the Black male students; I'm not sure why that is – they all seem fine to me. I do see, though, how they treat them differently to how they treat us – they are more formal and over-the-top polite to them. With us, they are less so – but that could be because they just see us as timid Asian girls. The lecturers just look like they're doing this dance, the way they treat us, and they think we can't see it. There's absolutely nothing different about how the Black male students behave – there's no way they are being aggressive. By labelling them as aggressive, it gives them an excuse to have something against them, even though it's not really there.

When asked what she meant by a 'dance', Priya described how some white lecturers seemed to perform the role of being an inclusive lecturer, but in reality this was a pretence. Although they were never openly expressed, Priya felt she could detect the racist feelings of some lecturers *'behind their eyes'*.

Respondents also spoke about how White lecturers were conscious of not wanting to *appear* racist. They did this through 'strategic talk' – using language in such a way that it excluded ethnic minority students but could not be identified or defined as actually racist. Teun van Dijk, one of the founders of critical discourse studies, argues that strategic talk allows individuals to mask their racism because, given 'the strict social norms against ethnic prejudice, discrimination and racism, who wants to be considered a racist? People have or try to maintain a positive self-image of tolerant, understanding, cooperative citizens, on the one hand, and of kind persons on the other.'[65] In this way, White lecturers hide their racism in order to keep up the appearance of a university being a safe and inclusive space.

COPING MECHANISMS AND STUDENT SUPPORT

Respondents told me how they used different ways of coping with and combating racism. One strategy was self-exclusion. In the words of Farah, a Bangladeshi student:

> There is a sort of seating plan in all the seminars – and the lectures actually. It's not a formal seating plan; it's one the students have introduced and it has kind of stuck. So, yeah, you could say that I sit with the other

Asian girls, but that's because I like it and I want to sit with them. I'm not sure if it was deliberate but I just navigated towards them. It does make me feel more comfortable, though, because I know I won't be judged, I will be accepted, and there are things I won't have to explain about myself.

Moira, a Black student, concurred with this.

I find that I tend to mix more with the Black and Asian students. I don't know if that is something that I do consciously or not, but when I do it, I don't try and change it. It does make me feel more comfortable, though.

While self-exclusionary behaviour of this kind can be seen as a way of creating 'safe' and comfortable spaces for students, there existed more formal types of exclusion, practised by the higher-education institutions *themselves*. This took the form of stereotypical attitudes about ethnic minority students, which Afia, who was of Pakistani heritage, felt were based on the expectations academics had about model White, middle-class students compared with those from ethnic minority backgrounds, like herself.

I did mention to one of the lecturers that I wanted to go on and do a master's [*degree*], but she kind of responded to me in a shocking way – like how come you want to do a master's? I don't know if it was because she didn't think I was good enough or she thought I was just some Muslim girl who was going to get married. I think it might have something to do with me wearing a hijab. There's an assumption there already, that I will be getting married. But the White students got a different reaction. It's just assumed they would go on to do a master's.

The lack of academic support or encouragement that ethnic minority students received was thus based on stereotypical attitudes academics and other university staff had about them. Meanwhile, other students spoke about the advice they received from the careers service, in which advisers made similar assumptions based on what they thought ethnic minority students could achieve. Troy, who was discouraged from applying to do a master's degree, felt this reflected the negative assumptions made about Black students:

> I was very annoyed when the woman at the careers service said she wasn't sure if I should do a master's law-conversion course. What does she know about me? She doesn't know anything about me – all she sees is a Black male, and she uses that to make stereotypes about what I should and shouldn't be doing. That's the subtleties of racism that can knock your confidence. You could say it's actually a microaggression – so that I don't get above myself, if you like. Does she say that to the White students? I don't think she does, and she probably would say the same to some of the Asian girls, because she would assume they are part of a stereotype.

How racism operates in higher education provides an excellent illustration of how racism works in society as a whole: stereotypes of ethnic minority students are used to portray them as outsiders in relation to the acceptable White 'norm'. In the overwhelmingly White space of higher education, students experience White supremacy through the predominant identity of Whiteness. So, White students are able (and are encouraged) to feel comfortable in such an environment by contrast with ethnic minority students, who have to constantly adapt to normative White practices. Many respondents also felt that overt forms of racism had been exacerbated by events such as Brexit and the election of Donald Trump as president of the US in 2016. Fayola, who was a Black student, believed these events had a significant impact on racial issues globally and directly affected race and racism in higher-education institutions:

> Things have changed since we have had different political changes in society. We've had Brexit and we've had Trump. Those two things are important because they are saying something to society. The people who have voted for them are saying one thing – they are saying we don't like foreigners and we want to keep them out. And that doesn't just happen on our TV screens; it's what we see right here in the university. We can see that here because we only have one Black lecturer – who isn't even British – and we have no Asian lecturers. I've never been taught by an Asian lecturer, yet most of the students are from Black or Asian backgrounds, but there's no one we can identify with who teaches us. There must be something wrong there. Is it because they're not applying for the jobs? Or is it just because the universities don't want them here?

Events of this kind, on a global scale, are examples of how racism has become 'normalized' and 'legitimatized' both in higher education and society more generally. It was part of the daily reality that the students I interviewed encountered at university, mirroring their wider experience in the world at large.

Despite higher-education institutions signalling a 'commitment' to tackling race and racism, many respondents felt this was 'window dressing' that would result in very little change. In the words of Amrit, who was Indian:

> I feel the universities have to be **shown** to be doing something, but a lot of that is a show – they have to be seen to be doing something, otherwise they will be accused of being racist. But that is all it is, it's a show. I think the unis know they have to do something, so they *pretend* to do things to make a difference. But they don't make any real changes, so all the professors here are White. So what's really changed? How can they [*university leaders*] say they want to make changes and understand racism when they aren't making any real changes at all? [*original emphasis*]

TRANSITIONARY RACISM

As discussed above, equality of opportunity does not translate into equality of outcomes for ethnic minority students, and in this section I outline how my research demonstrates this. Respondents spoke about their future in relation to seeking employment or embarking on further study. In all of their responses, one thing was clear: despite many of the students excelling in their studies (some were on track to receive a 2:1 or first-class honours degree), they all felt they would continue to experience racism. Jerrard, who was Black, spoke of overtly racist practices in the labour market.

> Even though we have to work harder to get a good degree and we have to keep on aiming higher, we still won't be able to challenge or counter that racism we will get once we start to look for jobs. If we think it's bad here, it's much worse out there. I know that because my brother got a 2:1 degree and he's got a master's and still can't get a job – what's that all about? He gets shortlisted and goes to the interview and never seems to get anywhere. That's down to racism. Anyone who doesn't get that doesn't understand the racism that's out there.

Black students in particular felt they would be disadvantaged in the labour market and feared discrimination and unemployment. Despite anticipating leaving university with a good degree, they felt that this would not necessarily be reflected in their employment prospects. Troy felt that his race (rather than his qualifications) would be the determining factor in whether he would be employed after leaving university.

> Just because I think I'm going to do well in my degree doesn't automatically correlate with me getting a good job. Employers can do whatever they want: they can say they don't want to shortlist me; they can interview me but not give me the job. Even though I might have the qualifications, I think employers will pick White candidates above me. It's just the way it is. It's the silent way that racism works, they [*employers*] can't say they don't want you because you're a Black man. Then you look and see in their firms they don't employ any Black people, so what does that say about them and their company? It's the kind of racism that's obvious in some ways because

> you see these firms that are all White, but on the other hand they can use tactics to say they're not racist, like interviewing you and then just not giving you the job.

Many respondents discussed the type of racism they felt they would experience in the labour market as 'silent racism' or 'subtle racism', in which employers would be able to use ways of excluding ethnic minority candidates while hiding their racism. Valerie, who was Black, felt this would be relatively easy for prospective employers to do.

> It's very easy for employers to be racist, because they can do it in an underhand kind of way – so that it can be disguised. They can say, well, you don't have enough experience, or you won't fit in with us. These are all ways to say, well, we don't want you because you're not White. Your face doesn't fit. We want to keep our organization the way it is, and we don't want you to represent us. They will always find ways to exclude you. They have the power to exclude you, and if you're non-White and they don't want you, they can easily justify that – and it doesn't matter to them.

The South Asian students I spoke to felt they would be disadvantaged in the labour market due to their South Asian-sounding names. Parminder, who was from an Indian background, was aware her name might exclude her from certain jobs.

> I think having a name like Parminder doesn't really help, does it? I think they will take one look at my application and say, do we want an Asian girl working here?

CHAPTER 3

> Even though I could have a first-class degree, they would rather take the White girl called Emily or Jane or whatever. I think that happens a lot; they look at your name and you can't go any further because you don't fit their stereotypes of being a White girl. Firstly you look different because you're not White and secondly your name is too difficult for them to spell or say – so why would they bother? And they don't want their customers to feel awkward when they have to speak to you and say your name, so they [*employers*] will opt for the White girls and their easy names, which are easy to say and easy to spell.

Afia gave a similar response in relation to her Muslim identity.

> They will take one look at me and think, oh, she's a terrorist because she's wearing a hijab. They won't want to employ me, will they? I know they're not meant to discriminate and there are all these laws in place to say they can't; they still get away with it. If they didn't, then why are all the good jobs taken by White graduates? It's also the way employers want to represent themselves; they might think it's awkward having a girl with a hijab and that can be interpreted in many different ways. People see you first as a Muslim, then they see you as non-White and then you're a woman. It makes it more complicated for them and so the easy thing for them to do is to just reject you – and they can do that and get away with it.

Others suggested that this form of 'silent racism' would continue once they were in the workplace and beyond. Valerie went on to describe this as a 'disguise'.

> People can kind of hide their overt racism and replace it with being politically correct, so they are seen as polite and they can't be as open as they might want to be about their dislike of immigrants. In the workplace, people have to be careful because there are laws in place that you have to follow and you can get found out. But in other more private places, people will continue to be racist and just get away with it.

Jeannette, who was Black, expressed similar sentiments.

> Universities don't want to confront their own sense of being the White oppressors. They have all played a role in this, but they both want to deny it and perpetuate their own superiority at the same time. I think the universities have to think about their own role in imperialism and colonialism. They need to confront it and address it. By ignoring it, they can ignore racism and not think about it. If you look at some universities like Bristol and UCL, what do you think it's been built on? Where do you think the money came from and who do you think built it? It's all from colonialism and it's been built by slaves.

Students were aware of the colonial past of their own higher-education institutions and many felt that this history perpetuated White supremacy. Jeannette went on to say:

> We know our universities were involved in the slave trade. Those legacies will always be there and we will always be marginalized because of that.

Outsiders Within

Ethnic minority students will always be seen as outsiders in higher-education institutions, which is related to their continued marginal status *within* it. Through various practices and processes, higher-education institutions are able to preserve their own status without allowing ethnic minority students to challenge it. Within educational policy-making, according to David Gillborn, 'conventional forms of anti-racism have proven unable to keep pace with the development of increasingly racist and exclusionary education policies that operate beneath a veneer of professed tolerance and diversity'.[66] Normative hegemonic White practices not only exist in higher-education institutions, as ethnic minority students have found, but these follow them into the labour market. The students I interviewed were all too aware that, despite the equality legislation that is in place, employers would continue to discriminate against ethnic minority graduates, and that the insidiousness of the prevailing White culture would continue to protect White individuals and serve their interests. Thus, despite attempts to increase access to universities for students from marginalized backgrounds, ethnic minority students are still disadvantaged, because of their race and because they do not 'fit in' with normative White ways of *being* and *doing*.

CHAPTER 4
White Elites and Educational Advantage
'Once Privileged, Always Privileged'

Britain has always had a set of elites that run society, a state of affairs that has existed for generations. Elites hold power in all areas of society, from politics, the media, arts and culture to education and the judiciary. As they are a select group; they also have disproportionate access to significant advantages, including wealth, privilege and political power. Their existence assumes a social hierarchy in which the top positions are occupied by the most powerful and the lower ranks – those *beneath* the elite – by the least powerful. The mere existence of elites signifies an unequal distribution of power and control in relation to a society's distribution of resources,[1] and in such a society elites are often regarded as being *worthy* of occupying a superior position – not just by themselves, but by society as a whole.[2] With the power, capacity and potential to signal their elitism to their 'subordinates',[3] elites have the ability to control political, economic, cultural and social networks and the spread of knowledge, with far-reaching consequences.

Elitism exists in all aspects of British society – but especially in our education system. Educational privilege is a trajectory that starts at an independent, fee-paying private school and continues into higher education and beyond. Educational institutions such as these are still dominated by wealthy, White groups. Their privileged education enables them to dominate the most highly paid jobs in the labour market, rewarding pre-existing privilege with further status, money and power.

In this chapter, I aim to demonstrate how this system works. Through a process of White privilege, White groups are able to maintain and reproduce their positions of power in every area, thanks in huge part to the elite educational institutions that they attend. As a result, White elites continue to dominate our society to benefit themselves and people like them. By keeping insiders 'in' and outsiders 'out', and by distinguishing themselves from 'others', these elites perpetuate inequality in our education system and beyond.

Elite Private Schools

Since the 1950s, elite schools in the UK have been seen as the most important way to transfer power to the upper social classes as a means of controlling wealth. Attending an elite school (a highly selective school based on merit and/or wealth) was the pivotal way of perpetuating privilege and passing it on from one generation to the next, and the unique advantage thus acquired was used as a means of gaining access to elite higher education and/or elite employment. Elite schools the world over are considered elite because of their curricula (with access to a range of sporting, musical, artistic and creative activities), their role in maintaining and perpetuating elite networks, their physical character and location, and their demography.[4] These schools serve different elite groups, but it is mainly those with considerable wealth and status who are able to access them.

In the UK, independent fee-paying schools – or private schools – provide this elite schooling. Unlike state schools – which are funded through taxation – they charge tuition fees for their students to attend, and often involve entrance exams. The parents who choose to send their children to private school are in effect choosing to invest their financial resources into gaining more beneficial educational outcomes for their children. These schools are registered with the government but are not directly funded by them; they have greater flexibility in their teaching and do not have to follow the national curriculum. The Independent Schools Inspectorate (and Ofsted) inspect schools that are members of the Independent Schools Council, a body that represents independent schools in the UK. Private schools are routinely granted charitable status, allowing them to benefit from significant tax concessions that protects their financial security.[5]

The Charities Act (2011) defines a charity as an institution established for a charitable purpose and that provides benefit for the public good.[6] Private schools are granted charitable status on the basis that they are engaged in advancing education and by making provision for bursaries for poorer children.[7] This entitlement to charitable status is highly questionable, however, as there is little clarity about the amount of provision private schools provide for genuinely poor or underprivileged children. More significantly, perhaps, is the fact that the argument that private schools contribute to the public good seems entirely fallacious; the clear aim and intention of such schools is that wealthier parents are able to use their wealth to purchase better educational outcomes for their children.

Private schools have been criticized for benefiting the already privileged. In 2017, Michael Gove, the then secretary of state for education, accused private schools of being addicted to state subsidies and said that they should be deprived of their charitable status and made to pay business rates, just like other businesses. 'Charitable status, and the tax exemption it offers, is very far from the only way the state subsidises private education,' he went on to say. 'We taxpayers give free uniforms, weapons and rations to private school cadet forces, indeed we pay for the instructors and hand over £20 cash per cadet. The Eton Rifles are welfare junkies.' In Gove's view, wealthy parents were able to 'buy advantage' for their children, helping them to gain places at prestigious universities and go on to highly paid jobs, but access to wealth did not equal greater intelligence. The offspring of wealthy parents were not 'intrinsically more talented and worthy, more gifted and more deserving of celebration than the rest', yet those who had been privately educated were 'massively overrepresented in the highest ranks of politics, business, the media and sport'.[8]

In 2020–21 there were approximately 545,000 pupils attending independent fee-paying secondary schools compared with around 3,494,000 attending state-funded schools.[9] Around 6.5 per cent of the total number of schoolchildren in the UK, at both primary and secondary level, attend independent fee-paying schools.[10] In terms of ethnicity, 33.6 per cent of pupils across all state schools are from an ethnic minority background,[11] compared with 35 per cent for ethnic minority pupils who attend independent schools, according to the Independent Schools Council. While this latter figure suggests that this is comparable to the number of ethnic minority children in the general school population, it is misleading because it is skewed by an over-representation of international non-British students at private schools (45.5 per cent of students whose parents do not live in the UK and 54.5 per cent whose parents do).[12] This suggests that those ethnic minority students who attend private schools are more likely to be from abroad, international students who are part of a global elite with access to considerable wealth and connections, and for whom attending a private school is part of their journey of privilege.[13]

Attending a private school has a number of significant benefits that derive from an initial access to wealth. This includes the likelihood of doing better academically compared with someone attending a state school, even when prior attainment is taken into account.[14] There are a number of reasons for this, including smaller class sizes and more one-to-one support from teachers, together with more coaching and better preparation for exams. Private-school pupils also receive considerable help and mentoring in preparation for applying to Oxford or Cambridge and other 'high-tariff' universities, which instils confidence in them and the belief that they will succeed.[15] Students from private schools are thus more likely to attend university. According to the Independent Schools Council, 90 per cent of private-school pupils went on to gain a place at a university, with 51 per cent gaining a place at a 'Top 25 University', of which 5 per cent secured a place at Oxford or Cambridge.[16] Furthermore, eight private schools dominate Oxbridge admissions: Westminster School, Eton College, St Paul's School, St Paul's Girls' School, the Perse School, Magdalen College School, King's College School and Brighton College.[17] In addition, private-school students are able to develop social networks that give them access to future opportunities such as elite jobs with high earning potential.[18] This bolsters their already strong sense of entitlement, confidence and self-esteem.

Elite Universities

When we think of elite universities, names such as Oxford, Cambridge, Harvard, Stanford and MIT (Massachusetts Institute of Technology) come to mind, because they are recognizable brands.[19] These universities are elite because, in the words of Simon Marginson, an expert in education, they 'derive global predominance from their position within their own national/imperial systems'.[20] They have been described by some as the 'Global Super League'.[21] Such institutions maintain and display their globally elite status in many different ways. They benefit from large and excessive endowments from former alumni and these endowments may be linked to the admission of wealthy students. Indeed, their wealth is often reflected in the stunning architecture of their campuses. They also achieve consistently high positions in QS World University Rankings and *Times Higher Education* World University Rankings league tables. They tend to select students on the basis of competitive entrance requirements that reward specific characteristics and forms of cultural capital predominantly associated with children from wealthier families. The application process itself can deter or forestall potential candidates from state schools that lack the resources or requisite know-how to be able to help them apply to elite universities. In some cases, the different (earlier) deadline for applying to Oxford or Cambridge ahead of all other UK universities has been linked to students simply missing the deadline to apply.[22] Such restrictions on applying to specific elite universities are set against a background of students from poorer, working-class and ethnic minority families often choosing to study at their nearest 'local' university owing to financial and cultural constraints, often regardless of the reputation of the university.[23] By comparison, White middle-class students are more likely to have better access to information about the relative merits of different universities. They are also more likely to want to relocate and to view 'leaving home' as a natural process.[24] Such inequalities contribute to who attends elite universities and who does not.

According to Simon Marginson, these universities are not constrained by the competition for resources facing many universities: 'Largely autonomous, their agency freedom is enhanced by the globalisation of knowledge and their pre-eminence displayed in the web, global university rankings and popular culture. The global power of these institutions rests on the *subordination* of other institutions and nations.'[25] They do so by deliberately increasing their own power by ensuring they maintain their position at the top of the hierarchy. In 2020, Harvard's endowment funds stood at $41.9 billion.[26] In the UK, Oxford University has endowment assets worth £1.2 billion, but individual colleges have their own endowment assets amounting to £4.9 billion in total.[27] Despite these exceptional reserves of economic wealth, this is not what sets elite universities apart; rather, it is their selectivity and accumulation of knowledge that gives them the greatest advantage in terms of academic research.[28] Such universities maintain *power* and *status* in the world through their historic tradition, social cachet, wealth and financial status.

Gaining entry to such elite universities is both hugely competitive and potentially very lucrative. The value of degree qualifications from these institutions is recognized globally and is directly related to greater rewards, with students progressing to better-paid and higher-status employment. However, it is also widely known that the selection process is inequitable and favours wealthier students.[29] In the UK, the universities of Oxford and Cambridge have both been criticized for being dominated by White, middle- and upper-class students, many of whom have attended private schools. In 2017, the MP David Lammy accused Oxbridge of operating a system of 'social apartheid', drawing on data from 2015 that showed that nearly one in three Oxford colleges failed to admit a single Black British student. Similarly, Cambridge failed to admit a single Black student in six of its colleges during the same year.[30] I have noted before that this is indeed a system of educational apartheid, one that openly divides students into different groups by race and in which universities implement racist policies to preserve their institutional and economic standing.[31]

Recent data suggests that, in 2019, a total of 23,020 students applied to study at Oxford University, with 3,889 being offered a place, resulting in a total of 3,280 who were admitted. In the same year, the university admitted a total of 22.1 per cent of students from an ethnic minority background. If applicant figures are broken down by UK-domiciled ethnicity, in 2019, 76.9 per cent of students were White, compared with 2.1 per cent who were Bangladeshi/Pakistani, 3.2 per cent Black, 8.2 per cent mixed-heritage and 9.6 per cent Asian, with all of these percentages showing a slight year-on-year increase since 2015.[32] However, these numbers remain low particularly for Bangladeshi/Pakistani and Black students (who are also more likely to be disadvantaged in their schooling).[33] An explanation given by Oxford University for the low numbers (of all ethnic groups) is that ethnic minority students are more likely to apply for the most competitive courses compared with White students,[34] suggesting that if they applied for easier courses they would be more successful, which is clearly not the case. In 2020, the university introduced the 'Oxford Opportunity' campaign to help students from disadvantaged backgrounds to prepare for life at university once they have been offered a place at Oxford and made 100 offers under the scheme.[35] While this scheme is well intentioned, it does little to address the challenges that such students face once they enter the university (such as feelings of marginalization and social exclusion, as well as racism, classism and sexism).[36]

Despite the emphasis on diversifying admissions to elite universities in the UK and US, White students from wealthy backgrounds continue to dominate the intake. In the US, the lowest percentage of students admitted to Harvard University in 2020 were of African-American, Hispanic/Latino, Native American and Native Hawaiian ethnicity.[37] Harvard remains one of the most expensive universities in the world with full-time undergraduate fees of $51,904 per year in 2020. The standard total annual budget (including living costs such as food, rent and textbooks, in addition to fees) is estimated at $85,000.[38] (According to the US Census Bureau, the median annual household income in the US in 2020 was $67,521.[39])

Achieving equal access, and closing the gap between those who attend elite universities and those who do not, is a long process. At current rates of progress, according to Lee Elliot Major and Pallavi Amitava Banerjee, experts in social mobility, it would 'take 96 years for highly-selective universities in England to raise the participation rate for 18-to-30-year olds from the least advantaged areas to the existing participation rate for 18-to-30-year olds from the most advantaged areas'.[40]

In the UK, as well as in the US, the elite journey of privilege, as we have seen, begins at private schools and continues with entrance to elite universities.[41] Attending an elite university confers rewards of 'supreme value' that can be used in a global market.[42] It ensures that those who have attended elite universities have access to a transnational cosmopolitanism, helping such graduates to find high-earning employment in the global labour market.[43] Consequently, elite universities are breeding grounds where future world leaders can develop the social networks that enable them to succeed. Elite universities produce citizens of the world and those who graduate from them are able to use their degrees as recognized credentials the world over.[44] Such credentials enable White privilege and an elite ruling class to flourish. In the UK, this system has produced political leaders such as former prime ministers Tony Blair, David Cameron, Boris Johnson and Liz Truss and the current prime minister, Rishi Sunak; leading judges such as Alan Rodger and Vivien Rose; actors such as Emilia Fox and Hugh Grant; broadcasters such as Robert Peston and Michael Crick; and scientists such as Cyril Burt and Stephen Hawking – all of whom attended the University of Oxford.

Transitioning from Elite Universities into High-Status Employment

Attending an elite university has significant economic returns in the labour market, resulting in short- and long-term gains for graduates, and a diminished risk of downward social mobility.[45] When prestigious employers look for new recruits, they are more likely to select on the basis of *where* the applicant has received their degree and the types of social activities they have participated in.[46] Such overtly selective criteria are used to assess whether the applicant would have the relevant qualities to enable them to fit in with their organization. This results in a handful of small firms recruiting graduates who attended the *same* private schools and the *same* universities.[47] It is a hierarchical system that works to keep certain groups out, while ensuring others remain part of the selection process.[48] Inequalities in degree outcomes suggest that students who attend elite universities are more likely to gain greater returns from their degrees compared with those who attend non-elite or post-1992 universities.[49] They will earn more over their lifetime and receive greater rewards and benefits.[50] White, middle-class, privately educated students benefit the most from this process. They dominate elite universities and in turn go on to dominate elite jobs.[51]

In this sense there is a linear progression, in which the characteristics acquired by children owing to their social background and having been educated at private schools are rewarded first by attending elite universities and then by transitioning into higher-status employment.[52] According to the American anthropologist Jonathan Friedman, private schools and elite universities are in effect a 'breeding ground where the children of advantage congregate to gain first-rate instruction, receive informal lessons in high-culture tastes and behaviours, join key elite social networks and, above all, acquire high-status credentials'.[53]

Evidence of the reproduction of elites is seen in a recent report published in 2019 by the Sutton Trust and the Social Mobility Commission, which found that at the time of the 2017 general election 52 per cent of MPs went to a comprehensive and 19 per cent to a grammar school, while 29 per cent were privately educated, a figure that is four times higher than in the electorate they represent. Furthermore, over half (57 per cent) of the members in the House of Lords attended private school. In spring 2019, among members of the cabinet of the then prime minister Theresa May, 39 per cent attended private school compared with only 9 per cent of the shadow cabinet. Those who are in the most senior and powerful positions in society are more likely to have attended private schools, including 65 per cent of senior judges, 59 per cent of civil service permanent secretaries, 52 per cent of foreign and commonwealth diplomats and a significant number of high-profile members of the media. Of the most influential 100 news editors and broadcasters, 43 per cent went to private schools and 33 per cent went on to gain a place at Oxford or Cambridge.[54] Furthermore, all of these professions are more likely to be dominated by White, middle-class groups.

White Elites, White Privilege

Private schools continue to be dominated by White middle-class groups, who go on to access highly paid jobs in the labour market.[55] Students from elite universities who apply for prestigious jobs are acutely aware of the advantages and privilege associated with gaining entry into elite professions and also that inequalities around race and ethnicity play a role in that process.[56] When students apply for 'elite', high-status jobs, their understanding of 'skills' and 'talent' is based on their membership of an elite group, and they are able to align how they present themselves with their cultural norms of behaviour and acceptance. At private school, they are taught that they are the 'talented few' and this perception of privilege is reinforced in higher education and then through the recruitment processes of selective employers. Once they have entered elite employment, this carries with it significant emblematic power, sending a message that 'I am here because I am *worthy* of being here; I earned it'.[57]

Related to this, companies offering high-earning employment favour Whiteness and racialized norms associated with the *performance* of Whiteness. In my research, I found that that there is an expectation by employers that potential candidates conform to White norms both during and after recruitment. This affects the way candidates behave and speak, and the things they talk about; it rewards those who align themselves with White norms, and penalizes those who do not.

As we have now established, because elites have greater control of and access to resources from a young age, this paves their way to elite higher-education institutions, which in turn gives them access to further resources (financial or otherwise) to progress into high-earning employment. A key part of this, I would maintain, is access to and possession of White privilege, which ensures that Whiteness remains the dominant culture of the powerful, and that White groups are thus able to continue to control and dominate elite institutions. Ethnic minority individuals from a wealthy, privileged background (such as Prime Minister Rishi Sunak), though not White themselves, have access to such networks and connections. They 'perform' Whiteness in a way that enables them to fit in with their White peers and be included as part of the elite. However, within these groups it is still Whiteness (actually *being* ethnically White) that remains the predominant form of privilege.

Wealthy White groups are able to reproduce their privilege not just from one generation to another but through schools, universities and the labour market. The transformation of privilege takes place through social, cultural and economic advantages that individuals possess. Elite higher education *affirms* and *reaffirms* the presence of such advantages. Students attending elite universities continue to draw on their networks of belonging, meeting students who have attended the same private schools as they did and/or drawing on their parents' connections to establish friendships with others who are *like them*. Consequently, private schools play a significant role in fostering a sense of *entitlement* for White (and a small number of privileged ethnic minority) middle-class wealthy students who feel they have earned their right to attend an elite university. Attending a private school prepares students for this sense of entitlement; they are taught they are the best, the crème de la crème.

Elite Journeys to 'Castle' University

In this section I take a look at the views expressed by students attending an elite university in the UK, which I refer to as 'Castle'. The key aim of the study was to examine the educational trajectories of students who were studying at Castle,* to explore how and if race had an impact on their time there. Castle is described as 'elite': it regularly ranks in the top ten of the QS World University Rankings and is a recognizable elite university 'brand', known globally for the number of former presidents, prime ministers and Nobel Peace Prize winners among its alumni. I conducted thirty-four interviews with students from a range of different ethnic backgrounds of which nineteen had attended a private school.[58]

AN ELITE JOURNEY: 'IT'S NOT JUST ABOUT WHERE I CAME FROM; IT'S MORE ABOUT WHERE I'M GOING'

When respondents discussed their trajectory into elite higher education, they referred to their extensive knowledge of elite universities (such as ranking in league tables, reputation, wealth and location). For many of them, this sense of privilege stemmed from their upbringing. The majority had parents who were in professional occupations and some described themselves as 'fortunate'. Having already attended a private school, the students I interviewed regarded the transition into an elite university as 'natural', a way of reinforcing or opening up new connections and networks that would be seen as highly valuable in the future, particularly in relation to

---

* The name of the university and names of respondents are pseudonyms.

access to the labour market and high-earning jobs. They were aware of the advantages they had accrued from attending a private school. Stephen, a White student who had attended a private school, spoke about how his parents had invested financially in his education and expected him to go to Castle.

> Both my parents work in the financial sector and they assumed me and my sister would come to Castle and they worked hard for us to get here. We've both had a lot of support getting here. We went to private schools, we had tutors, we had music lessons. We went on European holidays, so we have done a lot. It meant that I had a lot of examples that I could draw on when I had my interview – my skiing holidays and the like – things I could talk about that would set me apart in some ways from the other candidates. We all knew we had to do that and it was seen as the normal thing for us to do and we just did it.

Jean, a White student who also went to private school, spoke about the support she received.

> My school was a really good school. I had lots of support. I had someone help me with my personal statement, prepare me for the interview. This all helped me a lot and, to be honest, if I didn't have that support, I don't think I would have made it. The teachers were clearly invested in getting some of us to apply to Castle and so they put a lot of effort into that and wanted us to do well. If that support wasn't there, I don't think me and the others who applied would have done it – so, yes, the school and the teachers were very supportive.

While respondents were aware that gaining entry into an elite university was not based on a level playing field. Ethnic minority students described the restrictions they had overcome to be accepted as a form of White exclusion. According to Ayesha, a Black student who went to a state school:

> Those White students who have come from privilege bring that White privilege with them and then they can use it for their own advantage. They end up mixing with people who are just like them and don't look outside of those groups. This then means they exclude us because we are not White and we don't come from the same backgrounds as them. You can see it when you start; they all navigate to other students who are like them and then you find out that they know the same people, their parents know the same people and they have the same networks and so stick to people who are like them. I suppose it makes them different and want to make sure they keep those connections and that feeling that they are part of that exclusive group, which those of us who went to state schools just don't have.

Other respondents also recognized this institutional privilege, including Jack, a Black student who went to a state school.

> The sense of White privilege is seen as linked to the institutional privilege. We all have that institutional privilege when we get here, but White students have it more because Castle is seen as White, so they fit in more and see it as something that's **normal** to them, whereas for us it is not the norm. If you are not White, then you are the ones who have to fit in to that White system of privilege – and

that is something that's unlikely to happen because we are not White, so we are unlikely to be accepted in that environment. [*original emphasis*]

Some respondents spoke about their encounters with privately educated students at Castle, particularly when they had first started at the university. As Becky, a Black student who attended a state school, observed:

I remember when we first started here at Castle and we had an induction day and all the White students seemed to flock together, but they were a particular **type** of student. They were the posh ones and then we find out that they all went to the same private schools and know the same teachers and each other's siblings. They all seemed to share this experience and they were proud of it. For those of us who didn't attend private schools, we just don't have those kinds of connections. [*original emphasis*]

The students I spoke to discussed different types of privilege and how it worked to benefit White groups and exclude ethnic minorities. Some discussed the ways in which economic privilege was flaunted and used as 'kudos'. Becky went on to say:

The White rich students show off about how rich their parents are, that they have aunts and uncles who don't have holiday homes – they have castles and luxurious yachts in the South of France. It's another world. They are not embarrassed by it, they flaunt it. They don't care that you might not be as privileged as they are; instead they use it as a **form of power**, like a tool, so that you know they are rich and they have been to private school.

> They remind you of it all the time. I think it's deliberately used as a microaggression, as a way of keeping you down so you know you're not as wealthy as they are, so you can and can't do certain things. It is used to make sure we know that we are not as good as them because we haven't been on holidays all around the world and our parents aren't as rich as they are. We are seen as poor, and I guess we are compared to them. But they look down on us because we are poor, even though we are all occupying the same place **here now**. [*original emphasis*]

Respondents' past schooling, therefore, was influential in how they achieved their status at Castle. White students who had attended private school brought with them a sense of privilege, instilled in them from an early age. Attending a private school gave them a shared identity with other private-school students, and at the same time distinguished them from their state-school peers. At private school, they 'learned the ropes', ways of *being* and *doing* that equipped them for life at Castle. Applying to Castle was a natural progression, an expectation from their teachers, parents and themselves. They were taught that such privilege was their *entitlement*.

While ethnic minority students were aware of their second-class status, White students were equally aware of their privileged position. Many White students used their Whiteness as a form of power to keep ethnic minority students *in their place*, particularly by excluding them from networks where White students congregated and felt a sense of belonging together, based on their shared connections and interests. To them, the elite environment of Castle is a *White* space, one that is theirs and one to which they are entitled as a right. As a result, White students *perform* their privilege – at Castle, it is the normal way of behaving and doing things. Their privilege is part of *who they are*, part of their *embodied* identity. Christopher, a White student who had attended a private school, described this as

> My identity – the way I speak and where I come from – is part of who I am. Yes, I know I have been to a really good school and now I am here at Castle – the best university in the world. I know I am from an upper-middle-class background, so I am privileged. But it's **who I am, it's what I am** and there's nothing I can do about it. I can't pretend to be something else that I'm not. So, I may as well get what I can from it, because I can't hide my identity and I can't hide my background. I feel that society wants me to be ashamed of who I am because I am rich and privileged, but why should I be? My parents have worked hard and I have worked hard to be here, so I should be proud of that. It's like being wealthy is something you should be ashamed about, but if you have worked hard for what you have and it's yours, why should you be ashamed of it? [*original emphasis*]

Despite acknowledging his own privilege, Christopher felt that ethnic minority students were complicit in perpetuating privilege by *attending* an elite university such as Castle.

> I know I am in a privileged position but I also think that Black students are also in a privileged position by being

here. They may not be White, but they are also reinforcing their own privilege by coming to Castle. I don't think they can have it both ways and complain about us having White privilege, when they are also part of that **system** of privilege. If they were against the notion of privilege so much, then they would fight against it and not come to the best university in the world. I think at least we [*White, privately educated students*] are candid about what we want and what we want to get out of the system. You can't have it both ways – you either buy into the system of privilege or you don't. It's as simple as that, and those of us who are here – regardless of our ethnic background and the advantages we have had – have bought into that system by simply being **here**. [*original emphasis*]

Some of the Black students that I spoke to felt that, at Castle, there was a certain type of privilege that was linked to a certain kind of '*intelligence*'. According to Jack, a Black student who went to a state school:

White students can manifest their intelligence in different ways. They can speak like the professors, they feel confident asking them for help, they don't feel intimidated by them and they can communicate with them. That's because they are like **them**; they can use that type of intelligence. So, in turn, the professors will respond to that in positive ways and judge that as being intellectual, whereas for some of us who have been to state schools and don't come from the same backgrounds and don't use the language that they [*White private-school students*] use, it can be a challenge. To me, it feels like that's a deliberate mechanism White students use to excel at Castle. [*original emphasis*]

These types of behaviour and social codes are perceived as signs of intelligence, when in fact they are simply expressions and performances of Whiteness. This gives White elites credibility, and enables them to maintain and reinforce their *superior* position at an elite university like Castle. By using their White identity in this way, White students (and their professors) perpetuate a certain kind of *idea* of intelligence, which rewards specific ways of behaving that *enact* White privilege, and projects this idea of intelligence to the educational establishment and society as a whole.

ELITE PRIVILEGE: 'I DESERVE TO BE HERE, BECAUSE I EARNED IT'

The majority of White students that I spoke to had a firm belief in meritocracy. They told me that they had worked hard for years to gain their place at Castle, and that their admittance was a reward for the years of 'hard graft' that got them there. Jamie, who was White and went to private school, said it was 'the natural thing to do' to go to Castle; it was the 'normal order of things'.

> I always knew I would come here; it was the done thing in my family. We all knew we were working to get here. Coming to Castle was the endgame of our educational journey. Once we got here, it was the beginning of a different journey. Castle is what I've been working for since I started school; it's what my family have invested in me.

> It's something I just knew would happen. But, ultimately, it was me who had to do the hard work and pass the exams, and that's what got me here.

Alex, a White student who had attended a private school, was similarly keen to stress that gaining a place at Castle was the result of hard work.

> I think if you work hard enough you can get here. I worked very hard to get my grades and made sure that I spent every waking hour on the things I needed to do to get a place here. Everyone can get a place here; you just have to make sure you put the hours in. Castle has a lot of people to select from and so you have to be the best of the best to actually get in. If you think about the people you are competing with, then you realize how good you have to be. It just takes lots of hard work and anyone who is committed to that goal will be able to achieve it.

Alex noted that he came from a family where both of his sisters had attended elite universities and his parents had sent him and his siblings to private school. But he was adamant that it was his hard work alone that got him in to Castle.

> We all wanted to go to Castle, and we knew if we worked hard enough we would get in. I think if I didn't put the work in and get the grades, I wouldn't have got in. It's the reward for all my hard work to be here. I know Castle is very competitive, but if you work hard enough you can get in.

Similarly, Rebecca who was White and attended a private school, and whose parents were both bankers, felt she had earned her right to be at Castle and was entitled to be there due to her hard work.

> So we know that Castle is the best university in the world. Those of us who are here know we have worked hard over a long period of time, and our reward is being here and getting a place here. I shouldn't be ashamed of it; I am very proud of it. I earned it. We are told we are the select few and we are told we are the crème de la crème of the intellectual world. And then after a while, you kind of think, well, I got in to Castle so I must be smart. You are told that all of the time here, and if you didn't believe it before, you certainly believe it when you're here because you are **taught** to believe it. [*original emphasis*]

These White students who attended private school believed in meritocracy and felt that the admissions system for Castle was, in Rebecca's words, 'fair and square'. They didn't question the admissions process – they believed that students were selected on their educational achievements alone. Instead, many placed the blame on individuals for not working hard enough to gain a place at Castle, rather than the structures of inequality that reinforced White privilege. John, who was White and attended a private school, was adamant that the system was fair.

> I think the system is fair – it has to be, doesn't it? I think, yes, you could say it is mainly White and perhaps with people who have attended better schools, but you can't blame the system itself for that. We live in a society that is unequal. Just because I and my friends happen to be

born into a family where we are more fortunate in some ways, it doesn't mean that you have to punish me for that and say I shouldn't go to Castle. I think if you work hard enough, you would get into Castle. Yes, it's competitive, but everyone has an equal chance to enter that competition. Those people who can't apply and those people who don't get in, don't get in because maybe they weren't clever enough in the first place. It is a rigorous process and, ultimately, they take the best people and that's it. It's not based on any type of discrimination. If you work hard and you get the grades, you can get in.

By believing in this idea of meritocracy, White students could justify their presence in this elite space. They were aware that Castle was dominated by White middle-class students, but they still had faith in the system to identify talent, separating the wheat from the chaff. As John went on to say:

I think we have to accept that there's inequalities and those inequalities may be based on ethnicity, class or money or whatever. But that's part of society, otherwise how will you get the best people to do the best jobs? Not everyone can be prime minister and not everyone can get into Castle. The system works to distinguish those who can and those who can't, and not everyone can – it's as simple as that, really.

John also emphatically felt that the reason that elite universities were predominantly White was not because of discrimination but because more White students *were able to apply* to Castle.

> You can't just simplify it like that; you have to think that more White students apply here and so more get in. It's mainly because Black students don't apply here in the first place. You also have to look at how many Black people there are in the population. If you look at it like that, then it's not discriminatory.

John's views are an excellent example of the kinds of opinions held by some White students at elite universities, views that often remain unchallenged during their educational journeys and beyond. The ethnic minority students that I interviewed, however, often questioned the notion of meritocracy. Despite acknowledging that the students at Castle were well educated and well qualified to study there, they didn't feel that everyone gained a place at Castle by simply being super-smart. In the words of Kirpinder, a British-Indian student, who went to a state school and was the first in her family to attend university:

> I think people like to think that it's all about how you work hard and you get in because hard work rewards you, but that's simply not the case. You have to think about all the support and help these White students have had. They've been to the best private schools, their mummies and daddies have helped them financially and they have access to so many things that has helped them get here. They are rich and they have connections. They didn't get in because they're super-smart; they got in because of all those extra things they've had them to help them along the way. They've been to schools where there are small classes and they have more books, more equipment and more of

everything. There were thirty students in my classes and we didn't get the same levels of support compared to them.

Kirpinder recognized that Whiteness and White privilege were fundamental to what Castle stood for and what it perpetuated.

> Castle is the epitome of Whiteness and White privilege. You just have to walk on campus and use your eyes and ears. You can see and smell the privilege. Castle are well aware of that and they want to continue it because they see it as a superior space and they want to preserve that space for themselves. They don't want state-school kids, they don't want Black or Asian kids and they certainly don't want poor kids coming here. And when you are from these backgrounds, you feel totally out of place and you are made to feel like that and reminded of your difference every day. I am the first in my family to go to university, and that in itself is used to exclude you, because I am surrounded by people all the time who tell me that their parents are doctors, lawyers, judges and the like, and my dad is a taxi driver – how do I tell them that? It makes you feel as though you can't say anything as they will judge you and so you feel like an imposter here.

Similarly, Monty who was of mixed Black and White heritage and from a state school, discussed the unspoken sense of White privilege at Castle.

> I can see it by the way all the same people from the same backgrounds hang out together. In some ways, it is the unspoken way that White privilege works – **it's just there**.

> You can't get away from it, and when you're part of that White space – that entitled space that some White students have – you are made to silently and sometimes overtly feel you are not part of that space because **you are not White**. [*original emphasis*]

Monty went on to describe the different ways in which he had experienced overt and covert racism.

> The ways in which White privilege works is through the translation of that privilege, and White students can use that to their advantage. When you are visibly seen as being an outsider because you are not White, then that is something that can be used against you. The comments that are sometimes made and assumed about you because you are not White, says you are not allowed to be part of **our** space. You are always made to feel that you don't belong in **their** White space. [*original emphasis*]

Ethnic minority students who gained a place at Castle did not want to be seen as a token individual to make up numbers. Jessica, who was also of mixed Black and White heritage and had attended a state school, expressed this as a process that was both inclusionary (by attending the university) and exclusionary.

> I don't want to be seen as a number that's contributed to an equality statistic – that's not why I'm here – but some White students look at you and think you're only here because they had to let in a number of Black students and you fit the mould. There is always that assumption that you're not here on your merit if you're Black. But that assumption

isn't made if you are White. That's the silent way in which White privilege and advantage works here at Castle.

Ethnic minority students recognized the 'privilege' associated with gaining a Castle degree, but were more measured in their accounts of how they fitted in with the institution. Some ethnic minority students spoke about 'keeping a low profile' at Castle. Farah, a British Pakistani student who went to a state school, used specific strategies to ensure she felt safe in the different environments at Castle.

> I have to make sure I mix with the right kind of people; not to say I don't mix with White students, but some of them just don't get it. If they don't recognize their own privilege, how are they going to understand how we [*ethnic minority students*] feel being here? They complain that too much attention is given to minority issues, yet they don't understand that these are the kind of issues that affect minority students. They are colour blind to their own privilege and are quick to dismiss it and talk about how **they** are disadvantaged. I don't understand it – they are the ones who are **the** most privileged. I have thought about it and think that maybe they feel threatened when they see more and more Black and Asian students on campus.
> [*original emphasis*]

As Jessica shows, some White students at Castle protected their elitism by creating their own hierarchies of difference and acceptance – by refusing to see their own privilege, and freezing out others from different backgrounds. When ethnic minority students enter the White space of elite higher education, they are automatically positioned as outsiders and are 'othered' because of both their race and class.[59] At the same time, ethnic minority students are less likely than their White peers to have access to the same level of economic and social resources before and during their course. Combined, this means that students like Jessica never fully integrate with their privileged White peers at universities like Castle, because these institutions continue to be predominantly White spaces, which esteem and value above all else *White privilege*.

AN ELITE FUTURE: 'IT'S MY TICKET TO SUCCESS'

The majority of students that I spoke to at Castle saw the value of attending an elite university and were aware of the advantages and opportunities it would bring. All the White students I interviewed said they would use their experience of attending an elite university to reinforce their already-existing contacts, as well as making new ones. Many respondents mentioned a 'closed' system of recruitment that applied to elite universities. Trudy, a student of mixed Black and White heritage and who had attended a state school, felt that the system of recruitment for graduate jobs at Castle and other elite universities was entirely exclusive. She also suggested that she, and other ethnic minority students, would still benefit from their attendance but framed this in terms of acquiring elements of Whiteness that correlated with exclusivity.

> Studying at Castle is like being part of a members-only club. That exclusive club is also White. You can just see how that exclusivity carries on, because you're pretty

> much guaranteed a good job if you have been to Castle. But that is also dependent on what you look like, so if you have been to Castle **and you are White**, you've pretty much made it. White exclusivity follows White exclusivity. [*original emphasis*]

Monty, a student of mixed Black and White heritage student who had attended a state school, also knew the value of gaining a degree from Castle.

> Of course I recognize the value of getting a degree from Castle, but that doesn't exclude other types of discrimination. Firstly, it doesn't rule out racism. Secondly, even though I will have a degree from Castle, it doesn't mean I won't experience racism when I apply for jobs, just because I've been to Castle. So, getting a degree from Castle is a bonus, but it doesn't exclude other types of discrimination.

Chris, a Black student who went to private school, also recognized this system of White privilege.

> Here at Castle, we have some real top law and banking firms who have conventions about the packages they can offer if you can get a job with them. It helps if you have done an internship in one of those companies; they know you and so they will hire you. It's always the same students – the White students who get in there first to secure their place because they have the connections anyway. They have a shoe-in and so get the jobs. It doesn't work like that for us; if we haven't got those connections, [*it's*] because our parents don't have those kinds of jobs.

Systems of elite privilege are reproduced not just through a student's educational trajectory, but also through routes *out* of higher education. Elite firms target elite universities because they know they can pick the 'best of the best' for their organizations. By doing so, they work to perpetuate a system of privilege reinforced by race and class; the 'best of the best' in effect being shorthand for 'people like us'. White students are confident that they will find elite employment through this process compared with students from ethnic minority backgrounds, because they possess the requisite intellectual, social and cultural know-how to perpetuate their own positions of advantage. Elite firms often disregard applicants from other universities, and by doing so, they ensure that their own sense of elitism is safeguarded. The linear progression from private school to elite university to a high-status profession by a particular cohort of wealthy, White students reproduces the White *classed* privilege of their families and social networks.

The Continuation of Privilege

From my interviews with students at Castle, we have seen how privilege reinforces and perpetuates *further* privilege. Many respondents were from families in which siblings, parents and grandparents had all attended the same, or similar, private schools and elite universities, and these families worked to preserve and perpetuate their elite status. They spoke about elite higher education as their ticket to success that would enable them to have high earning potential in the top jobs. This final result would be the culmination of years of parental investment to reproduce White privilege through their children. While at elite universities, these students are hungry for success to ensure their hard work pays off. As a result, White privilege is passed on from generation to generation through wealth and access to social and cultural capital.

The White students I spoke to saw themselves as different, as the chosen few, not just in their superior academic abilities but in their whole sense of *who they are*, 'defined by a particular set of tastes, values and *being*', according to American sociologist Shamus Khan.[60] Sociologists Amy Binder and Andrea Abel, who have studied elite education, say that 'students are not simply positioned by their parents or their universities to reproduce high status. Rather, students actively *do* status reproduction of their own through acts of cultural distinction or symbolic boundary drawing.'[61] At elite universities, the White students' sense of 'who they are' is constantly affirmed and reaffirmed by their peers and their professors, who remind them they are the 'crème de la crème' – the chosen few who have been selected to occupy the elite space. Through this process, White students are active participants in the continuation and reproduction of their own privilege, while ethnic minority students are constantly reminded of their marginal and outsider status, because they do not fit in to the White space of elite privilege.

Whiteness and the performance of Whiteness work to maintain the status quo and leave systems of oppression unchallenged, allowing a sense of entitlement to flourish. As we saw above, White students at Castle used conscious and deliberate actions to keep ethnic minority students *in their place*. These intentional acts are forms of White supremacy that privilege the *already* privileged – and ensure that, despite studying at the same university, White students can feel very differently about their ability to occupy its space and capitalize on its benefits.

CHAPTER 5
Equality Whitewash
A Hierarchy of Oppression and the Performativity of Whiteness

Students are not the only ones who experience racial inequality in the education system. Academic staff also report regular occurrences of overt and covert racism, from both their colleagues and students. In order to understand the impact of racism in higher education, it is important to examine how staff are affected by it and the influence it has on career progression, promotional prospects and the academic curriculum.

Research suggests that racism and racist practices exist at all stages of employment for ethnic minorities in the education sector: this includes during recruitment, career progression and promotion, and access to equal and fair treatment at every stage.[1] These measurable inequalities indicate that higher education is far from an equal space, and it is White groups who benefit most from inhabiting it. Racism, exclusion and marginalization are experienced on a daily basis by ethnic minority groups in higher education, as part of the structural, institutional and individual forms of racism that remain deeply ingrained in the culture of higher education institutions, in both their policies and the behaviour of staff and students alike. This is borne out by the statistics as well as a plethora of qualitative evidence, including my own research.[2]

White men, followed by White women, are most likely to be professors and occupy the most senior roles in higher education, as Table 5 shows. White groups are also more likely to occupy senior managerial roles compared with ethnic minority groups, as shown in Table 6. The majority of senior managers are White, with only a minority from Black, Asian and minority ethnic (BAME – the term used by Advance HE[3]) backgrounds.

While there is ample evidence of racial inequality in higher education, policy-making has failed to address this, focusing instead on addressing gender inequalities, with racial injustice relegated to second place.

(White) Policy-Making

The Equality Act introduced in 2010 brought together all previous legislation on fighting discrimination into one single act, including the Equal Pay Act (1970), the Sex Discrimination Act (1975) and the Race Relations Act (1976). A key feature of the Equality Act is the inclusion of race as a protected characteristic, making it against the law to discriminate against anyone on racial grounds. (Other protected characteristics include age, disability, gender reassignment, marriage and civil partnership, pregnancy and maternity, religion or belief, sex and sexual orientation.) The Public Sector Equality Duty – the legal duty of public authorities to consider how their policies and decisions affect people who are protected under the Equality Act – was introduced to eliminate unlawful discrimination, harassment and victimization, advance equality of opportunity and foster good relations between people who share a protected characteristic and those who do not. All organizations to whom this duty and the Equality Act apply, including schools and higher-education institutions, are required to implement policies that demonstrate their commitment to race equality.[4]

While the Equality Act introduced race as a protected characteristic, which is a positive step, its significance as a form of inequality has been diluted because it is judged in relation to other protected characteristics. As a result, schools and higher-education institutions can appear to be addressing inequalities in general under the umbrella of 'equality, diversity and inclusion' while giving greater priority only to certain inequalities. In effect, the Equality Act has provided schools and higher-education institutions with a get-out-of-jail-free card whereby they can sidestep racial inequalities – which are often much harder to address – by appearing to tackle them through initiatives that address 'bullying' or 'harassment' more broadly, or that make demonstrable commitments to addressing other forms of inequality. Consequently, the Equality Act has been largely ineffective in addressing racial inequalities in schools and higher-education institutions. Instead, such policies, among others, have created a culture in which schools and higher-education institutions feel they do not need to directly tackle, or prioritize, racial inequalities that students (and staff) may experience – as we have seen in earlier chapters of this book. Instead, by giving other inequalities (such as gender) greater priority, this encourages the impression that racial inequality is a separate, minor issue, something that takes place in

Gender/ethnicity	No.	%
White female	5,385	25.6
White male	13,335	63.5
BAME female	575	2.7
BAME male	1,705	8.2
Total	21,000	100

Table 5
UK professors in higher-education institutions by gender and ethnicity, 2019–2020

Source: Advance HE, *Equality in Higher Education: Staff Statistical Report 2021* (London: Advance HE, 2021)

Gender/ethnicity	No.	%
White female	420	32.9
White male	775	60.5
BAME female	25	2.1
BAME male	55	4.5
Total	1,275	100

Table 6
UK senior managers in higher-education institutions by gender and ethnicity, 2019–2020

Source: Advance HE, *Equality in Higher Education: Staff Statistical Report 2021* (London: Advance HE, 2021)

unusual circumstances and only fleetingly, rather than at a systemic and structural level. As a result, when schools and universities attempt to address racial inequalities, they do so by meeting specific objectives that resolve the symptoms of racism, rather than tackling underlying racist practices. In effect, they treat such inequalities as a problem that can be resolved by a tick-box exercise, and, by doing so, present an *illusion* that racism is being dealt with.

The Performativity of Whiteness and Policy-Making

As evidenced by the Equality Act, new policies are sometimes created by government to be *seen* to be addressing large-scale inequalities in our society. These kinds of policies are often *performative* – they stand more for what they represent rather than resulting in any meaningful change. Such performativity is widely identified as an outcome of a marketized education system, one that focuses on the *reputation* of an institution – which is measured via deliverables and proving it has ticked the right box – rather than addressing day-to-day inequalities in the workplace.[5] The aim of these targets is to assess productivity, the value or worth of an individual or an organization in the education sector, and how well they are engaging with addressing racial and other inequalities that are part of the system, in order to entice new students and academics to their institution. But instead, these deliverables are simply performative and tend to form part of the publicity in presentations at major events or in glossy publications or formal policy documents that choose to tell a narrative of progress that does not necessarily represent any significant change.

Furthermore, while new policies may be introduced at the national level to change wider patterns of social behaviour in the education system, how the policy is delivered at the local level varies from institution to institution. One example of this is the Race Equality Charter.

The Race Equality and Athena Swan Charters

Within this marketized framework of higher education – a direct result of the introduction of student fees and the creation of the Office for Students (as discussed in the previous chapter) – policy-making has become focused on a culture of accountability, based on setting targets and meeting performance expectations. Race equality has become part of this, and through the performance and enactment of race policies, higher-education institutions have been able to display their 'excellence' on tackling racial inequality both internally and externally. This standard of excellence is measured by investing in policies such as the Athena Swan Charter (Swan standing for Scientific Women's Academic Network) and the Race Equality Charter (REC), both of which demonstrate how such excellence is defined in relation to equality, diversity and inclusion.

The Athena Swan was introduced in 2005 to encourage more women to study STEMM subjects (science, technology, engineering, maths and medicine), in response to the low numbers of women in STEMM-related academic careers. The REC was introduced in 2016 to tackle racial inequalities in higher education, such as increasing the number of ethnic minority staff, addressing the awarding gap and pay gap, and

CHAPTER 5

a Eurocentric, predominantly White curriculum. Higher-education institutions in the UK must apply to become members of the Athena Swan and REC and must then apply for an award up to three years after becoming a member. Based on their targeted self-assessment framework and level of progress, they may receive a gold, silver or bronze award (in the case of the Athena Swan), or a bronze or silver award (in the case of the REC). These awards are based on the premise that they will improve the opportunities and learning experience of women and ethnic minorities, while at the same time enhancing the universities' reputation and status as part of promoting themselves to prospective students (and their parents) to encourage them to apply there.

As the REC was introduced just over a decade after the Athena Swan, institutions that apply for membership are more than likely already members of the Athena Swan or are applying for membership of it too. They will therefore be taking on equality work *in addition to* existing work on the Athena Swan, adding to already stretched workloads. Ironically, there is evidence to suggest that those individuals whom the charters are intended to support (women and ethnic minorities) are the very people who end up carrying out the equality work that is required to be successful in gaining the charters in the first place.[6] Women are disproportionately represented on self-assessment teams for the Athena Swan[7] and my research has shown that ethnic minority groups are more likely to be involved with REC work, with an expectation from White staff that 'race work' is the responsibility of their ethnic minority colleagues.[8]

On the other hand, the introduction of the REC is a good

thing in principle as it has the potential to address racism in higher education, as current legislation, such as the Equality Act (2010), is failing to do so. Race is the main priority of the charter (unlike the Equality Act), which provides a forum in which difficult and uncomfortable discussions can take place, not just about racist practices in higher-education institutions, but also about changing cultural practices and addressing structural, institutional and individual racism. However, my research has found that more financial investment and time for university staff is needed if the charter is to make a marked difference or any impactful change in higher education.[9]

While there have been significant advances in promoting equality, notably gender equality, to advance the position of women in higher-education institutions, this has often masked continuing racial inequality. Initiatives set up to promote gender equality have been used as a smokescreen by higher-education institutions to suggest that they are focusing on addressing *all* forms of inequality. In addition, my research shows that while gender inequalities are being tackled, with increased investment and better outcomes, this is at the expense of addressing or even acknowledging structural, institutional or individual forms of racism.[10] The REC provides universities with a measurable means of addressing racial inequalities in higher education, but membership is most often used as a public gesture, a way of *performing* inclusion, rather than committing to real change. So, as we shall see, while universities may have the achieved the badge of REC membership, they still fail to tackle real racism in their own organizations, such as addressing the low ethnic minority achievement awarding gap or the lack of any ethnic minority professors.

CHAPTER 5

Inequalities in Higher Education: Gender vs Race, and Performing and Enacting the Race Equality Charter

In this section, I focus on two pieces of my research that examine how effective the Athena Swan and REC have been in achieving gender and racial equality in universities today. I've chosen to spotlight these two pieces of research to show you, through their example, how racial inequalities in education often lose out to other equality agendas, such as gender, and how a hierarchy of oppression (in which one type of inequality is considered more important than another) can slowly form, with concerns relating to gender often overshadowing those about race. I carried out fifty-five interviews* across two projects with equality and diversity officers and members of self-assessment charter award teams at different universities in the UK.[11] The first study specifically examined the effectiveness of the REC in tackling racial inequality and the second compared the charter with the Athena Swan to explore how gender and racial inequalities were addressed. The studies focused on the different impact and effects of gaining a successful charter award in different higher-education institutions, including post-1992, Russell Group, Million Plus and non-affiliated institutions.[12]

A HIERARCHY OF OPPRESSION

A significant finding from the research of the first study demonstrates that the work and commitment that goes into

---

* The names of respondents are all pseudonyms.

'doing diversity' are often overlooked, not appreciated and rarely rewarded by senior managers. I found that diversity work does not contribute to other significant measures of university success, it is rarely accounted for in workloads and is not linked to promotional objectives. Some of the staff I spoke to were reluctant to invest their time and energies into yet *another* equalities charter. Consequently, these higher-education institutions chose to focus their efforts on improving access to STEMM subjects for women by applying for membership of the Athena Swan, rather than the REC. The work involved in applying for both was viewed as *too* demanding, *too* time-consuming and not worth investing in. The findings from my research suggest that this precedence of gender over race is seen as a plausible justification for *not* applying for or investing in yet another award. As a result, equalities work is seen as *gender* work.

Juliet, who was White and worked in a post-1992 university, spoke about this in terms of the effect it would have on her own workload and that of her colleagues.

> We've been working really hard for years, firstly to make sure we were successful in getting Athena Swan and then in making sure we kept it. There's been a lot of work that's gone into that – a lot of work that has taken me away from my own research – and impacted on adding a burden to all the teaching I have to do. People here have been saying we should go for the Race Equality Charter, but they don't know how much work is involved in that – in collecting all the data and the actual application. And I don't think we have money for it at the moment.

CHAPTER 5

Because of her experience of already having applied for the Athena Swan, Juliet was aware of the amount of work needed for the REC application. She approached it with a sense of fatigue and as something that her institution needed a break from.

> I feel very tired about all of these processes. When the REC has been mentioned, I do have to take a deep breath and wonder whether it's worth it, why another one? What difference is it going to make to what we are already doing? We are already addressing lots of different areas in Athena Swan anyway – there is a lot of data we have on intersectionality anyway, so we can just focus on that.

Similarly, John who was Black Caribbean and worked in a Russell Group university, also spoke about the workload associated with applying for the REC but emphasized the *importance* of applying for it none the less.

> When the Race Equality Charter is mentioned, it is always mentioned **in relation to** Athena Swan and the amount of work that needs to be invested in it. I think we are all aware of the amount of work, but it [*the REC*] should not always be compared to Athena [*Swan*], because it's similar but at the same time it's very different. When Athena was first mentioned, there was no reference to the amount of work it would involve – and we all knew it would affect our workloads, but this is always mentioned in relation to the Race Equality Charter. [*original emphasis*]

John was acutely aware that his university was keen to apply for the REC because it wanted to be recognized as an institution that took issues of equality seriously, and achieving the badge of membership was part of that accolade.

> You know when the university wants the accolade of saying we have the Race Equality Charter, then they have to invest in it and they have to put money into it. They want to show the outside [*world*] that they are serious about race equality, but that also has to take place in the time and money they put into it. The time puts people off because it means they are under a lot of pressure to do it [*i.e. work for the* REC] and if it fails, then they will be the ones to blame and it would be seen as, 'You spent all this time on it, and you didn't get it.'

What is clear is the work invested in applying for the Athena Swan (in terms of both time and financial commitment) always comes *before* the institution has either become a member of the REC or has applied for the award. This inadvertently fuels a reluctance to work towards applying for yet *another* award and thus focusing on another form of inequality: racism, in this instance. Consequently, addressing racial inequality falls through the cracks and is always a lower priority.

A SINGLE EQUALITIES CHARTER?

Due to these competing priorities, including competition for funding, some respondents suggested that having a single equalities charter would overcome the problem by addressing the unequal allocation of resources, which tends to arise when an individual senior manager (such as a vice-chancellor or pro-vice-chancellor) is passionate about tackling a particular type of inequality. Some staff suggested that a single equalities charter should be all-encompassing and include different inequalities. Angela, who was White and worked in a Russell Group university, believed that a single equalities charter would be more inclusive.

> It would be better if there was one single charter that we could focus on, and if that charter covered everything – gender and race, and disability and sexuality – that would make things easier. It would be more inclusive and there would be less of the argument of where the investment should go. All the different inequalities have to be addressed; we can't say one is more important than another – that just ends up creating resentment among colleagues. There's also the work that goes into putting the applications together, and if we do these all at the same time, the work would all go into one submission and all the investment could go into that.

However, others felt that a single equalities charter would be used to shift the focus away from race and direct it back to inequalities regarded as more important by their universities, such as gender (or sexuality, or disability, or trans rights). In addition, the danger of a single equalities charter diluted the importance of addressing all forms of racism, structural, institutional and individual, in higher-education institutions. As Adrian, who was of mixed Black and White heritage and worked in a post-1992 university, observed:

> If you have one single equalities charter, then the main focus on race would be lost in the conversation, and there would always be that narrative that we get now – that people

> would just ignore race and keep on talking about gender – as they do now. The conversation about race would get lost in the wider framework. I think that has the potential to be very dangerous because it would mean racism would never be addressed. Even if it is only being addressed on the surface, at least we are having the conversation. I think it would also make it much easier for universities to easily disguise their disinterest with race. They could just say they are addressing it, when in reality, conversations about race will just disappear. I think it could be dangerous and take us back to where we were ten years ago.

Farah, who was British Pakistani and worked in a plate-glass university (one founded in the 1960s), took a similar view.

> We want the specialist interest in race, because of the risk of it being ignored. We don't want to dilute race amongst all the other characteristics. It's taken us a long time to have the Race Equality Charter and I think we should be focusing on that, and on that alone. If not, we are just saying we are going back to what it used to be like, and if that happens it will be the same old story. White women will fight for gender rights – like they always have done in history – and we will just be ignored and our discrimination will be at the back of the queue of inequalities again. So, no, I definitely don't think we should have a single equalities charter; that would be the wrong thing to do.

These responses show how respondents fell into two schools of thought: some felt that addressing racial inequalities alongside other issues would be the most inclusive way forward, while others believed that addressing racism as a specific inequality in its own right was crucial. However, given the history and chronology of addressing gender inequality in higher-education institutions, and the more established and easier conversations that have taken place (and continue to take place) about advancing gender equality, race is unlikely to be prioritized in an already overcrowded equalities arena.

A COMPETITION OF INEQUALITY: WHO GETS MORE?

From my interviews with academic staff, it became clear that not all respondents felt that there was enough time, money or space to address racial inequalities alongside other competing concerns. Priya, who was British Indian and worked in a Russell Group university, described this as an excuse by senior staff for *not* investing in inequalities such as racism.

> There's always a conversation first about money and time. How can we put more money and time in the Race Equality Charter when we have invested it all in Athena Swan. Conveniently, the university doesn't have any money left. I think this is done on purpose; it's done so that they can control what the outcomes are. If you have the Race Equality Charter, there are objectives and outcomes you have to reach and you are held accountable to that. But if the university says we don't have enough money for it, then they don't have to apply for it and so can carry on focusing on gender and not be held accountable for race.

Meanwhile, Julie, who was White and worked in a post-1992 university, was concerned that other marginalized groups were missing out because of the focus on race.

> You have to focus on everything if you say you are addressing inequalities. In terms of our protected characteristics, we are doing lots for women and ethnic minorities, but what about the other marginalized groups? What about disabled staff and trans staff? It does anger me sometimes that we have done lots of work on gender already and now we want to focus on race, when there are other groups who are just ignored.

While Julie was acknowledging the needs of women and ethnic minorities, she was also suggesting that we need to leapfrog race and focus on the needs of other marginalized groups. Meanwhile, according to other respondents, introducing racism as another inequality to focus on was not justified. According to Janet, for example, who was White and worked in a post-1992 university:

> I think there is a greater need to focus on gender than race, and that is more justified because there are more women – more than 50 per cent of the workforce – than ethnic minority people who are working in higher education. So we [*the university*] can easily justify why we are focusing more on gender than race, it makes sense to do so.

This idea that gender is a larger catch-all and thus a less contentious subject is clear in the comments made by Lisa, a member of staff who was of mixed Black and White heritage and worked in a post-1992 university.

> People are much more comfortable talking about generic things like childcare because that affects **everyone**, doesn't it? It's easier for them to talk about that than about race – people get very uncomfortable and don't want to go there. If they don't talk about it, it kind of means they don't have to confront institutional racism and what is going on in their own institution. So, they just brush it aside and focus on more general things that make them feel better. [*original emphasis*]

Such remarks illustrate how the perceived constraints on time, money and attention ensure that the higher-education sector prioritizes what is considered to be a universal issue, such as childcare, which applies to *all* women who choose to have children, rather than race, which only focuses on the issues faced by ethnic minority women. This approach is problematic because it is suggests that the needs of one marginal group are more important than the other, because of their size – which completely overlooks what makes groups marginalized in the first place. It also fails to acknowledge how questions of race and racism exacerbate gender inequalities, and how such characteristics intersect with each other. Consequently, uncomfortable discussions about confronting structural, institutional and individual racism are sidestepped and racial inequalities continue to be ignored in the higher-education sector.

Location, Location, Location

Geographical location also played a part in how staff perceived the significance of racial inequality in education, and how relevant they thought the REC was to their university.

According to Jane, for instance, who was White and worked in a post-1992 university:

> The universities are all applying for the Race Equality Charter and it's like a competition as to who gets it first and who can demonstrate they have the badge. But I think we have to stop in our tracks a little bit here. I think that we need to question, does every university really have to apply for it? Is it necessary and why are they doing it? If we look at our campus here, and our area, we're not ethnically diverse by any means – both inside and outside the university – so you have to ask the question, what's the point of wasting time and energy if we don't have ethnically diverse places? It has to all be relative. We could end up investing too much time, energy and, more importantly, finance when we have to question, do we as an area that has no minorities really need to be thinking about investing in something that could be very time-consuming and expensive? I think you have to ask that question.

Meanwhile, Martin, who was White and worked in a post-1992 university, suggested that geographical location mattered less when addressing gender inequalities compared with racial issues.

> You shouldn't just apply for the REC because it's just another thing for the university to apply for. The emphasis and importance of race is going to be different for different institutions. There are some places, like ours, where the numbers of BAME [*Black, Asian and minority ethnic*] people in the population and the university itself is very

low, compared to the general population, and it will be very different to somewhere like London, Manchester or Birmingham, say, so your focus will be very different. But then it makes more sense to focus on gender and address those inequalities, because pretty much wherever you go, you know there are going to be the same numbers and proportions of men and women in the staff and student population. These present different challenges, but the logical decision is to address the gender imbalances.

To these respondents, the idea of investing in the REC and addressing racial inequalities in universities that were either predominantly White, or located in predominantly White areas of the UK, was seen as a waste of time and an unnecessary risk, a gamble in terms of the investment of time and money. This becomes a self-fulfilling prophecy, where those uninterested in issues of racial inequality do not want to invest in tackling them either. According to Deborah, who was White and worked in a Russell Group university:

> There has to be some consideration from the judging panels [*panels that grant charter membership*] about location. Some universities have applied for the Race Equality Charter and their submissions have been really good but they have been unsuccessful and they have been in areas where they are small towns and there is no big population of non-White people. Our university itself is very White and it reflects the area, which is also very White, but what happens is then the university is penalized because of this. But what can they do? They can't change the demographics. So, if you are located in an area that is mainly White, you

will find it harder to be successful, and it begs the question: should you really be investing and applying for it?

This focus on geographical location presents a fallacious justification for not tackling racial inequalities at White academic institutions. It clearly disadvantages students and those working in these universities who are not White, because it disregards them, and thus allows racism to flourish.

It also ignores the fact that many students and academic staff in the UK are geographically mobile, and so the connection to the local population is a false one. Most British students move from their hometown to go to university, and many higher-education institutions invest heavily in marketing themselves in the global higher-education marketplace as diverse institutions attractive to both British and international students. As a result, many of these universities, including all Russell Group and other elite universities, rarely have strong links within their immediate locality; they attract students nationally and internationally willing to travel to study in their towns and cities. Far from being local, therefore, universities are defined by their engagement in a competitive global marketplace. In these circumstances, the claims of providing an education for a predominantly White market suggest that the institutions themselves *assume* that Whiteness is the default position and are therefore active in generating the conditions in which racism remains ingrained in their institutional ethos. The emphasis on geographical location simply works to justify the *irrelevance* of race.

These respondents also demonstrated the wider perception of gender inequality as a universal issue, while racial inequality is not. Tackling racial inequality is seen as being valid and worthy *only* when racial diversity *already exists* and is a key feature of the institution. Consequently, higher-education institutions that are White-only spaces, and which tend to be *more* exclusive and elite (as discussed in the previous chapter), work to reinforce the illusion that they represent the normal, natural, given state of affairs, and they should only be more diverse if they are *already* diverse in the first place. These views justify the failure to address issues of race and racial inequality and the persistence of White privilege in higher-education institutions, and reaffirms the perception that racial discrimination is not a general form of inequality in our university system, but one that instead only affects some people in some places.

PERFORMING, SHOWCASING AND ENACTING THE RACE EQUALITY CHARTER

A significant finding from my first study was how the REC was used as a way of broadcasting how the universities appeared to be tackling racial inequality. Respondents spoke about how, when their institutions had decided that they would become members of the REC or had submitted their application, there was often quite a bit of publicity. These universities invested considerable time and money in high-profile launches, often with famous ethnic minority speakers endorsing the inclusivity of the institution in question. Universities deployed different measures for showcasing their involvement in the REC: by recruiting diversity champions from different departments, for instance, setting up a race action group or introducing seminars on Black history and culture. My study indicated that these measures were introduced mainly by White senior managers and endorsed by vice-chancellors and pro-vice-chancellors.

On the whole, respondents were positive about this investment in and commitment to charter membership, particularly when the charter was supported by the vice-chancellor and had their seal of approval. Linda, who was Black and worked in a Russell Group that held a REC award, commented:

> When you have senior managers showing how serious they are about the charter, then this makes a real difference. If you have someone from the top, such as the actual vice-chancellor – which is what we had – then that directly shows the importance and seriousness attached to it. We had a launch that included the VC [*vice-chancellor*] and the director of HR [*human resources*]. It was a big event and showed that this was serious and we are going to take it forward. I think this made other colleagues realize that this was serious and we were going to move forward with these issues and we were going to have conversations about race. That has made a difference.

Other respondents, however, were not so positive about such showcasing. Some suggested that it was a 'false charade' that was based on a performance by the vice-chancellor and White senior managers, one that was carefully stage-managed for maximum impact, rather than a process that would contribute to achieving key objectives to address structural, institutional and individual forms of racism. This sense of performance was related to who took the credit for being awarded REC membership and who did the 'hard graft'

CHAPTER 5

to achieve it. As touched on already, despite being supervised by White senior managers, the groundwork involved in applying for the charter is mainly the responsibility of ethnic minority staff.[13] Because of their backgrounds, ethnic minority staff are expected to participate in taking the charter forward and consequently they are the ones held accountable if it is unsuccessful. According to Annette, who was Black Caribbean and worked in a Russell Group university that held an REC award:

> I have noticed that when new ways of looking at race are introduced, then the burden always falls on the shoulders of BME [*Black and minority ethnic*] people. They are the ones who end up having to do all the hard work that goes into the [REC] application. It shouldn't be seen as their responsibility to do it just because they are from a BME background. If we are going to address what the university is going to do about tackling racism, then this has to be done by everyone, at every level. It is not the sole responsibility of BME staff. There is an automatic assumption that because you are not White, then you will be interested in equality stuff, but some BME people are simply not interested in it. There is also an assumption that because you are not White, you are carrying out research on social justice issues. Again, this is not always the case and universities must think about their own assumptions about who does this research and who does not. Those assumptions are themselves part of the racism.

It is a common assumption made by White senior managers and colleagues that ethnic minority staff are the ones most likely to be able to understand racism, and hence should carry out the work needed to make a successful REC application, in effect to try to resolve a problem that is not of their own making. Yet ethnic minority staff are not necessarily in a senior enough position to have the power to make any significant changes to policies or practices or to initiate investment in addressing racial inequalities. Because of this, significant change only takes place when it might benefit the institutions or White senior managers themselves, and usually through interest convergence (as we saw in Chapter 1). If changes take place that threaten the position of White senior groups, they are unlikely to be implemented. Only those changes that result in insignificant small steps, which appear inclusive on the surface – such as introducing an ethnic minority speaker series or staff group – are implemented. In this way, the interests of powerful White groups are protected, at the expense of ethnic minority groups who have little or no power within the White hierarchical structures in higher-education institutions.

All ethnic minority respondents raised concerns about the amount of work required by them to attain membership of the REC and how this was often not acknowledged or rewarded. This was in contrast to the high-profile public support given to White senior managers from vice-chancellors for investing in the scheme. This kind of performativity focuses on gaining the badge, of being successful in achieving the status of REC membership, rather than the *delivery* of specific outcomes related to addressing issues of race and racial inequality across the whole higher-education institution. Instead, this *performance* of racial inclusion is used to demonstrate the university's commitment to enhancing diversity. Charter membership is proudly displayed on university websites and prospectuses to sell the university as inclusive in order to attract fee-paying students. The actual *enactment* of the charter then becomes little more than a public-relations exercise used to enhance the reputation of the institution, rather than a strategy to deliver change and real *outcomes*. According to Jackie, who was Black Caribbean and worked in a non-affiliated university that was a member of the REC:

> When we are doing all the work that goes with the REC, we have to be mindful of **what** it's for and **who** it's for. It's to make changes in the university, it's to address racism in the different structures and processes, such as in recruitment and promotion, and to address things like the reporting structures if people experience racism. Sometimes the endgame gets lost and people become more obsessed in getting [*membership of*] the charter and saying, 'Look at us we're inclusive, we've got the Race Equality Charter,' rather than thinking about what it's really **for**. We have to be very careful that the REC is used to make changes and differences. We have known about the racism in universities for a very long time, years pass and nothing changes. Maybe we have to think that the REC is an opportunity for change, but we have to ensure that it results in real differences rather than just another accolade the university can say they have achieved. [*original emphasis*]

A number of respondents were sceptical about what would happen if their institutions managed to attain REC membership. Some respondents felt that once their institutions were successful in gaining charter membership, discussions about race would be forgotten, resulting in measures only being implemented as a simple 'tick-box' exercise. As Pat, who was Black African and worked in a Russell Group university that had REC membership, commented:

> The thing I think we have to think about when we consider the Race Equality Charter is the long-term benefits of it. We can't think that we've got it and then can move on. It has to be about making changes that are long-lasting and show that we have used it for improvement. I can see it becoming something that we've got and then we can sort of rest on our laurels and do nothing about race. It could become something that we have achieved and then something else comes along to take its place. That is the real danger. It has to be something that carries on all the time and doesn't just stop because you have the award. That is going to be the real challenge. Race has to be seen as something that is embedded in the whole structure of the university, rather than being assigned to a specific department like EDI [*equality, diversity and inclusion*].

The REC could be a great way to enact race policy, to ensure that tackling racial inequalities in education becomes a key priority of universities around the country. This should be about ensuring long-lasting change in addressing racial inequalities in the higher-education sector by all groups (and not just those from ethnic minority backgrounds), but in reality, however, and as we have seen, it is ethnic minority staff who are the ones who shoulder the burden – and who are allocated the role of collecting data and conducting the research to deliver and submit the REC application – rather than there being an expectation that *all* staff should participate. In my research, I have questioned whether these kinds of policies are used to implement real change in relation to racial discrimination, and whether they make any concrete difference to the lives of ethnic minority groups.[14] The failure to link wider structural inequalities, such as the lack of ethnic minority professors or vice-chancellors, to the kinds of struggles ethnic minorities face at universities suggests that all these policies can only create a rhetoric of change, or only reinforce already-existing racial inequalities, which renders such policies unfit for purpose.[15] The REC creates a rhetoric of inclusion that fails to address racial inequalities because it leaves the status quo intact. Instead, it continues to perpetuate White privilege and White supremacy by reinforcing processes of exclusion and marginalization to keep ethnic minority people *in their place*.

MORE PERFORMATIVITY: TICKING THE BOX AND PAYING 'LIP SERVICE'

The Race Equality Charter is a good example of how racial inequality is addressed in higher-education institutions, which pay lip service to the idea but do not necessarily back it up with genuine action, leading to better outcomes. Many respondents felt that their institutions were not entirely honest in their goals for applying for charter membership. According to Jane, who was Black Caribbean and worked in a post-1992 university that was not a member of the charter:

> I wonder whether this all just a song and dance element to what the institution is really going to do in terms of making changes. Are they just paying lip service and doing this because other institutions are doing it and they don't want to be left out? That is often the way that universities work: when they see other competitive universities doing one thing, they all think they should be doing the same thing. In this way, it's not really for the real benefit of making a difference; it's about doing it because others are doing it – and then that in itself becomes the song and dance element because it's just about conforming.

There is a clear divergence between the public narratives communicated by higher-education institutions about addressing racial inequalities and the actual changes implemented in individual departments and faculties. Work on race equality that has made a difference has often been going on for years without any need for REC membership, usually conducted by ethnic minority staff. As Janice, who was of mixed White and Black heritage and worked in a post-1992 university that was a member of the charter, observed:

> There are a lot of us here in the department that have already been doing work in the area [*of race and racism*] so we know all the data and we have the evidence. Now the charter is being used to say the university is doing work on race, when some of us have been doing it for many years. To me, that feels very insulting, as if the work we have been already doing is either not seen as important or not valued enough, but then it is only valued when it is related to getting a public badge for it. The university has

> known about the work I do for years but it has never been seen as important or even acknowledged. If anything, it has been seen as something that is about a minority group that they're not interested in. It only becomes interesting when the university think they can gain from it and get something from it. Other than that, it just totally gets ignored.

As Janice indicates, work on issues of race and racism is rarely acknowledged or seen as important by institutions and White senior managers. However, some respondents said they would use the REC to formalize their research so that it could be seen as legitimate and worthy. According to Jyoti, who was British Indian and worked in a post-1992 university that was not a member of the charter:

> The REC has just made these issues [*race and racism*] more formal, more in the public arena. We now have a policy that takes these things into consideration, but it's nothing new. We have known about these inequalities for a long time. But the key difference now is having [*membership of*] the charter, which means that universities must be held accountable for their actions and explain what they have done to improve things. I hope that means that they can take our research seriously and use it in a good way to make an informed decision about the types of things that go on, like the real racism that we have in this university. Using proper research that has been around for years to inform the process of change means the decisions are coming from a proper research base – and that is something that rarely happens with

research on race. And that is a bigger problem because research on race is not seen as having any priority.

As Jyoti says, the REC may not address the bigger problem of racial discrimination in education, but instead it could become a tool to measure and document all the good work on research into race that is already taking place and give it official recognition. While higher-education institutions like to signal that they are addressing racial inequalities (such as investing financially in the REC), such efforts are rarely little more than a publicity stunt and will never be the driver of real change: instead, it is the work and research by people like Jyoti, and longer-term commitment by the university, that hold the key to making equity possible.

Playing the (White) Policy Game

Equality initiatives in higher-education institutions such as the Athena Swan and REC are clearly important frameworks for tackling different types of inequality. REC membership is important because it has encouraged higher-education institutions to begin to have challenging conversations about inequality. However, the chronology of the Athena Swan and the REC, the latter having been introduced eleven years after the Athena Swan, has meant that the race is regarded as a lower priority by comparison with gender. As we have seen, higher-education institutions are eager to publicize their efforts to address different inequalities, citing their investment in the Athena Swan. By drawing on this narrative, there is little incentive to make further investment in the REC. When charged with tackling racial injustice, higher-education institutions display an overt apathy and fatigue, preferring to address what are perceived to be universal inequalities such as those relating to gender, rather than to race. When race and gender become conflated, race is minimized and lost in the wider picture, and when the topic is discussed, it is only done so *after* discussions about gender. By combining work on race and gender inequalities, higher-education institutions can *demonstrate* that they are addressing these issues, when in fact they are perpetuating a system of White privilege that in this case prioritizes gender.

In addition, because the Athena Swan came before the REC, the latter creates an additional workload for staff and necessitates an increase in investment that is already stretched in terms of time and money. The response to this from higher-education institutions is to adopt economizing strategies such as combining work on race and gender and taking the view that race is not as necessary, vital or urgent an issue as gender. The deployment of economizing strategies in the name of efficiency is in effect a backwards step in terms of addressing racial inequalities. Instead, what is needed is greater investment in resources and recognition of the workload associated with the REC and other diversity projects. The REC itself should lead to wider institutional and cultural change (as has been demonstrated by the enactment of the Athena Swan), rather than becoming a simple 'tick-box' exercise. Furthermore, membership of the REC should be linked to research funding, so that all higher-education institutions invest in addressing racial inequalities, rather than just those whose senior managers are passionate about such issues.

Applying for REC membership and successfully gaining a charter award is an example of policy-making that works to benefit systems of White supremacy and White privilege. While the REC provides a nationwide scheme by which higher-education institutions may demonstrate a formal commitment to addressing issues of race and racial inequalities, enactment of the REC by individual institutions is something that should be measured, with specific targets to be met. Indeed, it would be regarded as progressive if charter members could be seen to have met their stated goals, such as tackling the number of ethnic minority staff on zero-hours contracts, closing the pay gap between ethnic minority and White staff and ensuring that the curriculum is more diverse rather than Eurocentric and predominantly White. However, this is not the reality. The same inequalities persist year after year. Instead, the REC is used by higher-education institutions as a smokescreen to reinforce the notion that the 'race problem' can be solved by a single initiative whose aim is to gain an award. The badge appears to demonstrate success while failing to address racism in any form, whether structural, institutional or individual. Implementation of the charter thus merely reproduces existing patterns of inequality, as *enactment* of the policy is about gaining an award rather than addressing the actual problem. The performativity and enactment of the REC becomes a ritual, a dance, a to-ing and fro-ing without addressing racial inequalities in any concrete way. This deliberate ritual works for the benefit of higher-education institutions, which reinforce normative practices and ideologies to uphold a system of White supremacy that benefits White groups.

CHAPTER 6
Race Equality Training
For Whose Benefit?

Anyone working in schools and higher-education institutions will be aware of the term *diversity*, generally nested in the triad of equality, diversity and inclusion (EDI). It is a recurrent buzzword that can seem imbued with a great deal of positive meaning, while also feeling slightly ambiguous and ill-defined. It is not always clear how equality, diversity and inclusion are differentiated in an educational setting, but they tend to be the focus of training courses run by schools and universities for their staff. However, as I aim to show in this chapter, the positive attributes of 'diversity' are often unmatched by real action or results. And, in addition, a policy of 'diversity' is often a means by which institutions can 'perform' a commitment to promoting racial equality while simultaneously doing little or nothing to encourage real change. If anything, 'diversity' is a performative tool that effectively maintains White racial hierarchies.

In this chapter, I focus on how EDI training works for the benefit of organizations rather than addressing the issues that prevent ethnic minority academics from progressing in higher education. I examine how, under the umbrella of EDI, training programmes are designed to focus on systems, institutional change and the 'development' of future ethnic minority leaders within a deficit model – which places the blame on individuals for their lack of achievement rather than addressing the faults and failures of an education system that prevented them from achieving their full potential in the first place. This training is premised on ethnic minority staff becoming more adept at navigating systemically racist institutions, rather than addressing underlying institutional racism itself. In this context, diversity work is used to maintain rather than dismantle the status quo, so that White groups continue to occupy positions of power, thus perpetuating a system of Whiteness and White supremacy.

Diversity?

The main drive behind diversity training is to promote equal opportunities. Diversity work encompasses a wide range of different approaches for addressing inequalities in the workplace, with the aim of creating an inclusive and representative workforce. It tends to focus on organizational processes rather than the personal experience of staff, with an emphasis on performance-related outcomes.[1] In terms of race-equality training, improving the outcomes for ethnic minority staff in higher education tends to be based on pre-existing ideas of success. The evidence of some groups doing less well in the workplace is understood to be a deficiency in which they are required to perform better, and diversity training is intended to give them the tools to enable them to succeed. As a means of tackling institutional racism, this approach is deeply flawed, however: ethnic minority groups are effectively being trained to mirror successful White behaviours in settings in which racism is the norm. At the same time, the promotion of diversity initiatives within the workplace suggests that the institution is committed to promoting equal opportunities.

Perhaps the greatest irony of diversity work in education is that it often falls on the shoulders of marginalized groups, adding to their workload.[2] In terms of issues of race and racism, and as we have seen with the Race Equality Charter, it is often ethnic minorities who are identified as best placed to 'solve' the diversity problem.[3] This work impacts on the time ethnic minority staff can spend on activities that affect career promotion and progression, including, in higher education, conducting research and publishing it, applying for funding and attending conferences and building professional networks. In a similar vein, ethnic minority students are also more likely to seek out ethnic minority staff for academic and emotional support, adding to already over-burdened workloads. I have argued that such work is not acknowledged, it is time-consuming and emotionally draining, and has little or no effect on career progression.[4] A significant change is needed in academia to give recognition to such work in performance reviews for career progression and promotion. If not, ethnic minority staff will continue to have to engage in work of little personal benefit that obscures genuine inequalities in order to promote a positive *public* image.

Training Programmes: The Solution?

Schools and higher-education institutions are not obliged to publish data about their training plans, making it difficult to collect exact figures on the numbers of diversity training programmes. However, anecdotal evidence from head teachers and vice-chancellors suggests that, since the Black Lives Matter protests in 2020, there has been a significant increase in the number and different types of training programme available for ethnic minority staff to support them in advancing their careers. Such programmes are cast as the 'solution' to the 'problem' of racism. Their increasing popularity seemingly correlates with shifts in public opinion and a desire within the education sector that schools and universities are seen to be inclusive organizations.

In the UK, ethnic minority academics are noticeably underrepresented in senior roles and often seen as outsiders in the predominantly White space of higher education.[5] Alongside widespread evidence of structural, institutional and individual forms of racism in higher-education institutions, research suggests that ethnic minority academics require greater support to reach their full career potential.[6] This has led to the introduction of new training programmes across higher education, used to challenge existing systems and support future ethnic minority leaders in their career trajectories. Such programmes tend to be promoted as a means by which ethnic minority staff can develop strategies to improve their leadership skills and be supported in reaching senior, leadership roles. They tend to adopt traditional methods, such as mentoring and coaching or providing access to professional networks for career advice, which have been shown to benefit career advancement.[7] A form of mentoring used in universities has been the pairing of senior White leaders with junior ethnic minority staff.[8] One problem with such initiatives is that they are based on a normative White perspective. Very few of these programmes consider the different experiences of ethnic minority staff and thus fail to acknowledge the impact of structural, institutional and individual racism on the career aspirations of ethnic minority staff members. Furthermore, they are largely premised on ethnic minority staff learning strategies that work for White groups negotiating systemically racist White institutions.

Similar targeted training programmes have been shown to have a significant impact on advancing the careers of women in terms of networking and developing positive strategies.[9] However, these gender-focused programmes often overlook the specific needs of ethnic minority women. My research has found that when ethnic minority women have attended such programmes, they have encountered racism and reported feelings of frustration and a lack of understanding of their needs.[10] The following sections explore research I conducted to examine whether such training programmes are useful in supporting the career progression of ethnic minority staff.

Routes to (White) Leadership

I carried out thirty interviews with ethnic minority staff who had attended training programmes specifically designed to support their career progression to senior roles at two Russell Group universities: Tower and Riverdale.* I conducted fifteen interviews at each university, with both academic and administrative staff. The study considered whether the training programmes were effective in achieving their aims and objectives in addressing the specific needs of ethnic minority staff, and whether the programmes offered the best advice

---

* The names of the universities and respondents are all pseudonyms.

for advancing their careers. The programme at Tower University addressed how ethnic minority staff could become leaders in higher-education institutions, and was targeted at ethnic minority staff who wished to progress to senior leadership roles. Riverdale University, meanwhile, ran a residential course that also taught strategies for career progression for ethnic minority staff, and which included a mixture of coaching and mentoring and reflexive practice (examining one's own thoughts and actions and learning from them).

THE VALUE OF TRAINING PROGRAMMES

There were mixed responses about the value of the training programmes. Some respondents felt they were very useful. They particularly enjoyed the information the programmes provided on how leadership worked and the different qualities and characteristics associated with it. Many felt that the programmes provided them with opportunities to make connections with other ethnic minority staff at a similar level within the organization. Some said the programmes helped them to increase their self-confidence and to see the value of emphasizing their strengths, skills and other abilities when applying for promotion to senior roles. As a result, they felt the time and financial investment in the training programme by their employers was worth it. As Steven, who was of mixed White and Black heritage and worked at Tower, observed:

> There are different aspects to leadership that I never thought about. This course has helped me to understand the theories behind how leadership works and what behaviours are associated with that. It also means that I can

think about that in my own behaviour at work and see how I can change it so that it reflects the correct leadership style that I need to follow to get promoted. There are certain ways of doing things that work and I don't think that I have been doing that before. Knowing about the different leadership theories and how they work can make you think about your own leadership style and how it fits in with what you are trying to achieve, whether that is going for a promotion or applying for a senior role.

Others noted how the training highlighted the behavioural aspects of leadership. Janice, who was Black Caribbean and worked at Riverdale, described this as adapting to specific behaviours.

I think there are ways of behaving that require you to show leadership, and not everyone knows how to do that. This has helped me to understand how to use that way of behaving in ways that show I am a leader and I can lead and so people will look at me that way and then see me – in their mind – as a leader. I didn't know about them before and this course has helped me to understand them and use them in my own career trajectory. There are certain things that you have to understand and be able to do if you want to take on a specific leadership role. There are different ways of **being** a leader and you have to choose which works best for you, in terms of the type of role you want to take on in the future. [original emphasis]

Although both Steven and Janice enjoyed the leadership training, it is interesting that both attributed their lack of career progression to a style of leadership that did not conform to the way recommended by the training programme. This suggests that the training assumed that a style of behaviour – unfamiliar to them both – was better than their own styles of leadership, and thus assumed that they were lacking or *deficient* in some way in how they performed their roles.

Some respondents identified the mentoring aspect of the course as particularly useful, because it offered guidance on how to find a mentor and use their advice in specific ways to advance their careers. Paul, who was Black Caribbean and worked at Riverdale, felt that having a mentor was crucial when applying for promotion, but qualified this in terms of ethnicity.

> Mentors are very important, because they help you see things you don't see yourself and they help you think about what you can improve on to achieve that goal. I think the mentoring process can work really well, but I would prefer to have a mentor who had not only been through the promotion process themselves but was also someone who was from a Black background, so that they could understand the additional pressures of being Black and working in a university, and what that entails. Having someone from the same background as you is important, because they can identify with the struggles you have and you don't have to explain that to them. Whereas some people may simply not understand the struggles or even accept that they exist. So, for mentoring to work for me, it has to be someone who has that experience of being a senior person but also someone who understands the disadvantages we face as Black groups.

Paul's comments suggest that mentoring is effective not because it fills a deficit in someone's personal attributes, but because it enables them to identify successful strategies for challenging inequality in the workplace. Some respondents felt that the university should invest purely in mentoring rather than training programmes. In so doing, the university would signal an ongoing commitment to diversity rather than relying on one-off training initiatives. Tara, who was Black Caribbean and worked at Riverdale, felt that formal mentoring schemes would be beneficial for ethnic minority academics.

> I think greater investment in ways forward would be a good thing – rather than just sending us on a single course that they [*White senior managers*] think can just change everything. We don't have many supportive systems in place at my university. I know in other places they have formal mentoring schemes where you can choose your own mentor and that can make a difference. The university has to invest in this to ensure that it is done properly and, again, it cannot be a tokenistic exercise. If they want to make sure we are part of the university, then they have to ensure that we are supported. The mentoring I get is from people who are not in my university. Our university should invest in mentoring for their staff and ensure that it meets their needs; it is not doing that at the moment. I also they think should ask us what we want as support and the type of mentoring we want, because that would make a difference. I don't think that the same types of mentoring work for everyone and mentoring for

CHAPTER 6

minorities has to be mindful of the fact that racism plays a big part in our experiences at universities.

While mentoring has been shown to be effective for ethnic minority staff, having access to mentoring schemes is often dependent on *who* selects which staff should be mentored. In many ways, this reflects the wider patterns of diversity training. Participants at both Riverdale and Tower acknowledged that their selection to take part in their respective programmes was largely determined by their managers. In the context of mentoring, the selection of mentors and mentees reflects unconscious bias in the workplace. There is often a suspicion that those who control mentoring select those who are like them, people they can identify with, in order that similar people with similar backgrounds and traits continue to be represented in the workplace.

Female ethnic minority respondents were more likely to say the training programmes did not meet their expectations. They felt the programmes did not address the specific challenges ethnic minority *women* face when navigating the complexities of leadership as an ethnic minority woman. Many felt the programmes were too generic in their focus, and could apply to *all* women, rather than specifically meeting the needs of ethnic minority women. Respondents stressed how the programmes just added the term 'diversity' to make them appear more attractive and applicable to ethnic minority staff. According to Susan, who was Black Caribbean and worked at Tower:

> The programme gave you basic information that was too general and could literally apply to anyone who wants to

get promoted. It didn't address the difficulties and challenges associated with those difficulties for women who are not White. In some ways, it was kind of ignoring that aspect of getting ahead, but including it at the same time without giving it any real meaning or importance. From that perspective, you could just take the programme and anyone could do it. It's not really correct to sell it as being aimed at non-White staff. It hasn't been thought out very well because there is the assumption that you have to do these things and then you get promoted, but what about addressing the disadvantages that apply to me because I am a Black woman? These issues have not really been addressed; they have been sidestepped.

Training programmes aimed at ethnic minorities did not address race, class and gender as multiple areas of oppression, and equated issues of race and racism with gender inequalities. Indeed, some elements of the programme were copied from gender equality training. This is doubly problematic. First, it fails to acknowledge race and racism as a specific issue. Secondly, as Priya, a British Asian who works at Tower, noted, the gender training on which it was premised was based largely on the experiences of White women.

The leadership perspective on this course feels very much like it's addressing the needs of White, middle-class or working-class women and the barriers they face to promotion. It doesn't really address our needs as Black or Asian women. It is written from the framework that the norm is White women who need to be promoted and so their needs are being met. I think it's a bit dishonest because it's sold to us in a way that it is directed to us as people of colour, but at the same time it completely ignores that aspect. The trainers mentioned racism once at the beginning and, even then, it felt like they didn't really have that knowledge that's needed to understand how that works in universities. I think that part of the course is really lacking. There needs to be more thought and acknowledgement given to the fact that our experiences are not as simple as just thinking about gender; they are more complex than that, and this includes race, and on top of that some of us are working class, so that is an additional disadvantage.

From Priya's perspective, the programme was sold on a false promise, as gender and the experiences of women were in fact prioritized over those of race. Other participants discussed the impact of their gender and class on their racial identity, further restricting their chances of reaching senior roles. Not only are training programmes, and the university policies that underpin them, designed without taking account of intersecting identities, but they also often appear to derive from training geared to White women. The structures of gendered Whiteness are not questioned, hence the programmes are used to *perpetuate* normative White practices. In my research, I have highlighted the importance of using an intersectional approach in order to establish how multiple inequalities combine to affect women's progress in higher-education institutions in different ways, and the significance of their past history in understanding how ethnic minority staff perceive academia.[11] Consequently, training programmes must always bear in mind how intersecting identities affect career progression and promotion, in order to redress power imbalances, past and present, to help ethnic minority academics achieve their full potential.

Developing Strategies for Career Progression

While the programmes give participants advice on how to develop strategies for advancing their careers, such as expanding networks and increasing their visibility in their organizations, these do not include strategies for dealing with racism. David, who was Black Caribbean and worked at Tower, felt that a lack of understanding of the lived experience of racism in the workplace led to training that acknowledged racism but without doing much to tackle it.

> The course did touch on how microaggressions exist in the workplace, but at the same time they didn't tell us what we can do about them. It was kind of like – they are here and they exist, and that's it. So we can't really do much about them. The strategies they told us about like networking didn't really address how race comes into play. It was all done from a White perspective. I think the danger of these courses is that they simply ignore that microaggressions affect everything we as Black academics do in universities. We need to know how to deal with them, call them out, how to complain about them and to understand that these are the issues – the real day-to-day issues – that we experience, and what they're saying in some ways by not giving us solutions is that there's nothing we can do about them, and that is very depressing. So it means nothing will change.

Similarly, other respondents felt that the programmes did not address structural racial inequalities. Devi, who was British Indian and worked at Tower, felt that this reflected a lack of understanding of the issues that ethnic minority academics have to deal with every day.

> The training sessions gave us different strategies but it didn't really address those real inequalities which exist – like the fact that there are few minority vice-chancellors and the things we need to do to address those real problems. It was a bit naïve of the trainers to think that just coming to this course will change the way things operate and that we will just get promoted. The structures will remain the same and won't change. Even if we make changes ourselves, it doesn't mean those changes will be taken in a serious or sympathetic way, because the system will remain the same. We have to work from the basis that we have to somehow change the system. That is the bigger question that we can't do by attending a training course. I think that this is what needs to be addressed and just coming on a course like this isn't going to solve the bigger issues. But by having this course, it means that [*White*] senior managers can think they are doing something to address the issues, but in reality I don't think that things will change that much.

The programmes at both universities assumed that attending them would solve the specific inequalities faced by their ethnic minority staff. However, this does not necessarily translate into an engagement with the structural, institutional and individual forms of racism experienced by participants

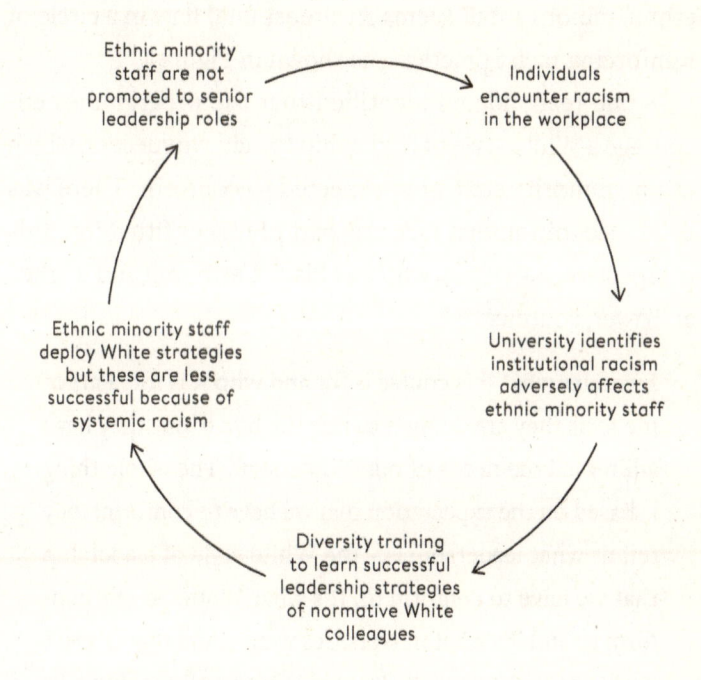

Figure 1
Patterns of Reinforcing Racism in Higher Education

- Ethnic minority staff are not promoted to senior leadership roles
- Individuals encounter racism in the workplace
- University identifies institutional racism adversely affects ethnic minority staff
- Diversity training to learn successful leadership strategies of normative White colleagues
- Ethnic minority staff deploy White strategies but these are less successful because of systemic racism

and which most believe are the cause of their marginalization. The same evidential patterns of racism are also presumably at the heart of investment by both universities in diversity training. The programmes' failure to challenge or question how racism impacts on the career opportunities of ethnic minority staff seems an almost fatal flaw in a circle of reinforcing racist practices, as shown in Figure 1.

Some respondents identified that the programmes encourage a White style of leadership to achieve success, which ethnic minority staff were expected to conform. There was little recognition that race was part of this or fitted into this perspective. As Angela, who was Black Caribbean and worked at Tower, commented:

> I wonder what this course is for and **who** it is for? Part of me feels they are doing it to tick the box to say they have addressed the needs of non-White staff. The whole thing is based on the expectation that we have to conform; they tell us what leadership is – the White style of leadership that we have to conform to. It's what White people conform to and it's what universities want – and that doesn't work for us because we're not White and we don't fit into that mould. It's difficult to know how we can move beyond that and change it. We need managers of colour in those top places but they only get there by conforming to what it means to be White, but I think once they are there, then we can look up to them and think this is a non-White style of leadership and these are our role models. But how do we get there in the first place? That's the real challenge. It's a difficult one for me, because whilst I want

to get promoted for my career and want to be successful in a leadership role, I know at the same time that I am adhering to a White style of leadership and I have to do that and conform to that model to be accepted and to progress in my career. It is a real challenge because you have to buy in to that White way of **behaving** which is considered acceptable and promotable. [*original emphasis*]

On the one hand, there is a recognition from White senior managers that there is lack of ethnic minority staff in senior roles and that they face specific barriers to reach those positions. On the other hand, policies and programmes are derived from the practices and procedures of White institutions. Programmes designed exclusively for ethnic minority staff are premised on identifying them as a group needing 'special' attention, yet even acknowledging this difference further marginalizes ethnic minority staff.

In the training programmes, networking is consistently promoted as a successful career strategy – which it is. However, networking is also a feature of the social preferences at play within an institution. Consequently, when universities are institutionally racist, the most powerful networks are those that have previously benefited from, and therefore retain an interest in, maintaining an institutionally racist status quo – so, for example, powerful university committees will continue to be represented by White academics who work to serve their own interests. These networks are constituent parts of a system that perpetuates racism. The assumption that ethnic minority groups will be able to access influential networks in the same way as their White colleagues does not take into account the networks of powerful individuals – with access to particular information and who serve on committees where important decision-making takes place – that form the connective tissue by which White groups ensure that they continue to occupy senior, decision-making roles.[12] Ethnic minority groups are less likely to have access to the same or similarly well-placed networks because these networks deliberately exclude them. Such networks control and reproduce what is considered the appropriate forms of 'knowledge' and 'behaviours' required to reach senior positions in White hierarchies that *they* control.

These training programmes are designed *not* to support and address the inequalities ethnic minority staff face when applying for senior positions, nor to challenge the dominant ideological structures, but instead are used by White senior managers (who, as we have seen in the statistics given in Chapter 5, are the majority of managers in the UK) to control and reproduce standards that reflect the normativity of Whiteness. As a result, ethnic minority staff are expected to adhere to Whiteness and White culture that marginalizes them as 'other'. Consequently, these training programmes give the impression of inclusion, while at the same time marginalizing ethnic minority staff and according little or no legitimacy or credibility to their experiences of racism in the workplace.

The programmes at Tower and Riverdale were run by ethnic minority trainers who were able to empathize with participants' experiences of racism. However, while respondents acknowledged that this was a positive thing, they also felt that by not including White staff (particularly senior managers) in the leadership aspects of training, this let them off the hook as it meant that there was no opportunity to discuss with White colleagues issues that affected ethnic minority staff. Adrian, who was Black Caribbean and worked at Riverdale, felt that there needed to be some recognition from White staff about how the system excluded ethnic minority staff from applying for promotion to senior roles.

> It is a good thing to have non-White trainers because they know where we are coming from, but at the same time it felt strange that there were no White academics in the room. They also need to be here and listen to what staff are saying and understand that they are the ones who need to make changes so that we can be included in **their** White systems. We work with **them** [*White academics*] every day and in some ways it doesn't really make sense to not include them in the conversation. By not having them here, it means they don't have to confront the systems they are part of, and they can simply ignore the racism. It also means they don't have to think about themselves, how they are part of the process, or the problem. I think that is very ignorant of the way the courses have been designed. And at the same time, it kind of excuses them from taking responsibility for what they are complicit in, and so gives them an easy ride. I think they should be here and listen to what we as minorities have to say about how universities continue to exclude us. It's easy for them as they can pass the buck and put the responsibility on minorities – who are the ones here running the course. It relieves them

CHAPTER 6

[*White senior managers*] of their responsibilities, because then they can say we have done something, but without themselves playing a part in that. [*original emphasis*]

The Cost of Diversity

A number of respondents noted the high cost associated with attending such diversity courses. For universities they are a substantial investment both in terms of the costs of the training itself and time not spent on usual work. And they not always worth the money, in the view of some respondents. As Farah, who was British Pakistani and worked at Riverdale, observed:

> It feels like these courses can be bought and sold, and so the real issues can be addressed by selling these courses and us minorities attending them. That makes me feel a bit uncomfortable and there has been a recent introduction of so many different diversity courses you can go on – it feels like everyone is going on the trend now. As a cynical person, I could say the companies are only interested in making money out of racism; they're not really interested in making changes. They can tick the box, but the system stays the same. It's like saying you can see this course, you can buy it and you can solve all the problems. The fact that these courses are **so expensive** is very revealing. It's a whole new money-making industry where the companies who run them are not necessarily thinking about changing anything; they are just thinking about the amount of money they get from them. I'm not sure how much they are, but they are about £800–£1,000 per

person – and that's a lot of money! It's just another way in which non-White people are being exploited, without any real changes happening to make things better for **us**. [*original emphasis*]

Some respondents felt that their higher-education institutions were 'passing the buck' by shifting the responsibility to 'trainers' who would solve their problems. In the words of Tara, who was Black Caribbean and worked at Riverdale:

> I sometimes think that the university spending all this money on sending us on different courses to try and make things better on diversity is really just missing the point. They make someone else do it, pay for it and then think that the problem is solved. We still have to go back to work, where the actual organization itself hasn't changed. I think they take a very simplistic view and in some ways it's like putting a sticking plaster on the problem without attempting to solve it. It has to be a long-term solution, rather than a one-off solution.

This is also emphasized in relation to 'throwing money' at addressing race, which is seen as a 'quick fix'. Rabina, who was British Pakistani and from Riverdale, felt that the economic investment in training programmes was based on higher-education institutions demonstrating their commitment to promoting racial equality, but without making any significant changes in their own day-to-day practices.

> By spending money on all these different things that we are told to do and go on, the university is showing they are spending money on **us** [*ethnic minorities*], but throwing

money at the problem doesn't solve it; it stays the same. It's also a way of the people offering training to capitalize on the situation – they have seen a gap in the economy and think, oh, we can draw up some new guidelines on how people can think about leadership and then target that to non-White people. So it's a win–win situation all around, except for us, because on Monday morning when we go back to work, what's really changed? [*original emphasis*]

Respondents who were sceptical of the training programmes criticized both their own higher-education institutions and the companies who delivered the training. As Adam, who was Black Caribbean and from Riverdale, commented:

The universities are contradicting themselves because they offer us training which they pay a lot of money for, but at the same time they don't change anything. I think the university is to blame for this and I also think the training companies are to blame – what are they really doing it for? Are they really concerned about getting more Black people into leadership roles, or are they more concerned about delivering their course and having the maximum number of participants so that they can make a profit of thousands of pounds? It's an industry that's very lucrative. It's more about making the money than making the changes.

Adam cited his mistrust of the economic motives of the training provider, but this *investment* by his university also signalled the economic value it placed on delivering the training. Having more ethnic minority staff in senior leadership positions has become increasingly important to universities, given that 94 per cent of senior managers are White.[13] They are under increasing public scrutiny about their ability to function as inclusive educational providers, not least because they are competing, as higher-education institutions, within a global market.[14] For universities the business case for diversity training is relatively simple and affordable. However, my research suggests that the training is delivered on a *one-size-fits-all* basis, and so the experiences of ethnic minority groups are homogenized. Different and individual experiences of racism do not have to be delineated in this process. The training approach assumes that the experiences of a Black working-class male academic researching neuroscience in a Russell Group university, for example, are broadly comparable with those of a middle-class female academic from an ethnic minority group teaching creative writing in a post-1992 university. Even more significantly, by drawing on prior examples of gender-equality training, it is also assumed that the needs of ethnic minority staff broadly correlate to those of White, middle-class women. Higher education in the UK is now a market in which race is increasingly treated as a commodity; it becomes ever more entwined within metrics that benefit university status rather than addressing racism on an individual and collective basis.

Race as a Commodity

The markets in which schools and universities compete determine to a large extent how they perform their institutional roles. This includes broad categories of their work, such as teaching and research, but also the less well-defined qualities associated with the ethos of an institution (or the values that underpin how it is run). In universities, these are often promoted in a very public way as *mission statements* or declarations of *aims and values*. The broader economic context in the UK – and beyond – has meant that, for at least the last twenty years, UK universities have shifted towards neoliberal values. As a result of the introduction of student fees and other changes, such as an increase in the number of zero-hours contracts and investment in campuses in countries with a questionable human-rights record, education seems to be increasingly delivered as a form of capitalist endeavour rather than as a public good, reflected in part in the use of rankings to measure and identify marketability. Race and ethnicity are positioned within this market as something that has value for the institution; demonstrable commitments to *equality, diversity and inclusion* are selling points need to be advertised within the marketplace. Racism, meanwhile, remains a fundamental characteristic of many universities, which seem on the surface to be addressing the issue, but, in reality, continue to produce greater rewards for White groups.

Here the concept of racial capitalism is critical. Racial capitalism is the process by which social and economic value is derived from an individual's non-White racial identity.[15] Within neoliberal economies, the development of policies and practices under the equality, diversity and inclusion (EDI) umbrella reinforces the commodification of racial identities. Institutional diversity is valued and therefore needs to be measurably demonstrated (even if the underlying intention is to avoid radical change). One means by which White institutions derive social and economic value from ethnic minority staff is through an investment in EDI. This allows the institution and its senior managers to make bold claims about their diversity in order to boost institutional value within the education markets in which they compete. White managers use EDI as a well-intentioned, rational ethos for initiatives that give recognition and assign value to the contribution of ethnic minority staff. In so doing, they commodify racism within the university in such a way that they themselves benefit.[16]

Law professor Nancy Leong argues that while the legal and social emphasis on diversity focuses on the need to address inequalities in society, it has in fact achieved the opposite. Instead, it has demoted ethnic minority people to the status of 'trophies' or 'passive emblems'.[17] White groups have always benefited from their Whiteness through White privilege and a system of White supremacy, and racial capitalism is just another way of exploiting ethnic minority groups.

While diversity training might exploit the value of ethnic minority staff as a form of capital to the benefit of White people, there is no reciprocal effect in the opposite direction. Despite attending training courses designed to fill a deficit, ethnic minority staff do not accrue any privileges from their non-Whiteness. By contrast, Whiteness consolidates its dominant position at universities, creating a racial hierarchy to which other groups (ethnic minorities) must conform, ensuring that they remain subordinate.

The institutional emphasis on diversity both requires ethnic minority groups to engage with the stereotypical views about their experiences of racism and their position in society and distracts employers and organizations from addressing the real problems of racial injustice. White groups thereby benefit from the racism experienced by ethnic minority groups because the commodification of racial identity does not entail any meaningful anti-discrimination work. This purely symbolic version of diversity provides an incentive for White senior managers and organizations to participate in developing diversity programmes and training, as it focuses simply on numbers and appearances and is only concerned with improving the *superficial appearance of diversity*. In so doing, it primarily benefits White groups.

Further evidence that diversity training is simply a form of publicity-seeking by institutions can be found in the moments when diversity becomes more significant and attempts to solve longstanding evidential problems around racism become more pressing. Following the murder of George Floyd in Minneapolis in 2020, as we saw earlier, there was a global outpouring of support for the Black Lives Matter movement, including protests across the UK. Universities appeared very attuned to this moment and promptly filled their websites and media feeds with expressions of support for #BlackLivesMatter and commitments to addressing racism. For a short period in the immediate aftermath of this moment there appeared to be much greater interest in the need for diversity training and events within universities. In her book *The Shock Doctrine: The Rise of Disaster Capitalism*, the Canadian author and social activist Naomi Klein discusses how significant moments in history – or 'shocks', as she calls them – such as wars, coups, terrorist attacks and natural disasters are seen as opportunities within neoliberal economies.[18] They are moments when the market can make incursions into a previously purely public domain within the economy, the chaos of the moment facilitating strategic interventions into markets previously operating for the public good rather than for private profit. The George Floyd murder and subsequent protests did not presage the forms of disaster capitalism Klein describes, but they did highlight the speed with which neoliberal universities could adapt and benefit from a shock to their economies. Much of the initial focus of the Black Lives Matter protests identified racism in universities, both in the present and also in historical links to slavery, and generated a great demand for action across many campuses. In retrospect, this seemed a short-lived moment, as universities effortlessly managed their public profile to align with the popular progressive politics of the time. Despite the abundant evidence of racism within universities, they remain adept at projecting a public image of progressive liberalism, exemplified in high-profile moments such as the Black Lives Matter protests or in their commissioning of diversity work and training. It is striking how universities consistently fill the pages of their promotional material with photographs of ethnic minority staff and students, even when there is clear evidence that they are under-represented at these institutions.

The focus on addressing diversity also signifies a retreat from any meaningful engagement with issues of race and racism; in effect, diversity is recognized, but oppression is ignored. The focus on diversity emphasizes inclusion, but at the same time it detracts from the serious business of addressing racial inequalities. Talk of inclusion then becomes a rhetorical victory for universities; the conditions that precipitate the need for diversity training are replaced with bold assertions about the creation of inclusive spaces. Inclusion becomes a narrative in which the university can choose which aspect of inclusion to focus on, such a small-scale immediate change, rather than transformational long-term reform. Diversity thus becomes a commodity, an asset that conceals the unequal relations of power underpinning the racial politics of academia. Consequently, universities invest in diversity initiatives rather than attempting to redistribute power and resources in their own organizations. Token diversity of this kind keeps power focused and concentrated in the hands of White senior managers. Instead, what is needed is a clear commitment to implementing genuine diversity, such as equal pay for ethnic minority staff, promoting them to senior roles and increasing the numbers of ethnic minority professors. A failure to address these inequalities means that higher education will continue to be preserved as a White space, reserved for Whites *only*.

As we have seen, higher-education institutions work from the premise that ethnic minority staff are the 'problem', lacking the necessary 'qualities' to 'fit in' with normative hegemonic White structures. This is seen as the obstacle, but one that can be 'fixed', primarily by investing in diversity training that, it is thought, will bridge the gap between ethnic minority staff and their White colleagues. While there has been some acknowledgement by higher-education institutions that racial inequality must be addressed, their approach is one that assumes that the system of higher education is already just and fair, and it is ethnic minority staff who should conform to the system. The greatest irony of this approach is that it works from the premise that there is a *need* to have such programmes in the first place. The existence of the training programmes reflects the recognition by higher-education institutions of structural, institutional and individual racism within the organization. Instead of addressing these issues, however, the programmes are used to applaud the success of institutions in demonstrating their commitment to EDI, and in the process diversity programmes become part of the very system that perpetuates racism and allows White supremacy to remain unchallenged.

In the neoliberal university, as this chapter has also explored, how issues of race and racism are managed is both commodified and racialized. Whiteness informs and reinforces *ways of being and doing*, so that ethnic minority groups are seen as the deficient ones, rather than the system itself that marginalizes and oppresses them through institutional racism. This situation is a reflection of wider society in the UK, in which powerful sections of the labour market remain White. While some changes have been made, influential sections of society, including the media, popular culture, government, the judiciary and elite universities remain predominantly White. Significant and wholesale change is needed to create an inclusive society and education system that no longer privileges Whiteness.

Conclusion

As we have seen throughout this book, racial inequalities continue to persist in all areas of education. Racism permeates all parts of society and is experienced by ethnic minority groups on a daily basis. It exists in all elements of culture. But it is only seriously addressed at particular historical flashpoints, such as the murder of Stephen Lawrence, which resulted in the Race Relations Amendment Act (2000) that provided a definition of institutional racism, and, more recently, the murder of George Floyd, which resulted in mass global Black Lives Matter protests. Yet despite the attention that racism has received during such moments, there has been little, if any, progress in the education system and beyond. They are quickly forgotten and the progress is short-lived; racism continues, business as usual. Examples of everyday racism appear daily in our media: in the recent cricket scandal in which Azeem Rafiq experienced racial harassment and bullying at a Yorkshire cricket club;[1] in football, where Crawley Town football manager John Yems was sacked on grounds of racism towards his players;[2] in government, where the majority of ethnic minority members of parliament reported experiencing racism on a regular basis from their colleagues;[3] in education, where a fifteen-year-old

Black girl was strip-searched by police officers at her school;[4] and in policy-making, such as the Windrush scandal, in which hundreds of Black Commonwealth citizens have been wrongly detained, deported and denied their legal rights.[5] Even war has a racial element. Tedros Adhanom Ghebreyesus, director-general of the World Health Organization, recently stated that humanitarian crises arising in war zones are not given equal attention because those suffering are not White and the world does not give the same attention to Black lives: 'I need to be blunt and honest that the world is not treating the human race the same way... some are more equal than others. And when I say this, it pains me. Because I see it. Very difficult to accept – but it's happening.'[6] Everything has a racial element.

Throughout the book, I have argued that, despite significant changes in public discourse and advances in policy-making, the condemnation of racial injustice in Britain today has served a largely symbolic function, relieved those involved from the need to match their rhetoric to action. In many ways, projecting the rhetoric of inequality is a smokescreen designed to protect the status quo. By drawing on the ideas of critical race theory, we can see how structural, institutional and individual racism continue to dominate the educational system in the UK. And we can see how educational policy-making and practice designed to be inclusive works instead to *deliberately* perpetuate White privilege and to disadvantage those from an ethnic minority background. In this way, policy responses to racial injustice may be shown to have actually contributed to maintaining the status quo rather than delivering a fairer, more equitable educational system. This has further marginalized those from ethnic minority backgrounds, and, as a result, issues of social justice remain unresolved. Specifically, racism in education is perpetuated because it is an embedded organizational principle of educational institutions. Such racial inequalities and disadvantages are not accidental; they are the deliberate means by which White groups maintain positions of power and privilege. In this concluding chapter, I will bring together previous arguments and, looking forward, explore ways of addressing racial injustices in education.

Challenging Racism: A Critical Approach

Appling a critical race perspective, I have examined how educational structures continue to perpetuate and reinforce racism and White supremacy. Drawing upon the analytical techniques of critical race theory, I have provided an analysis of racial and educational inequalities in the UK, using these methods to reveal how racism is endemic in educational institutions and to show how policy-making is little more than a performative exercise that benefits White groups and perpetuates a system of White supremacy. Despite claims of significant advances in educational policy-making, racism continues to persist in all areas of education. Meanwhile, the rhetoric of inclusion in education often disguises the fact that race, in practice, is an 'add-on' or an afterthought to other schemes that address inequalities of greater concern to White groups.

The overarching orientation of educational policy is to move towards practice and outcomes that benefit and maintain the privileged status of the White population. Ironically, initiatives that are deemed to be the most significant in tackling racial inequality often result in little or no change. These moments are often celebrated as evidence of real progress, of addressing the most difficult and uncomfortable aspects of racism. So, for example, small changes, such as putting up a statue or passing new laws that address racism, may suggest that racial inequality has been dealt with, but in reality these acts do little to contribute to genuine social change. Universities may make statements about high-profile scandals of racial injustice, such as Black Lives Matter, but they do little to address racism in their own organizations.

In the United States, as we saw in Chapter 1, Derrick Bell's analysis of the *Brown vs Board of Education* judgment, which was meant to end school segregation, showed how, instead, this law primarily benefited a range of White interests that did not remedy stark social injustices. In the UK, the Stephen Lawrence Inquiry provides similar evidence of how a high-profile policy intervention – the naming of 'institutional racism' as the reason why a racist murder went unpunished – can itself become a means of denying racism. By drawing upon the evidence of the Stephen Lawrence Inquiry, it has been possible for schools and universities (alongside many other institutions) to claim their anti-racist policies are framed by a post-racial 'moment' in which issues of race and racism are understood and no longer deemed significant.[7] While Black Lives Matter has changed the narrative by forcing higher-education institutions to acknowledge and address racism, at the same time it has sparked a backlash in which other groups (such as women and the White working class) feel they are the real victims of inequality. Contradiction-closing cases – in which landmark cases appear to advance the causes of racial injustice, thereby 'closing' the issue of race, but do little in reality – are a response to the most extreme incidents of racism, such as the complicity of the police in brutal racist murders, which are too prominent to be ignored. By publicly acknowledging their importance, they can be used as evidence in the future to suggest that racial injustices have been addressed.[8] Society, then, can point to the landmark case to show that racism has been dealt with, when, in reality, nothing has changed. According to Richard Delgado, an American legal scholar considered to be one of the key founders of critical race theory: 'Contradiction-closing cases . . . allow business as usual to go on even more smoothly than before, because now we can point to the exceptional case and say, "See, our system is really fair and just. See what we just did for minorities or the poor."'[9] Contradiction-closing cases such as the *Brown vs Board of Education* decision are unusual both because of the level of public recognition of racism and the seeming magnitude of the response. On a more mundane, day-to-day level, there are any number of interventions in schools and universities that produce the same outcomes. The outpouring of support by universities for Black Lives Matter for a brief moment when it was on-trend, or the amelioration of anti-racist policies within generic school behaviour codes in schools, all work to signal a higher level of commitment than genuine action. In this way, the reproduction of educational racism continues to perpetuate White supremacy, through policy-making and structural, institutional and individual forms of racism.

CONCLUSION

The Reproduction of Educational Racism

As we saw in Chapter 2, children from Black, Pakistani and Bangladeshi backgrounds are disproportionately more likely to be disadvantaged during their time in education.[10] From the moment an ethnic minority child starts at school, they are positioned as 'others' and 'outsiders'. They are more likely to be placed in lower sets, excluded from school compared with their White peers and labelled as academic failures by their teachers.[11] At school, they are taught an ethnocentric White curriculum by predominantly White teachers.[12] At the same time, ethnic minority teachers also report regular incidents of racism perpetrated by students and other teachers and find their professional careers are curtailed when they find they are unable to break through the glass ceiling, with few being promoted to senior roles.[13] It is therefore unsurprising that ethnic minority children also experience racism at school in the form of racist, derogatory language and stereotyping.[14] When White students use racial slurs and this is dismissed by the school as 'banter' or dealt with as a generic example of bad behaviour, of 'boys being boys', in which all parties are regarded as being equally culpable, this is because racism has been normalized in the school environment. At multiple levels – in policy, in the curriculum, in teachers' attitudes – racism is a given. It is *business as usual*.[15] Racist behaviour is legitimized. It is a powerful manifestation of White privilege that reinforces racial hierarchies so that ethnic minority students *know their place*.

Perhaps the most overt display of racism being reproduced within the education system can be seen in private schools.

White middle-class students are over-represented in private schools, particularly in terms of the number of students from the UK. They are more likely to receive high-quality teaching and gain access to a diverse range of extracurricular activities and greater resources compared with students at state schools. They are also more likely to gain a place at an elite university such as Oxford or Cambridge and enter a profession with high earning potential.[16] Elite universities reinforce inequalities by over-recruiting privately educated students, in part by adopting selection processes that privilege the behaviours and experiences of those students. There is a systemic logic to this process that excludes applicants on the basis of both race and class. The physical environment, the characteristics of students and teachers, and the demographics of private schools all correlate with those of elite universities. These universities are largely populated and managed by affluent, White groups socially connected to people like themselves in a range of powerful positions in the government, industry, business and the media; they select students from the same racial, cultural and socio-economic backgrounds because it protects *their* interests. When privately educated White students enter elite universities, they find themselves in a familiar environment that reflects their previous experiences; unlike ethnic minority students, who have to navigate the elite White space as outsiders. If we are serious about establishing a socially just society, we should abolish private schools, or at the very least strip them of their tax-exempt status.

Schools are not unique in reproducing educational racism. My research has found that ethnic minority students continue to face forms of racial exclusion and marginalization mirrored by their experiences at school. This affects their access to different types of institutions, their degree outcomes and career progression.[17] As we have seen, ethnic minority students are less likely than their White peers to leave university with a first-class degree or 2:1 and they are more likely to drop out of university.[18] They encounter racism on a daily basis from their peers and from academics, and are invariably required to study an ethnocentric curriculum centred on Whiteness.[19] Ethnic minority staff also report regular incidents of racism,[20] including when applying for promotion and in the recruitment process.[21] They are less likely to be professors, more likely to be employed on fixed-term contracts and to earn less than their White colleagues.[22] Far from being a liberal, progressive environment, higher education is a White space that perpetuates structural, institutional and individual racism.

As we saw in Chapter 3, policy-making in higher education has attempted to address various forms of inequality, but many of these initiatives have instead directly benefited White groups and/or have been used as performative exercises for their own benefit. While the Athena Swan Charter was introduced to advance the position of women in STEMM subjects, its main beneficiaries have been White women.[23] Policy initiatives such as the Athena Swan are intended to promote equality in higher education, yet they also create a smokescreen behind which universities can sideline issues of race and racism. The Athena Swan is deployed in evidence to suggest that higher-education institutions are addressing all forms of inequality, when in fact they are prioritizing gender inequalities. This has taken place at the expense of addressing structural, institutional and individual racism.

While the Race Equality Charter has gone some way to address this, it is regarded very much as a poor relation to the Athena Swan within higher-education institutions; one that is tarnished by association with additional workloads and a lack of financial resources that tend to adversely affect other equality work by staff members already stretched to the limit. One response has been to combine work on gender and race into one remit. In so doing, the distinctive issues of race and racism are conflated with other inequalities and often regarded as less significant than other specific inequalities, such as gender. This strategy is seen as progressive but, in reality, is a backwards step: the prioritizing of gender inequality reflects White assumptions that gender is more worthy of consideration and has a greater impact on a greater number of people than racial inequality. This argument ignores the fact that, for ethnic minority women, racism has a distinct and different effect upon their experience of gender inequalities compared with White women; and it ignores the fact that policy designed to address gender inequalities is derived from the experience of White women. When gender and race become conflated, race is essentially an add-on rather than an equally significant issue. This hierarchy of oppression is used to reinforce a system of White supremacy in which White women continue to benefit from policy-making but racial inequalities remain uncontested.

The REC, as we saw, is an interesting example of performative policy-making in which the process of applying for membership of the charter or for an award becomes a marketing exercise in which universities broadcast their commitment to addressing racial inequality. In a context of underlying

Whiteness and White privilege, universities are effectively required to perform the policy in order to *gain the award*, rather than addressing genuine racial inequality in their own organization. The performance is based on promoting a public image of inclusion evidenced by charter membership. Behind the scenes, meanwhile, it is expected that ethnic minority staff will shoulder the workload and additional burden of applying for membership, while senior, predominantly White, managers will get all the credit for their work. Despite being intended as a vehicle for genuine change, the REC is thus potentially both a means of reproducing inequitable conditions and of claiming that these conditions have been improved.

Higher-education institutions have attempted to address racial inequalities, such as the lack of ethnic minority senior managers and professors, by investing in diversity training programmes. As we saw in the previous chapter, these provide guidance on how to acquire the skills and qualities needed by ethnic minority staff to progress to senior leadership roles. As we have seen, many such training programmes are based on a deficit model that assumes that ethnic minority groups are the 'problem' and lack the necessary qualities to succeed. The solution is to send them on a training programme that operates within, and thus reproduces, White hegemonic structures. This approach assumes that higher education is an already equitable system, one that is just and fair, and ethnic minority groups must therefore adjust to fit in to the system. The training is designed to change their behaviours to align with White hegemony, despite this being the organizing principle of higher education that has caused them to be marginalized in the first place. By attending such training programmes, there is an assumption that they will be equipped with the (White) values needed to advance their careers. This approach perpetuates the view that ethnic minority groups are the problem and it is their responsibility to advance their careers and reverse racial inequality. These training programmes do not address racism specifically, nor the fact that the system is structurally unfair, but instead work to reinforce and perpetuate Whiteness as the norm.

The willingness of senior White managers and their organizations to invest in diversity training programmes is understandable, because it allows them to accrue social and economic value. Diversity training programmes are useful to universities because they present a superficial appearance of diversity and inclusion that suggests an attractive, marketable institutional ethos. Being recognizably diverse has value for an educational establishment wanting to expand into domestic and global markets that are increasingly non-White. In such an economy, race itself has become commodified, not least because anti-racist practice has to be recognizably 'performed' by a neoliberal university. Institutional interventions to increase diversity are often therefore a response to a particular 'moment' (such as a response to the Black Lives Matter protests), rather than a longstanding commitment to addressing racial injustice. They reflect communication strategies and marketing behaviours dictated by the market rather than an embedded ethos of anti-racism (or, for that matter, of education seen as a public good).

CONCLUSION

Dismantling Educational White Privilege

ADDRESSING RACISM

In order for schools and universities to make meaningful and significant changes, they must examine their role in perpetuating racism. At a basic level, educational institutions must address issues of race and racism consistently and with complete transparency. Ways of tackling these issues tend to come under the umbrella of equality, diversity and inclusion (EDI) and, as we have seen, the topic of race can become lost among other types of inequality deemed to be more worthy, such as gender. Educational institutions are able to 'tick the box' to demonstrate that they are meeting their EDI targets without actually addressing racial inequalities.

My research has consistently found that when ethnic minority staff and students experience racism, they do not feel confident about making a complaint because they fear they will not be taken seriously or adequately dealt with.[24] For ethnic minority staff to feel confident in the complaints process, clearly defined terms must be used in the relevant documents, such as the word 'racism' rather than 'harassment'. Many schools and universities see racism as an *individual* issue between students and members of staff, rather than an institutional and structural one in which their own organizations have a part to play. Schools and universities must identify racism in their organizations and take *institutional* responsibility for addressing it, in order to acknowledge their role in perpetuating White privilege and White supremacy. In addition to addressing racism, schools and universities need to record and monitor the extent of racial discrimination in their institutions. This data should be regularly analysed to identify patterns of racist activity. As we have seen, racism may take different forms, any of which may change over time, and too often institutions rely on a single event, such as the murder of George Floyd, or training programme in order to broadcast that racism is not a problem in their institution. To monitor racism accurately, clear and consistent terminology should be used to describe the experiences of ethnic minority groups. In the absence of clear terminology, it is difficult to measure their experiences, or make comparisons *across* different ethnic minority groups with regard to certain issues (such as the awarding gap or the lack of ethnic minority professors).

There is currently no requirement for schools and universities to have mandatory race equality training in place, and as such, White teachers at schools and White academics at universities have little or no understanding of how to deal with issues of race and racism. In order for race equality initiatives to be effective (such as the Race Equality Charter), these must be linked to applications for research funding. Universities that fail to invest in REC membership should not be allowed to apply for research funding and should be financially penalized. In schools, there should be an obligatory assessment of effectiveness within Ofsted reporting. Schools that are not implementing effective race equality measures should be classified as either requiring improvement or inadequate.

THE CURRICULUM

In schools, children are taught to value European history and culture in an environment in which the history and culture of other ethnic groups are at best ignored or treated as subordinate, or, at worst, demonized. In this way, White privilege and White supremacy are embedded in the school curriculum. In order to address racism in the curriculum, the history and culture other ethnic groups must be included at all levels of a child's schooling. Children must be taught to value diversity and inclusion and see their own history and culture represented at school. The curriculum must also include accounts that are critical of the UK's role as an imperial power, of colonialism and slavery. There should be an open acknowledgement that the UK actively oppressed ethnic minority people and that the effects are still felt today. A Eurocentric curriculum that centres only on the experiences of White groups sends a clear message to students from ethnic minority groups that their culture is not worthy and their history is unimportant. This is evidenced by the lack of ethnic minority groups represented in curriculum materials. Children's books are dominated by White characters[25] and the English literature curriculum does not include any books by ethnic minority writers.[26] As it stands, the curriculum contributes to racist perceptions because race is a social construct and is used to organize and create hierarchies of individuals based on their skin colour. In this system, Whiteness is judged as superior. The teaching of an ethnocentric curriculum is thus used to reinforce Whiteness and perpetuate a system of White supremacy.

While there have been some attempts by universities to decolonize or diversify their curriculum, progress on this has been piecemeal. What is clearly needed is for *all* educational institutions to work towards diversifying their curriculum; this should be the responsibility of *all* members of staff, rather than just those from ethnic minority groups. Schools and universities must devote time and money into diversifying their curricula, ring-fencing funding for the purpose, and focus on delivering specific and measurable outcomes – all of which must result in a properly diversified curriculum.

RECRUITMENT

As I have argued, schools and universities are predominantly White spaces. Teachers are more likely to be White and female, and ethnic minority staff are less likely to hold senior leadership roles (such as headships).[27] In order to make the teaching workforce more diverse, schools and universities must set targets for the numbers of ethnic minority staff they employ, including those in senior roles. They should make use of targeted advertising and networks to ensure that the appropriate groups are reached. Possible ways forward may include the introduction of the 'Rooney Rule'. Introduced in the US by the National Football League in 2003, and adopted in different versions by the Football Association in 2018 and the English Football League in 2019, the Rooney Rule guarantees individuals an interview if they are from an ethnic minority background.[28] It takes a similar approach to the Equality Act (2010), in which provisions are made to guarantee disabled applicants an interview. Schools and universities should also consider introducing name-blind applications for senior decision-making roles in order that ethnic minority people are not disadvantaged at the shortlisting stage. In addition, just as all-women shortlists are used in some organizations to increase female representation, so too should shortlists consisting of purely ethnic minority candidates be considered to increase ethnic minority participation.[29]

Students from ethnic minority backgrounds are less likely than their White peers to study for a PhD.[30] This has the effect of perpetuating academia as a predominantly White space. In order to address this, universities should consider ring-fenced bursaries for those from ethnic minority backgrounds to pursue a PhD. Higher-education institutions that have already introduced this, all in London, include UCL, Queen Mary, Birkbeck, London Metropolitan and Westminster. Such funding should be introduced by all universities to demonstrate their commitment to investing in increasing postgraduate participation by ethnic minority students.

INCLUSIVE EDUCATIONAL SPACES

In the US, historically Black colleges and universities (HBCUs) were established after the 1964 Civil Rights Act. There are currently 101 of these colleges and universities in the US, including both private and public institutions. Research has found that students of colour who attend them do better academically, feel more supported, have more appropriate role models and achieve better outcomes (such as greater financial success and well-being) once they have graduated, compared with students who do not attend them.[31] HBCUs do not start from the premise of a deficit model based on a stereotyped assumption linking ethnic minority culture with educational failure. It has been shown that the experience of attending one can be very positive. According to Zeus Leonardo and W. Norton Grubb, a professor of higher education, in such an institution students 'learn curricula, navigate the school climate and experience classroom pedagogies that raise their self-esteem and self-efficacy, much like White students in mainly White colleges and universities ... the point is that culturally relevant education does not sacrifice excellence for ethnic content. Cultural relevance *is* part of academic relevance.'[32] In addition, the US has for some time included graduate and postgraduate programmes on African-American or Black studies. While the HBCU model is unlikely to be adopted in the UK, given the different set-up in British universities, the lack of Black studies programmes within UK academia highlights a gap that could be filled more readily. To date, only one such degree course is available in the UK, at Birmingham City University. Introduced in 2017, it was the first to be offered in Europe and consists of a BA and an MA in Black studies.[33] Such courses diverge from ethnocentric White models of teaching and foreground the history of different ethnic minority people, thereby ensuring that their history and culture are valued rather than denigrated. A curriculum that embraces the culture of ethnic minority people gives credence and value to such history and helps to boost ethnic minority educational achievement and improve outcomes.

Furthermore, if universities are serious about addressing issues of race and racism, they must consider developing interdisciplinary university-wide research centres that focus specifically on race, and which include degree programmes on ethnic minority studies. These should be run by experts who not only conduct research on race but also teach it, using critical race theory to analyse issues of race and racism.

A university's commitment to racial issues should also include appointing ethnic minority staff to senior roles, including pro-vice-chancellors for equality, diversity and inclusion, with a clear remit of addressing racism. Currently, not all universities have such people in place. Instead, they tend to rely on vice-chancellors and senior staff members committed to equality, diversity and inclusion to address these issues on a more informal basis. Those universities that do employ individuals in such roles are sending a clear message that they are prepared to invest in promoting race equality and are taking these issues seriously. In addition, all departments should have 'race champions' to work with senior managers to ensure that race equality is included as a standing item on the agenda of all meetings, including those of the university executive board. It should not be assumed these roles must be filled by ethnic minority staff; one way of encouraging a broader base of interest in the work would be to open up these roles to everybody, and provide adequate resources and time for it. In so doing, a university would signal the importance of addressing racial inequalities within its broader aims. Adequately resourcing work that contributes to real change is also a means of ensuring that such appointments are not simply a 'tick-box' exercise.

Throughout this book, I have demonstrated how educational structures in the UK continue to perpetuate White privilege and disadvantage ethnic minority students. This is evidenced in the playground, classroom and lecture hall. It continues in the lack of representation of ethnic minority staff at the most senior levels in schools and universities. Existing educational structures are divisive and privilege certain groups over others. They are not meritocratic but premised on forms of exclusion. Social justice is not just a political matter; it is a moral issue that all governments should consider and place at the heart of their agendas. Radical measures are needed, such as a complete overhaul of our education system, implementing inclusive new strategies to reflect the view that education should be available to all. In this way, ethnic minority groups can be active participants, rather than passive recipients, in an educational system that is truly inclusive. Inequality in education impacts all areas of society, leading to inequalities in every aspect of it, from housing and income levels to access to the criminal justice system. Education is a fundamental aspect of the way society is run, and it can contribute significantly to social change. Educational equality matters not just for ethnic minority groups, but also for individual communities as well as the whole of Britain, because education is the vehicle by which social justice can be achieved. Every child, regardless of their race, is entitled to a decent education. We must work towards creating a socially just society that works for the many and not the few, because education is a right and not a privilege.

Notes

INTRODUCTION

1. Avtar Brah, *Cartographies of Diaspora: Contesting Identities* (London: Routledge, 1996).
2. Tariq Modood, '"Black" racial equality and Asian identity', *New Community*, 14:3 (1988), pp. 397–404.
3. Brah, *Cartographies of Diaspora*.
4. Kalwant Bhopal, *White Privilege: The Myth of a Post-Racial Society* (Bristol: Policy Press, 2018), p. 156.
5. Centre for Social Justice, *Facing the Facts: Ethnicity and Disadvantage in Britain* (London: CSJ, 2020); Patrick Butler, 'Nearly half of BAME UK households are living in poverty', *Guardian*, 1 July 2020, available at https://www.theguardian.com/society/2020/jul/01/nearly-half-of-bame-uk-households-are-living-in-poverty; Michael Marmot, Jessica Allen, Tammy Boyce, Peter Goldblatt and Joana Morrison, *Health Equity in England: The Marmot Review 10 years On* (London: Institute of Health Equity, 2020); and *The Lammy Review: An Independent Review into the Treatment of, and Outcomes for, Black, Asian and Minority Ethnic Individuals in the Criminal Justice System* (London: 2017), available at https://assets.publishing.service.gov.uk/government/uploads/system/uploads/attachment_data/file/643001/lammy-review-final-report.pdf.
6. House of Commons/House of Lords, Joint Committee on Human Rights, *Black People, Racism and Human Rights* (London: House of Commons, 2020).
7. See https://www.ethnicity-facts-figures.service.gov.uk/crime-justice-and-the-law/policing/stop-and-search/latest.
8. *Race Relations (Amendment) Act 2000* (Norwich: Stationery Office, 2000).
9. *Race Disparity Audit* (London: Cabinet Office, 2017).

NOTES

10. Bobby Duffy, Kirstie Hewlett, Rachel Hesketh, Rebecca Benson and Alan Wager, *Unequal Britain: Attitudes to Inequalities after Covid-19* (London: King's College, 2021).
11. See https://www.ons.gov.uk/peoplepopulationandcommunity/birthsdeathsandmarriages/deaths/articles/coronaviruscovid19relateddeathsbyethnicgroupenglandandwales/2march2020to15may2020#:~:text=Provisional%20analysis%20for%20the%20period,among%20males%20of%20White%20ethnic.
12. Nick Treloar, *Ethnic Inequalities are Playing Out Again in Covid-10 – How Can We Stop Them?* (London: Runnymede Trust, 2020), available at https://www.runnymedetrust.org/blog/ethnic-inequalities-in-covid-19-are-playing-out-again-how-can-we-stop-them.
13. Zubaida Haque, Laia Becares and Nick Treloar, *Over-Exposed and Under-Protected: The Devastating Impact of Covid-19 on Black and Minority Ethnic Communities in Great Britain* (London: Runnymede Trust, 2020), available at https://www.runnymedetrust.org/publications/over-exposed-and-under-protected.
14. Ibid.
15. See https://www.bbc.co.uk/news/uk-england-london-52905787.
16. The Attainment 8 score is used for measuring achievement in GCSEs by adding up points scored across all eight subjects. This is covered in more detail in Chapter 2.
17. See https://www.ethnicity-facts-figures.service.gov.uk/education-skills-and-training/11-to-16-years-old/a-to-c-in-english-and-maths-gcse-attainment-for-children-aged-14-to-16-key-stage-4/latest.
18. Young Men's Christian Association, *Young and Black: The Young Black Experience of Institutional Racism in the UK* (London: YMCA, 2020).
19. Ibid.
20. David Gillborn, 'The White working class, racism and respectability: victims, degenerates and interest-convergence', *British Journal of Educational Studies*, 58:1 (2010), pp. 2–25.
21. Nick Treloar and Halima Begum, *Facts Don't Lie: One Working Class: Race, Class and Inequality* (London: Runnymede Trust, 2021), available at https://www.nhsbmenetwork.org.uk/wp-content/uploads/2021/04/Facts-Dont-Lie-2021-Begum-Treloar-.pdf.
22. *The Equality Act 2010* (Norwich: Stationery Office, 2010).
23. Bhopal, *White Privilege*, p. 156.
24. See https://explore-education-statistics.service.gov.uk/find-statistics/school-workforce-in-england.

25. Zubaida Haque and Sian Elliott, *Visible and Invisible Barriers: The Impact of Racism on BME Teachers* (London: Runnymede Trust, 2019), available at https://neu.org.uk/sites/default/files/2023-02/Barriers%20Report.pdf.
26. Kehinde Andrews, *The New Age of Empire: How Racism and Colonialism Still Rule the World* (London: Penguin Books, 2022).
27. Bhopal, *White Privilege*.
28. Advance HE, *Equality in Higher Education: Students Statistical Report 2021* (York: Advance HE, 2021).
29. Wouter Zwysen and Simonetta Longhi, 'Employment and earning differences in the early career of ethnic minority British graduates: the importance of university career, parental background and area characteristics', *Journal of Ethnic and Migration Studies*, 44:1 (2018), pp. 154–72.
30. Kalwant Bhopal *The Experiences of Black and Minority Ethnic Academics: A Comparative Study of the Unequal Academy* (London: 2016).
31. Advance HE, *Equality in Higher Education: Staff Statistical Report 2021* (York: Advance HE, 2021).
32. *The Stephen Lawrence Inquiry: Report of an Inquiry by Sir William MacPherson of Cluny* (Cm. 4262, 1999), p. 49 (paragraph 6.34).
33. Audrey Kobayashi and Linda Peake, 'Racism out of place: thoughts on whiteness and an antiracist geography in the new millennium', *Annals of the Association of American Geographers*, 90:2 (2000), pp. 392–403, at p. 393 (original emphasis).
34. Derrick Bell, *Faces at the Bottom of the Well: The Permanence of Racism* (New York: Basic Books, 1992).

CHAPTER 1: A CRITICAL RACE PERSPECTIVE

1. *Commission on Race and Ethnic Disparities: The Report* (London: 2021), available at https://assets.publishing.service.gov.uk/government/uploads/system/uploads/attachment_data/file/974507/20210331_-_CRED_Report_-_FINAL_-_Web_Accessible.pdf.
2. Kimberlé Crenshaw, 'The first decade: critical reflections, or "A foot in the closing door"', *UCLA Law Review*, 49 (2002), pp. 1343–73, quotation on p. 1361.
3. David Gillborn, *Racism and Education: Coincidence or Conspiracy?* (London: Routledge, 2008).

NOTES

4. Kevin Hylton, 'How a turn to critical race theory can contribute to our understanding of "race", racism and anti-racism in sport', *International Review for the Sociology of Sport*, 45:3 (2001), pp. 335–54; John Preston, *Whiteness and Class in Education* (Dordrecht: Springer, 2007); and Paul Warmington, *Black British Intellectuals: Multiculturalism's Hidden History* (London: Routledge, 2014).
5. Devon W. Carbado, 'Critical what what commentary: critical race theory: a commemoration: afterword', *Connecticut Law Review*, 43:5 (2011), pp. 1595–26.
6. Noel Ignatiev, *How the Irish Became White* (New York: Routledge, 1995).
7. Bell, *Faces at the Bottom of the Well*.
8. Ibid., p. 194.
9. Charles W. Mills, *The Racial Contract* (New York: Cornell University Press, 1997), p. 17.
10. Bell, *Faces at the Bottom of the Well*, p. x.
11. Derrick Bell, '*Brown v. Board of Education* and the interest-convergence dilemma', *Harvard Law Review*, 95 (1980), pp. 518–33.
12. Gillborn, *Racism and Education*.
13. Peggy McIntosh, 'White privilege and male privilege: a personal account of coming to see correspondences through work in women's studies', in Richard Delgado and Jean Stefancic (eds), *Critical White Studies: Looking Behind the Mirror* (Philadelphia: Temple University Press, 1997), pp. 202–91, quotation on p. 291.
14. Cheryl Matias, Kara Viesca, Dorothy Garrison-Wade, Madhavi Tandon and Rene Galind, '"What is critical whiteness doing in OUR nice field like critical race theory?" Applying CRT and CWS to understand the white imaginations of white teacher candidates', *Equity & Excellence in Education*, 47:3 (2014), pp. 289–304, quotation on p. 209.
15. Ruth Frankenberg, *White Women, Race Matters: The Social Construction of Whiteness* (Minneapolis: University of Minnesota Press, 1993), p. 1.
16. Derrick Bell, *Ethical Ambition: Living a Life of Meaning and Worth* (New York: Bloomsbury, 2002), p. 238.
17. Zeus Leonardo, *Race, Whiteness, and Education* (New York: Routledge, 2009), p. 169.
18. Leonardo, *Race, Whiteness, and Education*, p. 170 (my emphasis).
19. Robin DiAngelo, *White Fragility: Why It's So Hard for White People to Talk About Race* (Boston: Beacon Press, 2018), p. 22 (my emphasis).
20. Bhopal, *White Privilege*, and Richard Delgado and Jean Stefancic, *Critical Race Theory: An Introduction*, 2nd edn (New York: NYU Press, 2012), both provide an excellent summary of critical race theory.

21. Cheryl Harris, 'Whiteness as property', *Harvard Law Review*, 106:8 (1993), pp. 1707–91, quotation on p. 1715.
22. Zeus Leonardo and Alicia Broderick, 'Smartness as property: a critical exploration of intersections between whiteness and disability studies', *Teachers College Record*, 113:10 (2011), pp. 2206–32.
23. Kimberlé Crenshaw, 'Demarginalizing the intersection of race and sex: a black feminist critique of antidiscrimination doctrine, feminist theory and antiracist politics', *University of Chicago Legal Forum* (1989), pp. 139–67, and idem, 'Mapping the margins: intersectionality, identity politics, and violence against women of color', *Stanford Law Review*, 43 (1991), pp. 1241–99.
24. Crenshaw, 'Demarginalizing the intersection of race and sex', p. 149.
25. Crenshaw, 'Mapping the margins', p. 1243.
26. Floya Anthias and Nira Yuval-Davis, *Racialised Boundaries: Race, Nation, Gender, Colour and Class and the Anti-Racist Struggle* (London: Routledge, 1992), and Avtar Brah and Ann Phoenix, 'Ain't I a woman? Revisiting intersectionality', *Journal of International Women's Studies*, 5:3 (2004), pp. 75–86.
27. Nira Yuval-Davis, '"Situated intersectionality": a reflection on Ange-Marie Hancock's forthcoming book', *New Political Science*, 37:4 (2005), pp. 637–42, quotation on p. 638.
28. Kalwant Bhopal, 'Confronting White privilege: the importance of intersectionality in the sociology of education', *British Journal of Sociology of Education*, 41:6 (2020), pp. 816–20.
29. Tom Wall, 'The day Bristol dumped its hated slave trader in the docks and a nation began to search its soul', *Guardian*, 14 June 2020, available at https://www.theguardian.com/uk-news/2020/jun/14/the-day-bristol-dumped-its-hated-slave-trader-in-the-docks-and-a-nation-began-to-search-its-soul.
30. Ben Habib, 'Of course black lives matter, but so do British values and heritage', *Telegraph*, 10 June 2020, available at https://www.telegraph.co.uk/politics/2020/06/10/course-black-lives-matter-do-british-values-heritage/.
31. Nesrine Malik, 'Despite being vilified in the rightwing media, Black Lives Matter will endure', 20 September 2020, available at https://www.theguardian.com/commentisfree/2020/sep/20/black-lives-matter-rightwing-media/.
32. Archie Bland and Jessica Elgot, 'Dissatisfied Tory MPs flock to ERG inspired pressure groups', *Guardian*, 11 November 2020, available

NOTES

at https://www.theguardian.com/politics/2020/nov/11/dissatisfied-tory-mps-flock-to-erg-inspired-pressure-groups.

33. Ibid., and National Trust, *Interim Report on the Connections Between Colonialism and Properties Now in the Care of the National Trust, Including Links with Historic Slavery* (Swindon: NT, 2020).

34. Edward Malnick, 'Museums told to stop pulling down statues or risk funding cuts', *Telegraph*, 26 September 2020, available at https://www.telegraph.co.uk/news/2020/09/26/museums-told-stop-pulling-statues-risk-funding-cuts/.

35. Mattha Busb, 'Up to a third of National Trust's historic homes have slave trade links', *Guardian*, 15 August 2020, available at https://www.theguardian.com/uk-news/2020/aug/15/up-to-a-third-of-national-trust-historic-homes-have-slave-trade-links.

36. See https://www.conservatives.com/news/boris-johnson-read-the-prime-ministers-keynote-speech-in-full.

37. Kemi Badenoch, *Black History Month*, Hansard, vol. 682 (20 October 2020), cols 1011–1022, at col. 1012, available at https://hansard.parliament.uk/commons/2020-10-20/debates/5B0E393E-8778-4973-B318-C17797DFBB22/BlackHistoryMonth.

38. Ibid., at col. 1011.

39. Sally Weale, 'Ofsted chief resists calls to make England school curriculum more diverse', *Guardian*, 1 December 2020, available at https://www.theguardian.com/education/2020/dec/01/england-ofsted-chief-resists-calls-to-make-curriculum-more-diverse.

40. Teach First, *Missing Pages: Increasing Racial Diversity in the Literature We Teach* (London: 2020).

41. Bell, *Faces at the Bottom of the Well*.

42. Ibid.

43. *Commission on Race and Ethnic Disparities*, p. 8.

44. Ibid.

45. Ibid., p. 55 (my emphasis).

46. See https://assets.publishing.service.gov.uk/government/uploads/system/uploads/attachment_data/file/1026735/E02682727_CP_524.pdf.

47. *Commission on Race and Ethnic Disparities*, p. 36.

48. Ibid., p. 46.

49. Ibid., p. 130.

50. Ibid., p. 19.

51. Farzana Shain, 'Navigating the unequal education space in post 9/11 England: British Muslim girls talk about their educational aspirations and educational futures', *Educational Philosophy and Theory*, 53:3 (2021), pp. 270–87.

52. Rajeev Syal, 'No 10 race adviser Samuel Kamusu resigns', *Guardian*, 1 April 2021, available at https://www.theguardian.com/politics/2021/apr/01/no-10-race-adviser-resigns-day-after-uk-structural-racism-report-published.
53. Serina Sandhu, 'Race report: author listed as contributor says he was absolutely not contacted by race commission', *iNews*, 1 April 2021, available at https://inews.co.uk/news/race-report-curator-listed-as-a-contributor-says-he-was-absolutely-not-contacted-by-race-commission-938503.
54. Nosheen Iqba, 'Downing Street rewrote "independent" report on race, experts claim', *Guardian*, 11 April 2021, available at https://www.theguardian.com/uk-news/2021/apr/11/downing-street-rewrote-independent-report-on-race-experts-claim.
55. Runnymede Trust, 'Statement regarding the report from the Commission on Race and Ethnic Disparities', 31 March 2021, available at https://www.runnymedetrust.org/news/statement-regarding-the-cred-report-2021.
56. Ibid.
57. David Olusoga, 'The poisonous patronising Sewell report is historically illiterate', *Guardian*, 2 April 2021, available at https://www.theguardian.com/commentisfree/2021/apr/02/sewell-race-report-historical-young-people-britain.
58. See https://www.ohchr.org/EN/NewsEvents/Pages/DisplayNews.aspx?NewsID=27004&LangID=E) (my emphasis).
59. James Tapsfield, Jack Maidment and David Wilcok, *Daily Mail*, 31 March 2021, available at https://www.dailymail.co.uk/news/article-9422587/Landmark-report-urges-UK-look-race-amid-row.html.
60. Rod Liddle, 'We finally have proof that the lines dividing us are based on class not race', *Sun*, 31 March 2021, available at https://www.thesun.co.uk/news/14516018/rod-liddle-race-report/.

CHAPTER 2: SCHOOLS AND EVERYDAY RACISM

1. See https://www.ethnicity-facts-figures.service.gov.uk/education-skills-and-training/11-to-16-years-old/gcse-results-attainment-8-for-children-aged-14-to-16-key-stage-4/latest.
2. Gillborn, *Race and Education*, and Bhopal, *White Privilege*.
3. See https://explore-education-statistics.service.gov.uk/find-statistics/school-pupils-and-their-characteristics.

NOTES

4. Bhopal, *White Privilege*.
5. Gillborn, *Race and Education*.
6. See https://www.ethnicity-facts-figures.service.gov.uk/education-skills-and-training/11-to-16-years-old/gcse-results-attainment-8-for-children-aged-14-to-16-key-stage-4/latest.
7. As indicated earlier, Gypsy, Roma and Traveller (GRT) groups are the most disadvantaged in the education system at every stage of their educational careers. This is due to the racism they encounter on a daily basis, including a lack of support from teachers. For more on the ethnicity of GRT groups, see https://www.ethnicity-facts-figures.service.gov.uk/summaries/gypsy-roma-irish-traveller#:~:text=The%20Gypsy%2C%20Roma%20and%20Traveller%20group,-The%20term%20Gypsy&text=Gypsies%20(including%20English%20Gypsies%2C%20Scottish,from%20Central%20and%20Eastern%20Europe; see also https://assets.publishing.service.gov.uk/government/uploads/system/uploads/attachment_data/file/181669/DFE-RR043.pdf.
8. Gillborn, *Race and Education*; Bhopal, *White Privilege*; and David Gillborn, Kalwant Bhopal, Claire E. Crawford, Sean Demack, Reza Gholami, Karl Kitching, Dina Kiwan and Paul Warmington, *Evidence for the Commission on Race and Ethnic Disparities* (Birmingham: University of Birmingham CRRE, 2021), available at http://epapers.bham.ac.uk/3389/1/CRREBirmevidencetoCRED2020.pdf.
9. See https://www.ethnicity-facts-figures.service.gov.uk/education-skills-and-training/a-levels-apprenticeships-further-education/students-aged-16-to-18-achieving-3-a-grades-or-better-at-a-level/latest.
10. Becky Francis and Louise Archer, 'British-Chinese pupils' and parents' constructions of the value of education', *British Educational Research Journal*, 31:1 (2005), pp. 89–108.
11. Priya Khambhaita and Kalwant Bhopal, 'Home or away? The significance of ethnicity, class and attainment in the housing choices of female university students', *Race, Ethnicity and Education*, 18:4 (2013), pp. 535–66.
12. See https://www.ethnicity-facts-figures.service.gov.uk/education-skills-and-training/a-levels-apprenticeships-further-education/students-aged-16-to-18-achieving-3-a-grades-or-better-at-a-level/latest.
13. See https://www.ethnicity-facts-figures.service.gov.uk/workforce-and-business/workforce-diversity/school-teacher-workforce/latest.
14. Haque and Elliott, *Visible and Invisible Barriers*.
15. Ibid.

16. Kalwant Bhopal and Jasmine Rhamie, 'Initial teacher training: understanding race, diversity and inclusion', *Race, Ethnicity and Education*, 17:3 (2014), pp. 304–25.
17. Tambra Jackson, 'Perspectives and insights from preservice teachers of color on developing culturally responsive pedagogy at predominantly White institutions', *Action in Teacher Education*, 37:3 (2015), pp. 223–37.
18. William Smith, 'Campuswide climate: implications for African American students', in L. C. Tillman (ed.), *The SAGE handbook of African American Education* (Los Angeles: SAGE Publications, 2009), pp. 297–309, quotation on p. 298, and Marcos Pizarro and Rita Kohli, '"I stopped sleeping": teachers of colour and the impact of racial battle fatigue', *Urban Education*, 55:7 (2020), pp. 967–91.
19. Rita Kohli, 'Behind school doors the impact of hostile racial climates on urban teachers of color', *Urban Education*, 53 (2016), pp. 307–33.
20. Haque and Elliott, *Visible and Invisible Barriers*, p. 6.
21. Clare, Lynette, Gaby Atfield, Sally Barnes and David Owen, *Teachers' Pay and Equality: Online Survey and Qualitative Study* (Warwick: University of Warwick, 2016).
22. Eleanor Busby, 'Most Black and minority ethnic teachers say they face covert racism in schools', *Independent*, 20 January 2020, available at https://www.independent.co.uk/news/education/education-news/black-teachers-racism-schools-microinsults-nasuwt-poll-a9292036.html, and Nazia Parveen and Niamh McIntyre, 'Systemic racism: teachers speak out about discrimination in UK schools', *Guardian*, 24 March 2021, available at https://www.theguardian.com/education/2021/mar/24/systemic-racism-teachers-speak-out-about-discrimination-in-uk-schools.
23. David Batty and Nazia Parveen, 'UK schools record more than 60,000 racist incidents in 5 years', *Guardian*, 28 March 2021, available at https://www.theguardian.com/education/2021/mar/28/uk-schools-record-more-than-60000-racist-incidents-five-years; Nazia Parveen, 'Children "may lose out" due to lack of policy on racism in UK schools', *Guardian*, 28 March 2021, available at https://www.theguardian.com/education/2021/mar/28/children-may-lose-out-lack-policy-racism-uk-schools; and Department for Education, *Preventing and Tackling Bullying: Advice for Head Teachers, Staff and Governing Bodies* (London: DfE, 2017).
24. Gillborn et al., *Evidence for the Commission on Race and Ethnic Disparities*.
25. Young Men's Christian Association, *Young and Black*.
26. Ibid., p. 7.

NOTES

27. Niamh McIntyre, Nazia Parveen and Tobi Thomas, 'Exclusion rates five times higher for Black Caribbean pupils in parts of England', *Guardian*, 24 March 2021, available at https://www.theguardian.com/education/2021/mar/24/exclusion-rates-black-caribbean-pupils-england.
28. Emma Dabiri, 'Black pupils are being wrongly excluded over their hair. I'm trying to end this discrimination', *Guardian*, 25 February 2020, available at www.theguardian.com/commentisfree/2020/feb/25/blackpupils-excluded-hair-discrimination-equality-act.
29. Freia Schulz, 'British schools are institutionally racist: that must change fast', *Guardian*, 24 March 2021, available at https://www.theguardian.com/education/2021/mar/24/british-schools-are-institutionally-racist-that-must-change-fast.
30. LaGarrett King and Prentice Chandl, 'From non-racism to anti-racism in social studies teacher education: social studies and racial pedagogical content knowledge', in A. R. Crowe and A. Cuenca (eds), *Rethinking Social Studies Teacher Education in the Twenty-First Century* (New York: Springer, 2016), pp. 3–2.
31. Claire Alexander, Debbie Weekes-Bernard and Joya Chatterji, *History Lessons: Teaching Diversity in and through the History National Curriculum* (London: Runnymede Trust, 2015).
32. LaGarrett King and Keffrelyn Brown, 'Once a year to be Black: fighting against typical Black History Month pedagogies', *Negro Educational Review*, 65 (2014), pp. 23–43.
33. Ashley Woodson, '"What you supposed to know": urban Black students' perspectives on history textbooks', *Journal of Urban Learning, Teaching, and Research*, 11 (2015), pp. 57–65.
34. Ibid.
35. UK Government and Parliament, Petitions, 'Teach Britain's colonial past as part of the UK's compulsory curriculum', debated on 28 June 2021, available at https://petition.parliament.uk/petitions/324092.
36. Badenoch, *Black History Month*, Hansard, vol. 682, at col. 1011.
37. *Commission on Race and Ethnic Disparities*, p. 8.
38. David Batty, Narzia Paveen and Tobi Thomas, 'Hundreds of schools in England sign up for anti-racist curriculum', *Guardian*, 26 March 2021, available at https://www.theguardian.com/education/2021/mar/26/schools-england-anti-racist-curriculum.
39. See https://theblackcurriculum.com/.

40. Keffrelyn D. Brown, 'Race as a durable *and* shifting idea: how black millennial preservice teachers understand race, racism, and teaching', *Peabody Journal of Education*, 93:1 (2018), pp. 106–20.
41. Rita Kohli and Marcos Pizarro, 'Fighting to educate our own: teachers of color, relational accountability, and the struggle for racial justice', *Equity and Excellence in Education*, 49:1 (2016), pp. 72–84.
42. Tambra Jackson and Rita Kohli, 'Guest editors' introduction: the state of teachers of color', *Equity and Excellence in Education*, 49:1 (2016), pp. 1–8.
43. Brown, 'Race as a durable *and* shifting idea'.
44. Haque and Elliott, *Visible and Invisible Barriers*.
45. 'Nine out of ten teachers want anti-racism training', survey by Centre for Mental Health, 20 January 2023, available at https://www.centreformentalhealth.org.uk/news/nine-out-ten-teachers-want-anti-racism-training.
46. Bhopal and Rhamie, 'Initial teacher training'.
47. Marvin Lynn and Michael Jennings, 'Power, politics, and critical race pedagogy: a critical race analysis of Black male teachers' pedagogy', *Race Ethnicity and Education*, 12:1 (2009), pp. 173–96.
48. Leonardo, *Race, Whiteness and Education*.
49. Tara Yosso, 'Whose culture has capital? A critical race theory discussion of community cultural wealth', *Race, Ethnicity, and Education*, 8:1 (2005), pp. 69–91.
50. Christine Sleeter and Dolores Delgado Bernal, 'Critical pedagogy, critical race theory, and antiracist education: implications for multicultural education', in James A. Banks and Cherry A. McGee Banks (eds), *Handbook of Research on Multicultural Education*, 2nd edn (Hoboken, NJ: Jossey-Bass, 2003), pp. 240–58.
51. Bhopal, *White Privilege*.
52. Zeus Leonardo and Norton Grubb, *Education and Racism: A Primer on Issues and Dilemmas* (New York: Routledge, 2019).
53. Dolores Bernal, Enrique Alemán Jr and Andrea Garavito, 'Latina/o undergraduate students mentoring Latina/o elementary students: a borderlands analysis of shifting identities and first-year experiences', *Harvard Educational Review*, 79 (2006), pp. 560–86.
54. Julia Johnson, Marc Rich and Alan Cargile, '"Why are you shoving this stuff down our throats?": preparing intercultural educators to challenge performances of White racism', *Journal of International and Intercultural Communication*, 1 (2008), pp. 113–35.

55. Jennifer Simpson, Angelique Causey and Levron William, '"I would want you to understand it": students' perspectives on addressing race in the classroom', *Journal of Intercultural Communication Research*, 36 (2007), pp. 33–50, and Julia Johnson and Archana Bhatt, 'Gendered and racialized identities and alliances in the classroom: formations in/of resistive space', *Communication Education*, 52 (2003), pp. 230–44.
56. Bhopal, *White Privilege*.
57. Kalwant Bhopal and Martin Myers, *Elite Universities and the Making of Privilege: Exploring Race and Class in Global Educational Economies* (London: Routledge 2023).
58. Ann Miller and Tina Harri, 'Communicating to develop white racial identity in an interracial communication class', *Communication Education*, 54 (2005), pp. 223–42.
59. Bhopal, *White Privilege*.
60. Yosso, 'Whose culture has capital?'.
61. Martin Myers and Kalwant Bhopal, 'Racism and bullying in rural primary schools: protecting White identities post Macpherson', *British Journal of Sociology of Education*, 38:2 (2017), pp. 125–43.
62. Ann Ferguson, *Bad Boys: Public Schools in the Making of Black Masculinity* (Michigan: University of Michigan Press, 2000), p. 19.
63. Pierre Bourdieu *Masculine Domination*, trans. Richard Nice (Stanford: Stanford University Press, 2001), p. 1 (my emphasis).
64. Eduardo Bonilla-Silva and Tyrone Forman, '"I am not a racist but . . .": mapping white college students racial ideology in the USA', *Discourse and Society*, 11:1 (2000), pp. 50–85, quotation on p. 78.

CHAPTER 3: HIGHER EDUCATION

1. Paul Bolton, *Higher Education Student Numbers*, House of Commons Library Briefing Paper No. 7857 (London: House of Commons Library, 2023).
2. The Dearing Report, *Higher Education in the Learning Society* (London: HMSO, 1997).
3. See http://news.bbc.co.uk/1/hi/uk_politics/460009.stm.
4. Stephen Ball, *The Education Debate: Policy and Practice in the 21st Century* (Bristol: Policy Press, 2008).
5. The Browne Review, *Securing a Sustainable Future for Higher Education: An Independent Review of Higher Education Funding and*

Student Finance (London: Department for Business, Innovation and Skills, 2010), p. 8.
6. *The Coalition: Our Programme for Government* (London: Cabinet Office, 2010).
7. Department for Business, Innovation and Skills, *Higher Education: Students at the Heart of the System* (Norwich: Stationery Office, 2011).
8. Higher Education Funding Council for England (HEFCE)/Office for Fair Access (OFFA), *National Strategy for Access and Student Success in Higher Education* (London: Department of Business, Innovation and Skills, 2014), p. 12.
9. Post-1992 universities are former polytechnics that were given university status after the Further and Higher Education Act (1992); they tend to focus on teaching rather than research.
10. Bhopal, *White Privilege*. Russell Group universities consist of twenty-four research-intensive universities that regularly score highly on league tables; they are known for their excellence in teaching and research – see https://russellgroup.ac.uk/about/.
11. The means-testing element applies to student maintenance loans. These presuppose that parents will contribute to their children's living costs to a greater or lesser extent depending on family income. In 2022, students whose annual family income was £25,000 or less received the full £9,706 loan. This was reduced to £4,524 for students with a family income of £62,311. If taking out the full loan, students from the poorest families would typically incur £5,182 additional debt for each year of study equivalent to £15,546 over a three-year degree, plus compound interest (which at the time of writing stood at a staggering 6.3 per cent).
12. Kalwant Bhopal, Martin Myers and Claire Pitkin, 'Routes through higher education: BME students and the development of a "specialisation of consciousness"', *British Educational Research Journal*, 46:6 (2020), pp. 1321–37.
13. *Fulfilling Our Potential: Teaching Excellence, Social Mobility and Student Choice* (London: Department for Business, Innovation and Skills, 2015).
14. Social Mobility Commission, *State of the Nation 2016: Social Mobility in Great Britain* (London: HMSO, 2016), p. 121.
15. Ibid., p. 102.
16. *The Office for Students*, House of Commons Library Briefing Paper No. 8924 (London: House of Commons Library, 2018).
17. Office for Students, *Regulatory Notice 1: Access and Participation Plan Guidance* (London: OfS, 2019).

NOTES

18. Universities UK, *Black, Asian and Minority Ethnic Attainment at UK Universities* (London: Universities UK, 2019).
19. Bhopal, *White Privilege*.
20. Vikki Boliver, 'Exploring ethnic inequalities in admission to Russell Group universities', *Sociology*, 50:2 (2016), pp. 247–66.
21. Advance HE, *Equality in Higher Education: Students Statistical Report 2021* (London: Advance HE, 2021).
22. Bhopal, *White Privilege*.
23. Advance HE, *Equality in Higher Education: Students Statistical Report 2021*.
24. Ibid.
25. Ibid.
26. Equalities and Human Rights Commission, *Tackling Racial Harassment: Universities Challenged* (London: EHRC, 2019).
27. Kalwant Bhopal, *The Experiences of Black and Minority Ethnic Academics: A Comparative Study of the Unequal Academy* (London: Routledge, 2016), and idem, *White Privilege*.
28. Universities UK, *Changing the Culture: Two Years On* (London: Universities UK, 2020), p. 4.
29. David Batty, 'UK universities condemned for failure to tackle racism', *Guardian*, 5 July 2019, available at https://www.theguardian.com/education/2019/jul/05/uk-universities-condemned-for-failure-to-tackle-racism.
30. Bhopal, *The Experiences of Black and Minority Ethnic Academics*.
31. Ibid., and Bhopal, *White Privilege*.
32. Sally Weale, 'UK universities perpetuate institutional racism, report says', *Guardian*, 24 November 2020, available at https://www.theguardian.com/education/2020/nov/24/uk-universities-perpetuate-institutional-racism-report-says.
33. Mike Wade, 'Dozens of St Andrews students complain of racism', *Times*, 23 November 2020, available at https://www.thetimes.co.uk/article/dozens-of-st-andrews-students-complain-of-racism-fxssbs3vk.
34. See https://www.ucl.ac.uk/play/ucl-talks/why-isnt-my-professor-black.
35. See http://www.dtmh.ucl.ac.uk/videos/curriculum-white/.
36. See https://itooamoxford.tumblr.com/.
37. Ibid.
38. See https://www.itv.com/news/meridian/2021-06-10/oxford-lecturers-boycott-oriel-college-over-cecil-rhodes-statue-decision.
39. See https://rmfoxford.wordpress.com/.
40. See https://www.gold.ac.uk/racial-justice/commitments/.

41. Sara Ahmed, 'The nonperformativity of antiracism', *Meridians*, 7:1 (2006), pp. 104–26, quotation on p. 105.
42. Frantz Fanon, *The Wretched of the Earth*, trans. Constance Farrington (New York: Grove Press, 1963), pp. 21–8.
43. Ibid., pp. 27–8.
44. David Batty, 'Only a fifth of universities say they are "decolonising" the curriculum', *Guardian*, 11 June 2020, available at https://www.theguardian.com/us-news/2020/jun/11/only-fifth-of-uk-universities-have-said-they-will-decolonise-curriculum.
45. Bhopal and Myers, *Elite Universities and the Making of Privilege*.
46. Marie Battiste, *Decolonizing Education: Nourishing the Learning Spirit* (Saskatoon, SK: Purich Publishing, 2013).
47. Derrick Bell, *Race, Racism and American Law* (Boston: Little, Brown & Co., 1980).
48. Bhopal, *White Privilege*.
49. Kalwant Bhopal, *Asian Women in Higher Education: Shared Communities* (Stoke-on-Trent: Trentham Books, 2010).
50. Claire Crawford and Ellen Greaves, *Socio-Economic, Ethnic and Gender Differences in HE Participation* (London: Department for Business, Innovation and Skills, 2015).
51. Kathleen Henehan and Helena Rose, *Opportunities Knocked: Exploring Pay Penalties Among UK's Ethnic Minorities* (London: Resolution Foundation, 2018).
52. Laurence Lessard-Phillips, Vikki Boliver, Maria Pampaka and Daniel Swain, 'Exploring ethnic differences in the post-university destinations of Russell Group graduates', *Ethnicities*, 18:4 (2018), pp. 496–517.
53. Tariq Modood and Nabil Khattab, 'Explaining ethnic differences: can ethnic minority strategies reduce the effects of ethnic penalties?', *Sociology*, 50:2 (2016), pp. 231–46.
54. Anthony Heath and Valentina Di Stasio, 'Racial discrimination in Britain, 1969–2017: a meta-analysis of field experiments on racial discrimination in the British labour market', *British Journal of Sociology*, 70:5 (2019), pp. 1774–98.
55. Zwysen and Longhi, 'Employment and earning differences in the early career of ethnic minority British graduates'; Christian Dustmann and Francesca Fabbri, 'Language proficiency and labour market performance of immigrants in the UK', *Economic Journal*, 113:489 (2003), pp. 695–717; and Carolina Zuccott, 'Do parents matter? Revisiting ethnic penalties in occupation among second generation ethnic minorities in England and Wales', *Sociology*, 49:2 (2015), pp. 229–51.

NOTES

56. Modood and Khattab, 'Explaining ethnic differences'.
57. Corrado Giulietti, Christian Schluter and Jackline Wahba, 'With a lot of help from my friends: social networks and immigrants in the UK', *Population, Space and Place*, 19:6 (2013), pp. 657–70.
58. Malcolm Brynin, Mohammed Shamshul Karim and Wouter Zwysen, 'The value of self-employment to ethnic minorities', *Work, Employment & Society*, 33:5 (2019), pp. 846–64.
59. Christian Dustmann, Albert Glitz and Uta Schonberg, 'Referral-based job search networks', *Review of Economic Studies*, 83:2 (2016), pp. 514–46.
60. Wouter Zwysen, Valentina Di Stasio and Anthony Heath, 'Ethnic penalties and hiring discrimination: comparing results from observational studies with field experiments in the UK', *Sociology*, 55:2 (2020), pp. 263–82.
61. Henehan and Rose, *Opportunities Knocked*.
62. Yaojun Li, 'Against the odds? A study of educational attainment and labour market position of the second generation ethnic minority members in the UK', *Ethnicities*, 18:4 (2018), pp. 471–95.
63. Trades Union Congress, *Is Racism Real?* (London: TUC, 2017).
64. Zwysen and Longhi, 'Employment and earning differences in the early career of ethnic minority British graduates'.
65. Teun A. van Dijk, *Prejudice in Discourse: An Analysis of Ethnic Prejudice in Cognition and Conversation* (Philadelphia: John Benjamins, 1984).
66. David Gillborn, 'Critical race theory and education: racism and anti-racism in educational theory and praxis', *Discourse: Studies in the Cultural Politics of Education*, 27 (2006), pp. 11–32, quotation on p. 26.

CHAPTER 4: WHITE ELITES AND EDUCATIONAL ADVANTAGE

1. Shamus Khan, *Privilege: The Making of an Adolescent Elite at St. Paul's School* (Princeton: Princeton University Press, 2010).
2. Bhopal and Myers, *Elite Universities and the Making of Privilege*.
3. John Scott, 'Modes of power and the re-conceptualisation of elites', *Sociological Review*, 56:1 (2008), pp. 29–34.
4. Rubén Gaztambide-Fernández, 'What is an elite boarding school?', *Review of Educational Research*, 79:3 (2009), pp. 1090–128.
5. Roy Lowe, 'The charitable status of elite schools: the origins of a national scandal', *History of Education*, 49:1 (2020), pp. 4–17.
6. *The Charities Act 2011* (Norwich: Stationery Office, 2011).

7. Catherine Fairbairn and Nerys Roberts, *Charitable Status and Independent Schools*, House of Commons Library Briefing Paper No. 05222 (London: House of Commons Library, 2019), and Julie Henry, 'Private schools "abuse charitable status" by giving discounts to affluent families', *Guardian*, 3 June 2018, available at https://www.theguardian.com/education/2018/jun/03/private-schools-abuse-charity-status-by-giving-discounts-to-richer-families.
8. Jonathan Owen, 'Private schools are "welfare junkies"', *Times Educational Supplement*, 24 February 2017, available at https://www.tes.com/news/gove-private-schools-are-welfare-junkies.
9. See https://explore-education-statistics.service.gov.uk/find-statistics/school-pupils-and-their-characteristics.
10. *ISC Census and Annual Report 2021* (London: Independent Schools Council, 2021).
11. See https://explore-education-statistics.service.gov.uk/find-statistics/school-pupils-and-their-characteristics.
12. *ISC Census and Annual Report 2021*.
13. Bhopal and Myers, *Elite Universities and the Making of Privilege*.
14. Francis Ndaji, John Little and Robert Coe, *A Comparison of Academic Achievement in Independent and State Schools* (Durham: Centre for Evaluation and Monitoring, Durham University, 2016).
15. Carl Cullinane and Rebecca Montacute, *Life Lessons* (London: Sutton Trust, 2017).
16. *ISC Census and Annual Report 2021*.
17. Sutton Trust/Social Mobility Commission, *Elitist Britain* (London: Sutton Trust, 2019).
18. Aaron Reeves, Sam Friedman, Charles Rahal and Magne Flemmen, 'The decline and persistence of the Old Boy: private schools and elite recruitment 1897 to 2016', *American Sociological Review*, 82:6 (2017), pp. 1139–66.
19. Martin Myers and Kalwant Bhopal, 'Cosmopolitan brands: graduate students navigating the social space of elite global universities', *British Journal of Sociology of Education*, 42:5 (2021), pp. 701–16.
20. Simon Marginson, 'Global field and global imagining: Bourdieu and worldwide higher education', *British Journal of Sociology of Education*, 29:3 (2008), pp. 303–15, quotation on p. 305.
21. 'The brains business', *The Economist*, 14 August 2018, available at https://www.economist.com/special-report/2018/08/14/the-brains-business.
22. Bhopal and Myers, *Elite Universities and the Making of Privilege*.

NOTES

23. Bhopal, *Asian Women in Higher Education*.
24. Anne-Marie Bathmaker, Nicola Ingram, Jessie Abrahams, Anthony Hoare, Richard Walle and Harriet Bradley, *The Degree Generation: Higher Education, Social Class and Social Mobility* (London: Palgrave Macmillan, 2016).
25. Marginson, 'Global field and global imagining', p. 305 (my emphasis).
26. See https://www.harvard.edu/about-harvard/endowment/.
27. See https://www.ox.ac.uk/about/organisation/finance-and-funding.
28. Marginson, 'Global field and global imagining'.
29. Sutton Trust, *Universities and Social Mobility: Summary Report* (London: Sutton Trust, 2021).
30. Richard Adams and Helena Bengstsson, 'Oxford accused of "social apartheid" as colleges admit no black students', *Guardian* 19 October 2017, available at https://www.theguardian.com/education/2017/oct/19/oxford-accused-of-social-apartheid-as-colleges-admit-no-black-students.
31. Bhopal, Myers and Pitkin, 'Routes through higher education'.
32. University of Oxford, *Annual Admissions Statistical Report* (Oxford: University of Oxford, 2020).
33. Bhopal, *White Privilege*.
34. University of Oxford, *Annual Admissions Statistical Report*.
35. See https://www.ox.ac.uk/admissions/undergraduate/increasing-access/opportunity-oxford.
36. Bhopal and Myers, *Elite Universities and the Making of Privilege*.
37. See https://college.harvard.edu/admissions/admissions-statistics.
38. See https://www.gse.harvard.edu/financialaid/tuition.
39. See https://www.census.gov/library/publications/2021/demo/p60-273.html#:~:text=Median%20household%20income%20was%20%2467%2C521,median%20household%20income%20since%202011.
40. Lee Elliot Major and Pallavi Amitava Banerjee, *Social Mobility and Elite Universities* (Oxford: Higher Education Policy Unit, 2019), p. 9.
41. Amy Binder, Daniel Davis and Nick Bloom, 'Career funneling: how elite students learn to define and desire "prestigious" jobs', *Sociology of Education*, 89:1 (2016), pp. 20–39.
42. Marginson, 'Global field and global imagining', p. 21.
43. Hiroki Igarashi and Hiro Sait, 'Cosmopolitanism as cultural capital: exploring the intersection of globalization, education and stratification', *Cultural Sociology*, 8:3 (2014), pp. 222–39.
44. David Baker, *The Schooled Society: The Educational Transformation of Global Culture* (Stanford: Stanford University Press, 2014).

45. Francis Green and David Kynaston, *Engines of Privilege: Britain's Private School Problem* (London: Bloomsbury, 2019).
46. UPP Foundation and the Bridge Group, *Social Mobility and University Careers Services* (London: UPP Foundation/Bridge Group, 2017).
47. Lauren Rivera, *Pedigree: How Elite Students Get Elite Jobs* (Princeton: Princeton University Press, 2015).
48. Joanne Moore, Louise Higham, Anna Mountford-Zimdars, Louise Ashley, Holly Birkett, Jo Duberley and Etlyn Kenny, *Socio-Economic Diversity in Life Sciences and Investment Banking* (London: Social Mobility Commission, 2016).
49. Linda Croxford and David Raffe, 'The iron law of hierarchy? Institutional differentiation in UK higher education', *Studies in Higher Education*, 40:9 (2015), pp. 1625–16.
50. Ian Walker and Yu Zhu, *University Selectivity and the Graduate Wage Premium: Evidence from the UK*, Discussion Paper No. 10536 (Bonn: IZA Institute of Labor Economics, 2017).
51. Paul Wakeling and Mike Savage, 'Entry to elite professions and the stratification of higher education in Britain', *Sociological Review*, 63:2 (2015), pp. 290–320.
52. Nick Drydakis, *The Effect of University Attended on Graduates' Labour Market Prospects: A Field Study of Great Britain*, Discussion Paper No. 9826 (Bonn: Institute of the Study of Labor, 2016).
53. Jonathan Friedman, 'Producing a global elite? The endurance of the national in elite American and British values', in Roland Bloch, Alexander Mitterle, Caterhine Paradeise and Peter Tobias (eds), *Universities and the Production of Elites: Discourses, Policies, and Strategies of Excellence and Stratification in Higher Education* (London: Palgrave Macmillan, 2018), pp. 327–47, quotation on pp. 327–8.
54. Sutton Trust/Social Mobility Commission, *Elitist Britain*.
55. *ISC Census and Annual Report 2021*.
56. Bhopal and Myers, *Elite Universities and the Making of Privilege*.
57. Rivera, *Pedigree*.
58. Respondents who participated in the study were from a range of different ethnic backgrounds: 24 students were White (19 had attended a private school and 5 had attended a state school); and 8 were from an ethnic minority background (3 were Black, 2 were British Indian, 1 was British Pakistani and 3 were mixed-heritage Black/White, and all but one student had attended a state school).

NOTES

59. Anthony Jack, *The Privileged Poor: How Elite Colleges are Failing the Disadvantaged* (Massachusetts: 2019).
60. Khan, *Privilege*, p. 368 (my emphasis).
61. Amy Binder and Andrea Abel, 'Symbolically maintained inequality: how Harvard and Stanford students construct boundaries among elite universities', *Sociology of Education*, 92:1 (2019), pp. 41–58, quotation on p. 53 (my emphasis).

CHAPTER 5: EQUALITY WHITEWASH

1. Trade Unions Congress, *Is Racism Real?*; University and College Union, *The Experiences of Black and Minority Ethnic Staff in Further and Higher Education* (London: UCU, 2016); and Bhopal, *The Experiences of Black and Minority Ethnic Academics*.
2. Kalwant Bhopal, Hazel Brown and June Jackson, 'BME academic flight from UK to overseas higher education: aspects of exclusion and marginalisation', *British Educational Research Journal*, 42:2 (2015), pp. 240–57; Bhopal, *The Experiences of Black and Minority Ethnic Academics*; idem, *White Privilege*; and Martin Myers, 'Racism, zero-hours contracts and complicity in higher education', *British Journal of Sociology of Education*, 43:4 (2022), pp. 584–602.
3. Advance HE, *Equality in Higher Education: Staff Statistical Report 2021*.
4. *The Equality Act 2010*.
5. Stephen Ball, 'Neoliberal education? Confronting the slouching beast', *Policy Futures in Education*, 14:8 (2016), pp. 1046–59,
6. Kalwant Bhopal and Claire Pitkin, '"Same old story, just a different policy": race and policy making in higher education in the UK', *Race, Ethnicity and Education*, 23:4 (2019), pp. 530–47.
7. Louise Caffrey, David Wyatt, Nina Fudge, Helena Mattingley, Catherine Williamson and Christopher McKevitt, 'Gender equity programmes in academic medicine: a realist evaluation approach to Athena SWAN processes', *BMJ Open*, 6:9 (2019), pp. 1–9.
8. Bhopal and Pitkin, '"Same old story, just a different policy"'.
9. Ibid.
10. Kalwant Bhopal and Holly Henderson, 'Competing inequalities: gender versus race in higher education institutions in the UK', *Educational Review*, 73:2 (2019), pp. 153–69.

11. A total of 10 interviews and 5 focus groups were conducted with respondents for the first study (Bhopal and Henderson, 'Competing inequalities') and 45 interviews were conducted for the second (Bhopal and Pitkin, '"Same old story, just a different policy"').
12. Million Plus is the association of modern universities with a focus on enterprise and employment as well as research and teaching – see https://www.millionplus.ac.uk/about-us/our-role. Non-affiliated universities that participated in my research did not fall into any of the formal categories of British universities and/or did not align themselves with any such formal groupings.
13. Bhopal and Pitkin, '"Same old story, just a different policy"', and idem, *White Privilege*.
14. Bhopal and Pitkin, '"Same old story, just a different policy"'; Bhopal and Henderson, 'Competing inequalities'; Bhopal, *White Privilege*; and Myers, 'Racism, zero-hours contracts and complicity in higher education'.
15. Myers, 'Racism, zero-hours contracts and complicity in higher education'.

CHAPTER 6: RACE EQUALITY TRAINING

1. Stephen Bramer, Andrew Millington and Stephen Pavelin, 'Corporate reputation and women on the board', *British Journal of Management*, 20 (2009), pp. 17–29.
2. Kalwant Bhopal, '"We can talk the talk, but we're not allowed to walk the walk": the role of equality and diversity staff in higher education institutions in England', *Higher Education*, 85 (2022), pp. 325–39.
3. Sara Ahmed, '"You end up doing the document rather than doing the doing": diversity, race equality and the politics of documentation', *Ethnic and Racial Studies*, 30:4 (2007), pp. 590–609.
4. Bhopal, *The Experiences of Black and Ethnic Minority Academics in Higher Education*.
5. Ibid.
6. Bhopal and Pitkin, '"Same old story, just a different policy"'.
7. Savita Kumra and Susan Vinnicombe, 'Impressing for success: a gendered analysis of a key social capital accumulation strategy', *Gender, Work and Organisation*, 17:5 (2010), pp. 521–46.

NOTES

8. Jacky Lumby with Marianne Coleman, *Leadership and Diversity: Challenging Theory and Practice in Education* (London: SAGE Publications, 2007).
9. Advance HE, *Onwards and Upwards? Tracking Women's Work Experiences in Higher Education* (London: Advance HE, 2016).
10. Kalwant Bhopal, 'For whose benefit? Black and Minority Ethnic training programmes in higher education institutions in England, UK', *British Educational Research*, 46:3 (2019), pp. 500–15, and idem, 'Success against the odds: the effect of mentoring on the careers of senior Black and Minority Ethnic academics in the UK', *British Journal of Educational Studies*, 68:1 (2020), pp. 79–95.
11. Bhopal, 'Confronting White privilege', and idem, 'Gender, ethnicity and career progression in UK higher education: a case study analysis', *Research Papers in Education*, 35:6 (2019), pp. 706–21.
12. Bhopal, *The Experiences of Black and Ethnic Minority Academics in Higher Education*.
13. Advance HE, *Equality in Higher Education: Staff Statistical Report 2021*.
14. Bhopal and Myers, *Elite Universities and the Making of Privilege*.
15. Nancy Leong, 'Racial capitalism', *Harvard Law Review*, 126:8 (2013), pp. 2151–226.
16. Affirmative action is one example of this in the US through which the legal approach to diversity has placed value on the identity of being a person of colour. However, the main beneficiaries of affirmative action have been White women (Gloria Ladson-Billings 'Critical race theory – what it is NOT', in Marvin Lynn and Adrienne Dixson (eds), *Handbook of Critical Race Theory in Education* (New York: Routledge, 2013), pp. 34–47). So, for example, in university admissions and graduation rates women of colour remain under-represented, whereas there has been the greatest increase in the numbers of White women since affirmative action was introduced – see https://www.pewresearch.org/short-reads/2014/03/06/womens-college-enrollment-gains-leave-men-behind/#:~:text=In%201994%2C%20among%20high%20school%20graduates%2C%2062%25%20of,while%20the%20rate%20for%20men%20remained%20the%20same.
17. Leong, 'Racial capitalism', p. 2156.
18. Naomi Klein, *The Shock Doctrine: The Rise of Disaster Capitalism* (London: Allen Lane, 2007).

NOTES

CONCLUSION

1. See https://news.sky.com/story/from-rafiq-to-vaughan-the-key-people-involved-in-the-racism-storm-engulfing-cricket-and-what-they-have-said-12460603.
2. See https://news.sky.com/story/crawley-town-fc-manager-john-yems-sacked-after-allegations-of-racism-towards-his-own-players-12606815.
3. See https://www.politico.eu/article/most-non-white-uk-mps-have-experienced-racism-study-itv/.
4. Nadeem Badshah, 'Met police urged to admit racism after strip-search of black girl in Hackney', *Guardian*, 1 April 2022, available at https://www.theguardian.com/uk-news/2022/apr/01/met-police-urged-to-admit-racism-after-strip-search-of-black-girl-in-hackney.
5. Amelia Gentleman, 'Windrush scandal caused by "30 years of racist immigration laws" – report', *Guardian*, 29 May 2022, available at https://www.theguardian.com/uk-news/2022/may/29/windrush-scandal-caused-by-30-years-of-racist-immigration-laws-report.
6. See https://www.aljazeera.com/news/2022/4/13/who-chief-says-world-treats-crises-differently-due-to-race.
7. Myers and Bhopal, 'Racism and bullying in rural primary schools'.
8. Gillborn, *Racism and Education*.
9. Richard Delgado, 'Rodrigo's committee assignment: a skeptical look at judicial independence', *Southern Californian Law Review*, 72 (1998), pp. 425–54, quotation on p. 445.
10. Department for Education, *Ethnicity Facts and Figures, GCSE Results (Attainment 8)*, 2021, available at https://www.ethnicity-facts-figures.service.gov.uk/education-skills-and-training/11-to-16-years-old/gcse-results-attainment-8-for-children-aged-14-to-16-key-stage-4/latest.
11. Bhopal, *White Privilege*.
12. Gillborn et al., *Evidence for the Commission on Race and Ethnic Disparities*.
13. Haque and Elliott, *Visible and Invisible Barriers*.
14. Batty and Parveen, 'UK schools record more than 60,000 racist incidents in 5 years'.
15. Delgado and Stefancic, *Critical Race Theory*.
16. Rivera, *Pedigree*.
17. Bhopal, *White Privilege*.
18. Advance HE, *Equality in Higher Education: Students Statistical Report 2021*.
19. Gillborn et al., *Evidence for the Commission on Race and Ethnic Disparities*.
20. Batty, 'UK universities condemned for failure to tackle racism'.

21. Equalities and Human Rights Commission, *Tackling Racial Harassment*.
22. Advance HE, *Equality in Higher Education: Staff Statistical Report 2021*.
23. Bhopal and Henderson, 'Competing inequalities'.
24. Bhopal, *The Experiences of Black and Minority Ethnic*, and idem, *White Privilege*.
25. Centre for Literacy in Primary Education, *Reflecting Realities: Survey of Ethnic Representation within UK Children's Literature 2020* (London: CLPE, 2021).
26. Historical Association, 'How diverse is your history curriculum?', *History Journal*, 26 June 2019.
27. See https://www.ethnicity-facts-figures.service.gov.uk/workforce-and-business/workforce-diversity/school-teacher-workforce/latest.
28. National Football League, 'NFL expands Rooney Rule requirements to increase diversity', *NFL.com*, 12 December 2018, available at https://www.nfl.com/news/nfl-expands-rooney-rule-requirements-to-strengthen-diversity-0ap3000000999110.
29. The all-women shortlist policy was first introduced by the Labour Party in 1993, with quotas that would mandate a certain percentage of women to be included on party candidate election lists.
30. Advance HE, *Equality in Higher Education: Students Statistical Report 2021*.
31. Dave Clayton, Melissa Leavitt and Nichole Torpey-Saboe, *The Significant Value of Historically Black Colleges and Universities* (Indianapolis: Strada Education Foundation, 2022).
32. Leonardo and Grubb, *Education and Racism*, p. 54 (my emphasis).
33. See https://www.bcu.ac.uk/social-sciences/research/identities-and-inequalities/research-clusters/black-studies.

Index

Page references in *italics* indicate images.

A

Abel, Andrea 155
'acceptable' and 'unacceptable' racism 50, 72-7, 101, 111-13
accountability, culture of 163
Adrian (staff member at Riverdale) 170-71, 209-10
Advance HE 93, 158
affirmative action 85, 262
Afia (Muslim student) 114-15, 120-21
agency, power of 46, 129
Ahmed, Sara 105
A-levels 17, 55-8, 71
Alex (White university student) 145
Algerian War of Independence (1954-62) 105
All Lives Matter 36
Amrit (Indian student) 117
Angela (Black staff member at Tower) 206-7
Angela (White staff member in a Russell Group university) 170
Annette (Black staff member in a Russell Group university) 180
Asian groups 3, 6, 201
- BAME (Black, Asian and minority ethnic) term and 8
- 'Black' term and 9, 44
- educational outcomes 44, 56
- female student stereotypes 10, 17*n*, 112
- labour market and 47, 96
- schools and 53, 56, 72, 77, 84
- 'South Asian' term 9, 10, 93, 119-20
- teachers 18-19
- university staff 116, 158, 201-2
- university students 92, 93, 94, 95, 112, 113-14, 115, 116, 119-20, 131, 149, 151
Athena Swan Charter 163-9, 172, 187-8, 228, 229
Attainment 8 score 17, 53-5
awarding gap 11, 95, 95*n*, 101, 104, 163-5, 233
Ayesha (Black student) 139

B

'bad behaviour', confusing racism with 51-2, 70, 78, 226
Badenoch, Kemi 37-9, 40, 66
BAME (Black, Asian and minority ethnic) 8, 44
- educational achievement 92-7, *92*, *94*
- labour market and 95, *96*, *97*
- university staff 158, *159*, *160*, 175-6
Banerjee, Pallavi Amitava 132
Bangladeshi heritage
- 'Black' term and 8-9
- educational outcomes 17, 44, 46, 51, 58, 92, 93, 94, 95
- educational racism and 226
- labour market and 96
- racism and 113-14
- university students 108, 109, 110*n*, 113-14, 131
'banter', dismissing complaints about racism as 10, 23, 52, 74, 75-6, 80, 81, 99, 226

INDEX

battle fatigue 61
Becky (Black student) 140
Bell, Derrick 26, 30, 39, 107; *Faces at the Bottom of the Well* 28–9, 30, 40
Binder, Amy 155
Birmingham City University 237
'Black' identity
– 'Black' term 8–10
– Black History Month and 37–8
– educational outcomes 17, 42, 53–8, 92, 93, 94, 95, 226
– historically Black colleges and universities (HBCUs) 236–7
– labour market and 96, 117–19
– Race Equality Charter and 168–71, 173–4, 179, 180, 182, 183, 194–5
– race equality training and 196–201, 203–4, 206–7, 209–10, 211, 212, 213
– racism and 63–7, 72–4, 79, 80–86, 101, 111, 112, 115–18
– university staff and 101–2, 168–71, 173–4, 179, 180, 182, 184–5, 196–201, 203–4, 206–7, 209–10, 211, 212, 213
– university students and 92, 93, 94, 95, 96, 101–2, 108, 109, 111, 112, 114, 115–19, 121, 130–31, 139–40, 142–51, 152–4, 158
Black, Asian and minority ethnic. See BAME
Black Caribbean heritage
– 'Black' term and 9–10
– Black History Month and 37–8
– educational outcomes 17, 42, 55, 58, 92, 94
– labour market and 96
– Race Equality Charter and 168–9
– race equality training and 197, 198, 199–201, 203–4, 206–7, 209–10, 211, 212
– racism in schools and 64, 72–4
– university staff and 168–9, 180, 182, 184–5, 197, 198, 199–201, 203–4, 206–7, 209–10, 211, 212
Black Curriculum campaign 67
Black feminism 9, 35
Black history 37–8, 60, 65, 178–9
Black History Month 37–8, 60, 65
Black Lives Matter
– backlash after protests 36–9, 224–5

– higher education and 23, 25, 36–9, 40, 105–6, 107, 194, 216, 217, 221, 225, 231
– race equality training and 194, 216, 217
– schools and 72, 75, 77, 85, 103
Black Student Society 9
Black studies 237
Black women 9, 34–5, 39, 47, 201. See also women
Blair, Tony 88, 132
BME (Black and minority ethnic) 8, 180
Bonilla-Silva, Eduardo 84–5
Bourdieu, Pierre 80–81
Brexit 116
Broderick, Alicia 34
Brown vs Board of Education 30–31, 224, 225
Browne Review 88
Butler, Dawn 38

C

Cambridge University 91, 127–8, 129, 130, 134, 227
Cameron, David 132
career progression, developing strategies for 203–10
Castle University, elite journeys to 137–55
charitable status 125–6
Charities Act (2011) 125
Chinese ethnic groups 42, 54, 55, 56, 57, 58, 59, 92, 94, 96, 109
Chris (Black student) 153
Christopher (White student) 142–3
civil rights 26, 28, 30, 65, 69, 236
Civil Rights Act (1964) 236
class 10, 26, 27, 41–4, 56, 87
– intersectionality and 34
– labour market and 109
– middle-class 35, 46, 83–4, 89, 129, 130, 133, 134, 142, 147, 201, 213, 227
– racism and 41–50
– schools and 42–50, 227 see also private schools
– training programmes and 201–2
– universities and 89, 129, 130, 132, 133, 134, 142, 147, 152, 154, 213
– White working-class 13, 14–15, 18, 43–4

INDEX

- working-class 11, 13, 14-15, 18, 43-4, 67, 89, 126, 129, 130, 201, 202, 213
Commission on Racial and Ethnic Disparities (CRED) report (2021) 26, 41-50, 66
commodity, race as a 213-19 .
Common Sense Group 37
Commonwealth 66, 134, 222
complicity 7, 52, 76-7, 85-6, 142-3, 209, 225
Conservative-Liberal Democrat coalition government (2010-15) 88
contradiction-closing cases 224-5
coping mechanisms 113-17
Coulson, Edward 36
covert racism 6-7, 15, 63, 93, 150, 157
Covid-19 pandemic 16-17, 19-20, 35-6, 101
Crawley Town 221
Crenshaw, Kimberlé 26-7, 34-5
criminal justice system 15-16, 36, 42, 239
critical discourse studies 113
critical legal theory 26
critical race theory (CRT) 21-2, 25-50, 222, 223, 225, 237
- 'Anti-American Propaganda', as 40
- Black Lives Matter protests backlash and 26, 36-40, 50
- Commission on Racial and Ethnic Disparities (CRED) report, critical race theory
- analysis of 26, 41-50
- critical race pedagogy 69-71
- curriculum and 68-71
- interdisciplinary university-wide research centres and 237
- interest convergence 22, 25, 30-31, 43, 107, 181
- intersectionality 4, 22, 25, 34-6, 43, 103, 168, 202
- key tenets of 22, 25, 29-36
- origins and definition of 13, 21, 26-9
- racial realism 22, 25-6, 29
- Whiteness, White supremacy and Whiteness as property and 21, 22, 25, 27, 29, 31-4, 40, 48-9

culture war 37, 50
curriculum 233-5
- Black Curriculum campaign 67
- critical race theory and 38, 39, 68-71
- decolonizing 38-9, 65-71, 101-7, 234
- elite schools and 124, 125
- higher education 25, 93, 98, 101-7, 157, 164, 189, 234-5, 236-7
- history teaching 19, 38-9, 65-9, 108, 233-4
- inclusive 65-9
- national curriculum 125
- schools and 19, 25, 38, 39, 51, 62, 65-71, 76, 85, 125, 226, 228, 233-4
- Whiteness and 228, 234
- White privilege and 68-9, 71
- White supremacy and 107, 121-2, 234

D

Daily Mail 49
David (Black Caribbean staff member at Tower) 203
Dearing Report (1997) 87-8
Deborah (White staff member in a Russell Group university) 176-7
declarations of aims and values 214
decolonization, curriculum 38-9, 65-9, 101-7, 234
Delgado, Richard 26, 225
Department of Education 37, 53, 55
Devi (British Indian staff member at Tower) 204
DiAngelo, Robin 33
Dijk, Teun van 113
direct racism 41, 63
disaster capitalism 216-17
diversity
- equality, diversity and inclusion (EDI) and *see* equality, diversity and inclusion (EDI)
- performative, rather than practical, tool 24, 167, 178-9, 191-3, 216-17
- policies of 18, 78, 191-3
- term 191
- training *see* race equality training
Dowden, Oliver 37

INDEX

E

economizing strategies, higher-education institutions 188-9
educational apartheid 129
elites, White. *See* White elites
endowment funds 128-30
English Baccalaureate 53
English Football League 235
entry rates, higher-education 87-9
Equalities and Human Rights Commission 16
Equality Act (2010) 16, 18, 158-9, 161, 162, 165, 235
Equality and Human Rights Commission (EHRC) 98-9
equality, diversity and inclusion (EDI) training 183, 191-2, 214-15, 219, 232. *See also* race equality training
equality policy-making. *See* policy-making
Equal Pay Act (1970) 158-9
'ethnic minority' term 10
everyday experiences of racism 4, 6, 7, 9, 15-17, 21, 22-3, 32
- 'banter', dismissing complaints about racism as 10, 23, 52, 74, 75-6, 80, 81, 99, 226
- coping mechanisms and student support 113-17
- higher education and 110-21
- media and 221-2
- polite racism 111-13
- schools and 51-86
- transitory racism 117-21
exclusion/expulsion, school 17, 64-5, 99, 114

F

fairness 45, 49
Fanon, Frantz 105
Farah (Bangladeshi student) 77, 113-14, 151
Farah (British Pakistani staff member in plate-glass university) 171, 210-11
favouritism 83-5
Fayola (Black student) 116
Ferguson, Ann 80

Floyd, George 36, 41, 73, 104, 105, 216, 217, 221, 233
Football Association 235
Forman, Tyrone 84-5
Friedman, Jonathan 134
Fulfilling Our Potential: Teaching Excellence, Social Mobility and Student Choice (green paper) 90

G

GCSEs 39, 42, 58, 71
gender 9, 10, 12, 13, 19, 22, 23, 158
- Athena Swan/REC and 166-78, 187-8, 201-2, 213, 228-9
- CRT and 26, 34, 35, 46
- gender reassignment 158
- UK Professors in higher education institutions by gender and ethnicity (2019-2020) 159
- UK Senior managers in higher education institutions by gender and ethnicity (2019-2020) 160
- *See also* women
Ghebreyesus, Tedros Adhanom 222
Gillborn, David 27, 31, 122
Gini coefficient 45
glass ceiling 61, 226
Goldsmiths Anti-Racist Action campaign 103-4
Gove, Michael 126
grammar schools 134
Grubb, W. Norton 236-7
Guardian 99-100, 106
Guinier, Lani 26
Gypsy/Roma students 17, 17n, 54, 55, 56, 57, 58, 64

H

Hackney Council 67
Harris, Angela 26
Harris, Cheryl 33
Harvard University 102, 128, 129, 131
health 15, 16, 42, 43
higher education 5, 7, 10, 11, 19, 21, 22, 23, 87-122, 124, 128, 135

268

INDEX

- Athena Swan Charter *see* Athena Swan Charter
- Black Lives Matter and 23, 25, 36–9, 40, 105–6, 107, 194, 216, 217, 221, 225, 231
- Browne Review and 88
- Conservative-Liberal Democrat coalition government and 88–9
- curriculum, decolonizing 101–7
- Dearing Report and 87–8
- elite universities 128–55
- entry rates/widening participation 87–9
- equality initiatives in 157–89. *See also individual imitative name*
- ethnic minority students experience of 91–3, 92, 122
- everyday experiences of racism in 110–21
- *Fulfilling Our Potential: Teaching Excellence, Social Mobility and Student Choice*
- and 90
- Goldsmiths Anti-Racist Action campaign 103–4
- Higher Education Funding Council for England and 89
- *Higher Education: Students at the Heart of the System* and 88–9
- 'I, too, am Oxford' and 'I, too, am Harvard' campaigns 102
- labour market, transitions from higher education into 107–10, 133–7, 152–4
- National Scholarship Programme 89
- Office for Fair Access and 89
- Office for Students (OfS) and 90–91, 100–101, 163
- outcomes for ethnic minority students compared with White students 93–8, 92, 94, 96, 97
- Race Equality Charter and. *See* Race Equality Charter
- race equality training and. *See* race equality training
- racism in higher-education institutions 98–101, 110–21
- 'Rhodes Must Fall' movement 102–3
- 'Skin Deep' project 102
- Social Mobility Commission report 90
- student fees and loans 88–9, 125, 131–2, 163, 214
- undergraduates *see* undergraduates
- White privilege and *see* White elites *and* White privilege

Higher Education Funding Council for England 89
Higher Education: Students at the Heart of the System (white paper) 88–9
Hillside School, interviews with pupils at 71–86
historically Black colleges and universities (HBCUs) 236–7
history, teaching of 19, 38–9, 65–9, 108, 233–4
House of Commons 15, 37, 43, 66
House of Lords 15, 37, 134
Hylton, Kevin 27

I

Ignatiev, Noel 28
income levels 14, 16, 28, 36, 45, 88, 89, 132, 239
independent fee-paying schools. *See* private schools
Independent Schools Council 125, 127
Independent Schools Inspectorate 125
Indian heritage 5
- 'Black' term and students of 8
- education outcomes and students of 42, 44, 55, 56, 92, 94, 96
- equality whitewash in higher education and 172, 186–7
- labour market and 96, 109, 119–20
- race equality training in higher education and 204
- racism in higher education and 112, 117, 119–20, 148–9
- racism in schools and 10, 73–4, 75, 81–2, 84

individual acts of racism 10, 11–12, 20, 27, 76–7, 107
inequality
- competition of 172–4
- deficit model of 46
- measuring 45, 46
institutional privilege 139–40

269

INDEX

institutional racism 12, 62, 225
- Covid-19 and 17
- CRED Report and 41, 42, 46, 47, 48–50
- CRT and 41, 42, 46, 47, 48–50, 222
- definition of 16, 20, 221, 224
- higher education and 98–9, 101, 111, 157, 165, 170, 174, 177, 179, 189, 192–3, 194,
- 195, 204–5, 207, 219, 228, 231
- race equality training and 192–3, 194, 195, 204–5, 207, 219, 231
- schools and 76–7

intelligence 126, 143–4
interest convergence 22, 25, 30–31, 43, 107, 181
intersectionality 4, 22, 25, 34–6, 43, 103, 168, 202
Irish Traveller groups 17, 17n, 55, 56, 57, 58, 64
Islamophobia 60
'I, too, am Oxford' and 'I, too, am Harvard' campaigns 102

J

Jack (Black student) 139–40, 143–4
Jackie (Black Caribbean staff member in a non-affiliated university) 182
Jamie (White student) 144–5
Jane (Black Caribbean staff member in a post-1992 university) 184–5
Jane (White staff member in a post-1992 university) 175
Janet (White staff member in a post-1992 university) 173
Janice (Black Caribbean staff member at Riverdale) 197–8
Janice (mixed White and Black heritage staff member in a post-1992 university) 185
Jayden (mixed White and Black ethnicity student) 79–80
Jean (White student) 138
Jeannette (Black student) 121
Jerrard (Black student) 117–18
Jessica (mixed Black and White heritage student) 150–52

John (Black Caribbean staff member in a Russell Group university) 168–9
John (White student) 146–8
Johnson, Boris 37, 41, 48–9, 132
Julie (White staff member in a post-1992 university) 173
Juliet (White staff member in a post-1992 university) 167–8
Juliette (White and Indian heritage student) 73–5, 77–8
Jyoti (British Indian staff member in a post-1992 university) 186–7

K

Khan, Shamus 155
Kirpinder (British-Indian student) 148–9
Klein, Naomi: *The Shock Doctrine: The Rise of Disaster Capitalism* 216–17
Kobayashi, Audrey 20–21

L

labour market 7–8, 14, 19, 26, 36, 43, 56
- elite White groups and 23, 124, 132–4, 135–6, 138–9, 219
- Pakistani or Bangladeshi background and 46
- transitioning from higher education into 90, 91, 95–6, 107–10, 117–20, 122, 132–4, 135–6, 138–9
Labour Party 37, 38, 87–8
Lammy, David 130
Lawrence, Charles 26
Lawrence, Stephen 20, 221, 224
Leonardo, Zeus 32–4, 236–7
Leong, Nancy 215
Linda (Black staff member in a Russell Group university) 179
lip service, paying 184–7
Lisa (Black and White heritage staff member of in a post-1992 university) 173–4
location, racial inequality in education and geographical 174–8
London Metropolitan University 236

M

Macpherson report (1999) 20
Major, Lee Elliot 132
Malik, Nesrine 36
Marginson, Simon 128, 129
Martin (White staff member in a post-1992 university) 175-6
Marxism 37
May, Theresa 16, 134
McIntosh, Peggy 31-2
mentoring 127, 194-200
meritocracy 22, 70, 144-9, 238-9
Metropolitan Police 20, 47
Million Plus 166
Mills, Charles: *The Racial Contract* 29
Mirza, Munira 47
mission statements 214
MIT (Massachusetts Institute of Technology) 128
mixed-heritage identity
– A level attainment 56, 57, 58
– Attainment 8 scores 54, 55
– degree attainment 92, 94, 96
– exclusion rates 64
– labour market and 96
– Oxford University admissions 131
– racism and 74-5, 79
– teachers, percentage of 59
– university staff members 170-71, 173-4, 185-6, 196-7
– university student experience 149-51, 152-3
Moira (Black student) 114
Monty (Black and White heritage student) 149-50, 153
MPs 37, 134

N

National Association of Schoolmasters Union of Women Teachers 62
National Football League (NFL) 235
National Scholarship Programme 89
National Trust 37
neoliberal values 214, 216, 217, 219, 231
networking/social networks 109
– race equality training and 193, 194, 195, 203, 207-8
– White elites and 123, 124, 128, 132, 134, 136, 137-8, 139, 141-2, 154
New Labour 87-8
non-affiliated institutions 166, 182
N-word 73, 81

O

Office for Fair Access 89
Office for National Statistics 45
Office for Students (OfS) 90-91, 100-101, 163
Office of the High Commissioner for Human Rights 48-9
Ofsted 39, 125, 233
Olusoga, David 48
Omar (Pakistani student) 111-12
Oriel College, University of Oxford 103
'other', ethnic minorities seen as 46, 83, 85, 140, 208, 226
'outsiders', ethnic minorities seen as 6, 7, 10, 17n, 22, 52, 66, 71, 115, 122, 124, 150, 152, 155, 194, 226, 227
overt racism 72, 76, 93, 110, 116, 117, 121, 150, 157, 226-7
Oxford University 227
– deadline for applying to 129
– endowment assets 129
– ethnic minority background admissions rates 91, 102-3, 130-31
– 'I, too, am Oxford' campaign 102-3
– media and 133, 134
– 'Oxford Opportunity' campaign 131
– private school attendance and admissions to 127-8
– 'Rhodes Must Fall' in 105
– 'social apartheid' system 130

P

Pakistani heritage 8
– students with 17, 42, 44-5, 46, 51, 58, 77, 92, 93, 94, 95, 96, 108, 109, 110n, 111, 114, 131, 151, 226
– university staff members with 171, 210-12

INDEX

Parminder (Indian background student) 119–20
Pat (Black African staff member in a Russell Group university) 183
Patterns of Reinforcing Racism in Higher Education 205
Paul (Black Caribbean staff member at Riverdale) 198–9
pay 15, 19, 124, 126, 130, 135
– Equal Pay Act (1970) 158–9
– pay gap 108–9, 158–9, 163–4, 189, 218
Peake, Linda 21
performance
– diversity and 24, 113, 191, 223, 231
– policy-making and 162–6, 178–87, 189, 228–30
– privilege and 142–4
– REC and 178–87, 189, 229–30
– -related outcomes 192–3
– Whiteness and 135, 136, 142–4, 155–6, 162–6
PhD 236
plate-glass university 171
policy-making, (white) 5, 10, 13, 17–18, 19, 22, 23, 27, 30, 50, 52, 158–89, 222, 223, 225
– accountability culture and 163
– Athena Swan Charter *see* Athena Swan Charter
– competition of inequality and 172–4
– economizing strategies and 188–9
– Equality Act (2010) and 158, 161–2
– geographical location and 174–8
– money and time constraints and 172–4
– performativity of 162–3, 178–87, 229–30
– playing the (White) policy game 187–9
– Race Equality Charter (REC) *see* Race Equality Charter (REC)
– single equalities charter 169–72
– ticking the box/paying lip service 184–7
Policy Unit, No. 10 Downing Street 47
political leaders 132–3
post-1992 universities 89, 99, 106–8, 111, 133, 166–8, 170–1, 173–5, 184–7, 213
Preston, John 27
primary schools 6, 52–3
private schools 87, 90, 124–8, 130, 132, 133–46, 148–9, 153–4, 226–7
privilege. *See* White privilege

Priya (British Indian student) 81–2, 83–4, 112–13
Priya (British Indian staff member in a Russell Group university) 172–3, 201–2
professors 11, 19
– black and ethnic minority, lack of 101–2, 104, 117, 165, 184, 218, 228, 230, 233
– in higher education institutions by gender and ethnicity, UK 158, 159, 160
– white students and 143–4, 155
Public Sector Equality Duty 158–9

Q

QS World University Rankings 128, 137
Queen Mary, Birkbeck 236

R

Rabina (British Pakistani staff member from Riverdale) 211–12
Race Disparity Audit 16
Race Equality Charter (REC) 163–89, 229–30, 233
– performing, showcasing and enacting 166–89
– ticking the box/paying lip service 184–7
race equality training 191–219, 233
– behavioural aspects of leadership, highlights 197–8
– capitalist endeavour, delivered as form of 214
– career progression, developing strategies for and 203–10
– connections with other ethnic minority staff, opportunities to make 196
– cost of 210–13
– disaster capitalism and 216–17
– 'diversity' policy and 191–3
– equality, diversity and inclusion (EDI) training 183, 191–2, 214–15, 219, 232
– gender-focused programmes 195
– interviews with ethnic minority staff who attended 195–203
– mentoring and 194–200
– mission statements or declarations of aims and values and 214

INDEX

- neoliberal values and 214, 216, 217, 219, 231
- networking and 193, 194, 195, 203, 207–8
- normative White practices, used to perpetuate 202–3, 208
- number and types of training programme, increase in 193–4
- one-size-fits-all basis 213
- performance-related outcomes, emphasis on 192–3
- publicity-seeking by institutions, as form of 216
- race as a commodity and 213–19
- racial capitalism and 214–15
- racism and 192–5, 200, 203–10, 205, 213–19
- recognition from White staff and 208–9
- structural racial inequalities, failure to address 204, 206
- superficial appearance of diversity 216–17
- value of programmes 196–203
- White style of leadership to achieve success, encourage a 206–8
- women experience of 200–203
- workload of marginalized groups and 193

Race Relations Act (1976) 158
Race Relations (Amendment) Act (2000) 16, 221
racial capitalism 214–15
racialization 28
racial profiling 76
racial realism 22, 25–6, 29
racial stereotypes 10, 17, 20, 46, 61, 64, 76, 77–81, 83, 84, 112, 115–16, 226, 236
racism
- 'acceptable' and 'unacceptable' 50, 72–7, 101, 111–13
- addressing 10, 232–3
- Athena Swan Charter and *see* Athena Swan Charter
- 'bad behaviour', confusing with 51–2, 70, 78, 226
- 'banter', dismissing complaints about racism as 10, 23, 52, 74, 75–6, 80, 81, 99, 226
- Black identity and 63–7, 72–4, 79, 80–86, 101, 111, 112, 115–18

- bullying 63
- challenging 223–5
- class and 41–50
- coping mechanisms and student support 113–17
- covert 6–7, 15, 63, 93, 150, 157
- CRED report and *see* CRED report
- critical race theory (CRT) and *see* critical race theory (CRT)
- direct 41, 63
- education reinforces systems and structures of Whiteness and White privilege and 5, 14
- everyday experiences of *see* everyday experiences of racism
- higher-education and 10–13, 87–122
- institutional *see* institutional racism
- media and 221–2
- overt 72, 76, 93, 110, 116, 117, 121, 150, 157, 226–7
- polite 111–13
- Race Equality Charter and *see* Race Equality Charter
- race equality training and 192–5, 200, 201, 202, 203–10, 205, 213–19
- reproduction of educational 20–24, 225, 226–31
- schools and 51–86
- silent 119, 120
- structural *see* structural racism
- subtle 83, 119
- teachers and 10, 17, 17n, 51–2, 55, 56, 60–64, 76–81, 83–5, 226, 233
- transitory 117–21
- White elites and *see* White elites
- White privilege and *see* White privilege
- White supremacy and *see* White supremacy

Rafiq, Azeem 221
Rebecca (White private school student) 145–6
recruitment 64
- ethnic minority staff 62, 157, 182, 228, 235–6
- graduate 133–7, 152–4
- university student 106, 227
- *See also* labour market

273

INDEX

religious education 77
Rhodes, Cecil 102-6
'Rhodes Must Fall' movement 102-3, 105-6
Rhodes Scholarship 103
Riverdale University 195-213
Rohit (British Indian student) 75-6
Roma 17, 17n, 55, 56-8, 64
Rooney Rule 235
Runnymede Trust 18, 47, 61
Russell Group universities
 – ethnic minority students and 89, 91-2, 99, 111, 166
 – REC in 168-9, 170, 172-3, 176-7, 179, 180, 183
 – staff in 168-9, 170, 172-3, 176-7, 179, 180, 183, 195, 213
Ryan (Black Caribbean background student) 72-5

S

schools
 – 'banter', dismissing complaints about racism in as 10, 23, 52, 74, 75-6, 80, 81, 99, 226
 – CRED Report and 42-4
 – critical race pedagogy and 69-70
 – critical race theory and 38-9, 68-71
 – curriculum 65-9, 71, 85, 226
 – educational outcomes and 53-8, 54, 57
 – Equality Act and 161-2
 – everyday racism and 22-3, 51-86, 226
 – Hillside School, interviews with pupils at 71-86
 – primary schools 6, 52-3
 – private schools 87, 90, 124-8, 130, 132, 133-46, 148-9, 153-4, 226-7
 – Race Equality Training and *see* Race Equality Training
 – secondary schools 52-3, 71-2, 85, 126-7
 – segregation in US 30-31, 224
 – special schools 53
 – symbolic violence in 80-81
 – teachers *see* teachers
 – White elites, educational advantage of 124-56, 226-7
 – White spaces 18-19
Second World War (1939-45) 65
secondary schools 52-3, 71-2, 85, 126-7
Sex Discrimination Act (1975) 158
silent racism 119, 120
single equalities charter 169-72
'Skin Deep' project 102
slavery 12, 28, 29, 33-4, 36, 37, 48, 65, 67, 105-6, 121, 217, 234
social media 73, 76, 104
Social Mobility Commission 90, 134
socio-economic problems 28, 29, 30-31, 41-3, 46, 90, 108, 110, 227
South Asian heritage 9, 10, 93, 119-20
special schools 53
Spielman, Amanda 39
St Andrews University 101
Stanford University 128
STEMM subjects (science, technology, engineering, maths and medicine) 163-4, 167, 228
Stephen (White private school student) 138-9
Steven (mixed White and Black heritage staff member at Tower) 196-7
strategic talk 113
strip-searches 222
structural racism 12
 – Covid-19 and 17
 – CRED Report and 41, 46, 49-50
 – defined 20
 – everyday racism and 111, 157-8, 162
 – guidelines to address 62
 – higher-education and 101, 111, 157-8, 162, 165, 170-71, 174, 179, 189, 194, 195, 204-5, 219, 222, 225, 228
 – individual acts of racism and 76-7
student fees and loans 88-9, 125, 131-2, 163, 214
subtle racism 83, 119
Sun 49
Sunak, Rishi 132, 136
Susan (Black Caribbean staff member at Tower) 200-201
Sutton Trust 134
symbolic violence 80-81

INDEX

T

Tara (Black Caribbean staff member at Riverdale) 199-200
teachers
- critical race theory and 68-9
- curriculum and 65, 66, 67-8, 71, 226
- ethnic minority background 18-19, 25, 51, 58-60, 59, 71, 226, 235
- head teachers 18, 51, 58-60, 85
- racism and 10, 17, 17n, 51-2, 55, 56, 60-64, 76-81, 83-5, 226, 233
- recruitment process 64

The Forgotten: How White Working-Class Pupils Have Been Let Down and How to Change It (House of Commons report) 43-4
'tick-box' exercise 78, 106, 162, 183, 184-7, 188, 206, 210, 232, 238
Times Higher Education World University Rankings league tables 128
Tower University 195-210
training programmes, race equality. *See* race equality training
transitory racism 117-21
Travellers of Irish heritage 17, 17n, 55, 56, 57, 58, 64
Troy (Black student) 115, 118-19
Trudy (student of mixed Black and White heritage) 152-3
Trump, Donald 40, 116
Truss, Liz 132
Twitter 11, 12, 14, 10

U

UCL (University College London) 101-2, 121, 236
undergraduates 9-10, 111
- fees 131-2
- UK domiciled students by ethnic group and undergraduate qualifiers 94
- UK first degree undergraduate qualifiers by ethnic group (2019-20) 96
unemployment 15, 19, 95, 109, 118
universities. *See* higher education
Universities UK 98

University of Cape Town 102
University of Manchester 101
University of Oxford. *See* Oxford University

V

Valerie (Black student) 119-21

W

Warmington, Paul 27
wealth inequality 29, 30, 45, 89, 90, 123-31, 136, 137, 141, 154, 155
Westminster School 128
Westminster University 236
White elites, educational advantage and 123-55
- 'Castle' University, elite journeys to 137-55
- charitable status of private schools and 125-6
- continuation of privilege 154-5
- educational apartheid 129
- endowment funds 129
- ethnicity, independent schools and 126-7
- Independent Schools Council 125, 127
- Independent Schools Inspectorate 125
- intelligence and 143-4
- labour market and 23, 133-7, 152-4
- meritocracy and 144-9
- overt and covert racism and 150
- 'Oxford Opportunity' campaign 131
- performance of Whiteness and 135, 136
- political leaders and 132-4
- private schools and 87, 90, 124-8, 130, 132, 133-46, 148-9, 153-4, 226-7
- QS World University Rankings 128
- reproduction of elites 134
- ruling class 132-3
- schools and 23, 87, 124-8, 130, 131, 132, 133-4, 135, 136, 137-54, 227
- *Times Higher Education* World University Rankings league tables 128
- transitioning from elite universities into high-status employment 133-4

INDEX

- undergraduate fees and 131–2
- universities and 23, 89, 128–33, 137–55, 177, 219, 227
- White privilege and 135–6

White kids pretending to be Black 81–3

White Lives Matter 36

Whiteness 5, 7, 14, 20–21
- CRT and 22, 25–6, 31–4, 38, 39
- curriculum and 228, 234
- higher education and 116, 135, 136, 162–3, 177, 229–30
- performance of 135, 136, 162–3, 177, 229–30
- race equality training and 202, 208, 215, 219, 231
- schools and 52, 68, 70, 71, 76–7, 82, 86
- White elites and *see* White elites

White privilege
- CRED report and 44–5, 49, 52
- critical race theory and 21, 22, 31–4, 36–9
- curriculum and 68–9, 71
- dismantling educational 232–9
- educational policy-making/practice designed to deliberately perpetuate 5, 7, 14, 222–4, 225
- higher-education and 23, 101, 107, 178, 184, 188, 189, 215, 219, 222–4, 225, 230, 232–9
- Race Equality Charter and 178, 184, 188, 189, 230
- Race Equality Training and 215
- racism and 20, 70, 75–7, 80, 81, 82, 84–5
- schools and 36–9, 68–9, 70, 71, 75–7, 80, 81, 82, 84, 86
- White elites and *see* White elites

White Privilege: The Myth of a Post-Racial Society (Bhopal) 14

White spaces
- schools as 18, 61, 85, 235
- universities as 152, 235

White supremacy 20, 21–3
- CRED Report and 48–9
- critical race theory and 22, 25–6, 27, 29, 31–4, 40

- curriculum and 107, 121–2, 234
- educational structures perpetuate and reinforce 5, 25–6, 155–6, 223–5, 229, 232
- elite White groups and *see* White elites
- higher education and 23, 155–6, 192, 215, 219, 223–5, 229, 232
- race equality training and 192, 215, 219
- racism and 14, 15, 20, 21, 22, 80, 84–5, 116, 223–5
- REC and 184, 189, 229

White working-class 14, 18, 43–4

Windrush generation 67, 222

women
- all-women shortlists 235
- Athena Swan/REC and 163–4, 165, 167, 171, 173, 174, 176, 228–9
- Black women 9, 34–5, 39, 47, 201
- CRT and 34–5
- higher education equality policy-making, White women main beneficiaries of 13, 19, 163–4, 165, 167, 171, 173, 174, 176, 228–9
- higher education senior roles and 158, 159, 160
- race equality training and 195, 200–203, 219
- school students 10, 82, 93
- school teachers 60

working-class 14–15, 18, 43–4, 67, 89, 126, 201, 213
- White working-class 14, 18, 43–4

World Health Organization 222

Y

Yems, John 221
YMCA 63, 64–5
Yorkshire cricket club 221
Yuval-Davis, Nira 35

Z

zero-hours contracts 16, 19, 189, 214

INDEX

T

Tara (Black Caribbean staff member at Riverdale) 199–200
teachers
- critical race theory and 68–9
- curriculum and 65, 66, 67–8, 71, 226
- ethnic minority background 18–19, 25, 51, 58–60, 59, 71, 226, 235
- head teachers 18, 51, 58–60, 85
- racism and 10, 17, 17n, 51–2, 55, 56, 60–4, 76–81, 83–5, 226, 233
- recruitment process 64
The Forgotten: How White Working-Class Pupils Have Been Let Down and How to Change It (House of Commons report) 43–4
'tick-box' exercise 78, 106, 162, 183, 184–7, 188, 206, 210, 232, 238
Times Higher Education World University Rankings league tables 128
Tower University 195–210
training programmes, race equality. *See* race equality training
transitory racism 117–21
Travellers of Irish heritage 17, 17n, 55, 56, 57, 58, 64
Troy (Black student) 115, 118–19
Trudy (student of mixed Black and White heritage) 152–3
Trump, Donald 40, 116
Truss, Liz 132
Twitter 11, 12, 14, 10

U

UCL (University College London) 101–2, 121, 236
undergraduates 9–10, 111
- fees 131–2
- UK domiciled students by ethnic group and undergraduate qualifiers 94
- UK first degree undergraduate qualifiers by ethnic group (2019–20) 96
unemployment 15, 19, 95, 109, 118
universities. *See* higher education
Universities UK 98

University of Cape Town 102
University of Manchester 101
University of Oxford. *See* Oxford University

V

Valerie (Black student) 119–21

W

Warmington, Paul 27
wealth inequality 29, 30, 45, 89, 90, 123–31, 136, 137, 141, 154, 155
Westminster School 128
Westminster University 236
White elites, educational advantage and 123–55
- 'Castle' University, elite journeys to 137–55
- charitable status of private schools and 125–6
- continuation of privilege 154–5
- educational apartheid 129
- endowment funds 129
- ethnicity, independent schools and 126–7
- Independent Schools Council 125, 127
- Independent Schools Inspectorate 125
- intelligence and 143–4
- labour market and 23, 133–7, 152–4
- meritocracy and 144–9
- overt and covert racism and 150
- 'Oxford Opportunity' campaign 131
- performance of Whiteness and 135, 136
- political leaders and 132–4
- private schools and 87, 90, 124–8, 130, 132, 133–46, 148–9, 153–4, 226–7
- QS World University Rankings 128
- reproduction of elites 134
- ruling class 132–3
- schools and 23, 87, 124–8, 130, 131, 132, 133–4, 135, 136, 137–54, 227
- *Times Higher Education* World University Rankings league tables 128
- transitioning from elite universities into high-status employment 133–4

275

INDEX

- undergraduate fees and 131–2
- universities and 23, 89, 128–33, 137–55, 177, 219, 227
- White privilege and 135–6

White kids pretending to be Black 81–3
White Lives Matter 36
Whiteness 5, 7, 14, 20–21
- CRT and 22, 25–6, 31–4, 38, 39
- curriculum and 228, 234
- higher education and 116, 135, 136, 162–3, 177, 229–30
- performance of 135, 136, 162–3, 177, 229–30
- race equality training and 202, 208, 215, 219, 231
- schools and 52, 68, 70, 71, 76–7, 82, 86
- White elites and *see* White elites

White privilege
- CRED report and 44–5, 49, 52
- critical race theory and 21, 22, 31–4, 36–9
- curriculum and 68–9, 71
- dismantling educational 232–9
- educational policy-making/practice designed to deliberately perpetuate 5, 7, 14, 222–4, 225
- higher-education and 23, 101, 107, 178, 184, 188, 189, 215, 219, 222–4, 225, 230, 232–9
- Race Equality Charter and 178, 184, 188, 189, 230
- Race Equality Training and 215
- racism and 20, 70, 75–7, 80, 81, 82, 84–5
- schools and 36–9, 68–9, 70, 71, 75–7, 80, 81, 82, 84, 86
- White elites and *see* White elites

White Privilege: The Myth of a Post-Racial Society (Bhopal) 14

White spaces
- schools as 18, 61, 85, 235
- universities as 152, 235

White supremacy 20, 21–3
- CRED Report and 48–9
- critical race theory and 22, 25–6, 27, 29, 31–4, 40

- curriculum and 107, 121–2, 234
- educational structures perpetuate and reinforce 5, 25–6, 155–6, 223–5, 229, 232
- elite White groups and *see* White elites
- higher education and 23, 155–6, 192, 215, 219, 223–5, 229, 232
- race equality training and 192, 215, 219
- racism and 14, 15, 20, 21, 22, 80, 84–5, 116, 223–5
- REC and 184, 189, 229

White working-class 14, 18, 43–4
Windrush generation 67, 222
women
- all-women shortlists 235
- Athena Swan/REC and 163–4, 165, 167, 171, 173, 174, 176, 228–9
- Black women 9, 34–5, 39, 47, 201
- CRT and 34–5
- higher education equality policy-making, White women main beneficiaries of 13, 19, 163–4, 165, 167, 171, 173, 174, 176, 228–9
- higher education senior roles and 158, 159, 160
- race equality training and 195, 200–203, 219
- school students 10, 82, 93
- school teachers 60

working-class 14–15, 18, 43–4, 67, 89, 126, 201, 213
- White working-class 14, 18, 43–4

World Health Organization 222

Y

Yems, John 221
YMCA 63, 64–5
Yorkshire cricket club 221
Yuval-Davis, Nira 35

Z

zero-hours contracts 16, 19, 189, 214